Tales of Terror and the Supernatural

Tales of Terror and the Supernatural

WILKIE COLLINS

SELECTED AND INTRODUCED BY
Herbert van Thal

Dover Publications, Inc., New York

Bibliographical Note

This Dover edition, first published in 1972, is a new collection of short stories by Wilkie Collins, with a new introduction by Herbert van Thal.

International Standard Book Number

ISBN-13: 978-0-486-20307-2
ISBN-10: 0-486-20307-7

Manufactured in the United States by Courier Corporation
20307710
www.doverpublications.com

Introduction

Wilkie Collins was the elder of the two sons of the artist William Collins and his wife Harriet Geddess. He was born on the 8th January 1824, at 11 New Cavendish Street, London, and was educated at a private school in Highbury. On leaving, his father decided that he should go into commerce and arranged that he should be articled to a firm of tea-merchants. But he was a gay spirited young man who enjoyed life, and a business career was not for him. (Incidentally he was christened Wilkie because his father's close friend was the painter Sir David Wilkie). After a holiday in Paris he returned to enter Lincoln's Inn as a law-student. On the death of his father, he decided to write a "memorial" to him, and in 1848 a two-volume work was published, *Memoirs of the Life of William Collins, R.A.* It was a painstaking work and it sold some five hundred copies, giving Collins the necessary impetus to become a professional writer. He decided that an historical novel would give him the fame he was seeking. Undoubtedly inspired by Bulwer-Lytton's *Last Days of Pompeii* he wrote *Antonina, or the Fall of Rome.* It was a complete failure and today is totally unreadable. He never wrote another historical novel. Undaunted, he decided to write a travel book about Cornwall, then England's most remote county, for not even the railway had penetrated there. The result of this tour was *Rambles Beyond Railways: Notes in Cornwall Taken A-foot* (1851). It was, however, in 1851 that a great change was to come into Collins' life, for his friend Augustus Egg, R.A., introduced him to Charles Dickens. Collins and Dickens immediately took to one another and as a result their friendship was unbroken until Dickens' death some twenty years later. At that time Dickens was immersed in *Household Words;* it was therefore not unnatural that he should ask Collins to contribute. His first contribution was to be one of his most sinister tales, a story which has no recourse to the supernatural, "A Terribly Strange Bed," which appears in this volume. It was his second short story—his first had appeared a year before in *Bentley's Miscellany* called "The Twin Sisters." During 1852 he went on tour with Dickens' "Splendid Strollers," for Collins enjoyed acting as did Dickens. At the same time he was working on his first novel of contemporary life, *Basil*. It was a highly original work, especially for those days when so much offended "good taste." *Basil* is a story of love, hate and revenge, and had it been published in France, Collins would have been hailed as a new writer of the realistic school. But in England it was trounced by the critics for its realism. Collins as much as Dickens was continually stressing the many unjust laws, and Swinburne's "Wilkie! have a mission" was apparent in most of his works. But Collins was never cowed, and all his life fought for freedom of expression. The following year Collins accepted an invitation to go on a tour of Switzerland and Italy with Dickens and Egg. The trip was a considerable success despite the fact that Dickens was not an easy man with whom to travel, while Collins began to show the signs of ill-health which were to develop so appallingly for him in the later years of his life. The three were away over a year. Back in England acting had become of paramount interest, and in January 1855 Dickens suggested that Collins needed some permanent income and offered him the editorship of *Household Words,* which he accepted. He had in the meanwhile published in 1854 *Hide and Seek,* which was his first mystery novel. It was not by any means such a powerful work as *Basil,* and although it contains some brilliant characterization it was not particularly well received and again failed to make the author's name. Meanwhile Collins collected his stories for book publication, and a first volume appeared under the title *After Dark* (1856). These clearly showed he was a great master of the macabre story, and that he was only overshadowed by Poe and Sheridan LeFanu. Many of the stories in *After Dark* appear in this volume. Thus the afore-mentioned "A Terribly Strange Bed," "The Stolen Letter," a story in the same genre as Poe's "Purloined Letter," and "The Lady of Glenwith Grange," a moving and highly successful story of double identity told in Collins' most accomplished manner.

The same year also saw the publication of joint authorship with Dickens of one of the famous Christmas stories, "The Wreck of the Golden Mary." The second collection of Collins' short stories appeared in 1859—*The Queen of Hearts,* which contained many others of his best-known tales—"The Dream-Woman," "Fauntleroy," "Mad Monkton" and "The Biter Bit"—all of which are included in this volume. "The Dream-Woman" was revised into a longer tale and was republished in *The Frozen Deep and Other Tales* (two vols. 1874). These stories are amongst his best examples of the "Tales of Suspense."

The following year Collins was "a made man," for in August 1860 *The Woman in White* was published, and this novel was to become one of the most successful of its kind to be published in England. From being a man of modest means Collins became both rich and famous. In 1863 he was able to resign from *All the Year Round,* which Dickens had started after his quarrel with Bradbury and Evans over *Household Words.* After the enormous sale of *The Woman in White* it was no easy matter to satisfy his large and awaiting public with another novel of the same success. Although the novel that followed it, *No Name,*[1] was a tour de force it did not achieve the same success. *No Name* is a highly complex story about a girl who has been wronged of her heritage by nature of the fact that her parents were not married at the time of her birth. Apart from the sociological injustice which the book stresses, Collins created some remarkable characters, such as the heroine herself, no namby-pamby girl of the period. The amusing rogue Captain Wragge is one of Collins' most realistic portraits. Nevertheless Collins' reputation as a highly skilled novelist persisted. It was followed by *Armadale* (1866), an even longer and more complex story than its predecessors. The main character, Lydia Gwilt, is one of the most interesting of his long line of admirably drawn female characters, and the book holds one from chapter to chapter despite its involved plot and the fact that the 'secret' of the book is disclosed in the opening chapters. The last of Collins' four major works, *The Moonstone* (1868), is considered by Professor Oliver Elton to be his greatest work. It heralded the novel of detection, and its popularity was second only to *The Woman in White.* At first Dickens was greatly impressed, but a year later changed his mind and wrote William Gorman Wills "I quite agree with you about *The Moonstone.* The construction is wearisome beyond

---

[1] *No Name* has recently been re-published in the Doughty Library with an Introduction by the writer (N.Y.,Stein & Day, 1966).

endurance, and there is a vein of obstinate conceit"—yet *The Mystery of Edwin Drood* followed *The Moonstone!*[2]

Collins now enjoyed seeing his books dramatized, but equally his health began to fail. Although he was writing away as hard as ever none of his fifteen novels (the last was completed by Walter Besant) achieved the fame or quality of his previous works; yet *Man and Wife* (1870) and *Poor Miss Finch* (1872) are in the writer's opinion novels that have been grossly neglected. Collins never married, and his private life has always been as mysterious as the mysteries that envelop his own books! He was devoted to his mother, equally he was fond of gay living, and took himself off to Paris whenever he could, for he loved France. His mistress was one Caroline Elizabeth Graves, née Courtenay, who was the original of *The Woman in White,* and by her he had a daughter Hariette. He also lived for a while with Martha Rudd, by whom he had three illegitimate children who were given the name of Dawson.

The turning point in Collins' life was to be the death of Dickens on June 9th, 1870. Collins with his only brother, Charles Alston, attended the funeral. G. K. Chesterton wrote "In his capacity as editor [Dickens] made one valuable discovery. He discovered Wilkie Collins. Wilkie Collins is the one man of unmistakable genius who has affinity with Dickens; an affinity in this respect, that they both combine a modern and Cockney and even commonplace opinion about things with a huge elemental sympathy with strange oracles and spirits and old night. There were no two men in mid-Victorian England with their top-hats and umbrellas, more typical of its rationality and dull reform; and there were no two men who could touch them at a ghost-story. No two men would have more contempt for superstitions; and no two men could create the superstitious thrill."

The last years of Collins' life were indeed sad. More and more he had to rely on laudanum to kill the terrors of pain that he suffered, and finally he could swallow a wine glass full at a single gulp. Gradually he withdrew more and more from society until finally he lived the life of a hermit, yet by present-day standards of life he should have been in his prime, for he was only in his fifties when his health failed. One can only regret that modern medical skill was not available to him. Of the real man, his thoughts and

[2] See Robert Ashley: *Wilkie Collins,* p. 92 (London, Barker, 1952).

revelations will remain closed to us, as Kenneth Robinson has observed in his admirable biography of Collins. None of those close to him left any material about him—save Dickens, and he has left us only his letters to him; and they rarely reveal anything of Wilkie's own thoughts. Like his books his letters were in the main mostly of their business together. He kept no diaries. Yet one would have loved to have known more of him—he was obviously a charming man.

The selection of stories chosen here show Collins at all his most variable. The fault must be with the reader if he is not impelled to read them, for although they are melodramatic and are naturally redolent of their times, they are none the worse for that.

Herbert van Thal

London, 1972

Contents

The Dream-Woman

Chapter One

I had not been settled much more than six weeks in my country practice, when I was sent for to a neighbouring town, to consult with the resident medical man there on a case of very dangerous illness.

My horse had come down with me at the end of a long ride the night before, and had hurt himself, luckily, much more than he had hurt his master. Being deprived of the animal's services, I started for my destination by the coach (there were no railways at that time), and I hoped to get back again, towards the afternoon, in the same way.

After the consultation was over, I went to the principal inn of the town to wait for the coach. When it came up it was full inside and out. There was no resource left me but to get home as cheaply as I could by hiring a gig. The price asked for this accommodation struck me as being so extortionate that I determined to look out for an inn of inferior pretensions, and to try if I could not make a better bargain with a less prosperous establishment.

I soon found a likely-looking house, dingy and quiet, with an old-fashioned sign, that had evidently not been repainted for many years past. The landlord, in this case, was not above making a small profit, and as soon as we came to terms he rang the yard-bell to order the gig.

"Has Robert not come back from that errand?" asked the landlord, appealing to the waiter who answered the bell.

"No, sir, he hasn't."

"Well, then, you must wake up Isaac."

"Wake up Isaac!" I repeated; "that sounds rather odd. Do your ostlers go to bed in the daytime?"

"This one does," said the landlord, smiling to himself in rather a strange way.

"And dreams too," added the waiter; "I shan't forget the turn it gave me the first time I heard him."

"Never you mind about that," retorted the proprietor; "you go and rouse Isaac up. The gentleman's waiting for his gig."

The landlord's manner and the waiter's manner expressed a great deal more than they either of them said. I began to suspect that I might be on the trace of something professionally interesting to me as a medical man, and I thought I should like to look at the ostler before the waiter awakened him.

"Stop a minute," I interposed; "I have rather a fancy for seeing this man before you wake him up. I'm a doctor; and if this queer sleeping and dreaming of his comes from anything wrong in his brain, I may be able to tell you what to do with him."

"I rather think you will find his complaint past all doctoring, sir," said the landlord; "but if you would like to see him, you're welcome, I'm sure."

He led the way across a yard and down a passage to the stables, opened one of the doors, and, waiting outside himself, told me to look in.

I found myself in a two-stall stable. In one of the stalls a horse was munching his corn; in the other an old man was lying asleep on the litter.

I stooped and looked at him attentively. It was a withered, woebegone face. The eyebrows were painfully contracted; the mouth was fast set, and drawn down at the corners. The hollow wrinkled cheeks, and the scanty grizzled hair, told their own tale of some past sorrow or suffering. He was drawing his breath convulsively when I first looked at him, and in a moment more he began to talk in his sleep.

"Wake up!" I heard him say, in a quick whisper, through his clenched teeth. "Wake up there! Murder!"

He moved one lean arm slowly till it rested over his throat, shuddered a little, and turned on his straw. Then the arm left his throat, the hand stretched itself out, and clutched at the side towards which he had turned, as if he fancied himself to be grasping at the edge of something. I saw his lips move, and bent lower over him. He was still talking in his sleep.

"Light grey eyes," he murmured, "and a droop in the left eyelid; flaxen hair, with a gold-yellow streak in it—all right, mother—fair white arms, with a down on them—little lady's hand, with a reddish look under the finger-nails. The knife—always the cursed knife—first on one side, then on the other. Aha! you she-devil, where's the knife?"

At the last word his voice rose, and he grew restless on a sudden. I saw him shudder on the straw; his withered face became distorted, and he threw up both his hands with a quick hysterical gasp. They struck against the bottom of the manger under which he lay, and the blow awakened him. I had just time to slip through the door and close it before his eyes were fairly open, and his senses his own again.

"Do you know anything about that man's past life?" I said to the landlord.

"Yes, sir, I know pretty well all about it," was the answer, "and an uncommon queer story it is. Most people don't believe it. It's true, though, for all that. Why, just look at him," continued the landlord, opening the stable door again. "Poor devil! he's so worn out with his restless nights that he's dropped back into his sleep already."

"Don't wake him," I said; "I'm in no hurry for the gig. Wait till the other man comes back from his errand; and, in the meantime, suppose I have some lunch and a bottle of sherry, and suppose you come and help me to get through it?"

The heart of mine host, as I had anticipated, warmed to me over his own wine. He soon became communicative on the subject of the man asleep in the stable, and by little and little I drew the whole story out of him. Extravagant and incredible as the events must appear to everybody, they are related here just as I heard them and just as they happened.

Chapter Two

Some years ago there lived in the suburbs of a large seaport town on the west coast of England a man in humble circumstances, by name Isaac Scatchard. His means of subsistence were derived from any employment that he could get as an ostler, and occasionally, when times went well with him, from temporary engagements in service as stable-helper in private houses. Though a faithful, steady, and honest man, he got on badly in his calling. His ill luck was proverbial among his neighbours. He was always missing good opportunities by no fault of his own, and always living longest in service with amiable people who were not punctual payers of wages. "Unlucky Isaac" was his nickname in his own neighbourhood, and no one could say that he did not richly deserve it.

With far more than one man's fair share of adversity to endure, Isaac had but one consolation to support him, and that was of the dreariest and most negative kind. He had no wife and children to increase his anxieties and add to the bitterness of his various failures in life. It might have been from mere insensibility, or it might have been from generous unwillingness to involve another in his own unlucky destiny; but the fact undoubtedly was, that he had arrived at the middle term of life without marrying, and, what is much more remarkable, without once exposing himself, from eighteen to eight-and-thirty, to the genial imputation of ever having had a sweetheart.

When he was out of service he lived alone with his widowed mother. Mrs. Scatchard was a woman above the average in her lowly station as to capacity and manners. She had seen better days, as the phrase is, but she never referred to them in the presence of curious visitors; and, though perfectly polite to everyone who approached her, never cultivated any intimacies among her neighbours. She contrived to provide, hardly enough, for her simple wants by doing rough work for the tailors, and always managed to keep a decent home for her son to return to whenever his ill luck drove him out helpless into the world.

One bleak autumn, when Isaac was getting on fast towards forty, and when he was, as usual, out of place through no fault of his own, he set forth from his mother's cottage on a long walk inland to a gentleman's seat where he had heard that a stable-helper was required.

It wanted then but two days of his birthday; and Mrs. Scatchard, with her usual fondness, made him promise, before he started, and he would be back in time to keep that anniversary with her, in as festive a way as their poor means would allow. It was easy for him to comply with this request, even supposing he slept a night each way on the road.

He was to start from home on Monday morning, and, whether he got the new place or not, he was to be back for his birthday dinner on Wednesday at two o'clock.

Arriving at his destination too late on the Monday night to make application for the stable-helper's place, he slept at the village inn, and in good time on the Tuesday morning presented himself at the gentleman's house to fill the vacant situation. Here again his ill luck pursued him as inexorably as ever. The excellent written testimonials to his character which he was able to produce availed him nothing; his long walk had been taken in vain: only the day before the stable-helper's place had been given to another man.

Isaac accepted this new disappointment resignedly and as a matter of course. Naturally slow in capacity, he had the bluntness of sensibility and phlegmatic patience of disposition which frequently distinguish men with sluggishly-working mental powers. He thanked the gentleman's steward with his usual quiet civility for granting him an interview, and took his departure with no appearance of unusual depression in his face or manner.

Before starting on his homeward walk, he made some inquiries at the inn, and ascertained that he might save a few miles on his return by following a new road. Furnished with full instructions, several times repeated, as to the various turnings he was to take, he set forth on his homeward journey, and walked on all day with only one stoppage for bread and cheese. Just as it was getting towards dark, the rain came on and the wind began to rise, and he found himself, to make matters worse, in a part of the country with which he was entirely unacquainted, though he knew himself to be some fifteen miles from home. The first house he found to inquire at was a lonely roadside inn standing on the outskirts of a thick wood. Solitary as the place looked, it was welcome to a lost man who was also hungry, thirsty, footsore, and wet. The landlord was civil and respectable-looking, and the price he asked for a bed was reasonable enough. Isaac therefore decided on stopping comfortably at the inn for that night.

He was constitutionally a temperate man. His supper consisted of two rashers of bacon, a slice of home-made bread, and a pint of ale. He did not go to bed immediately after this moderate meal, but sat up with the landlord, talking about his bad prospects and his long run of ill luck, and diverging from these topics to the subjects of horse-flesh and racing. Nothing was said either by himself, his host, or the few labourers who strayed into the tap-room, which could, in the slightest degree, excite the very small and very dull imaginative faculty which Isaac Scatchard possessed.

At a little after eleven the house was closed. Isaac went round with the landlord and held the candle while the doors and lower windows were being secured. He noticed with surprise the strength of the bolts and bars, and iron-sheathed shutters.

"You see, we are rather lonely here," said the landlord. "We never have had any attempts made to break in yet, but it's always as well to be on the safe side. When nobody is sleeping here, I am the only man in the house. My wife and daughter are timid, and the servant-girl takes after her missuses. Another glass of ale before you turn in? No! Well, how such a sober man as you comes to be out of place is more than I can make out, for one. Here's where you're to sleep. You're our only lodger to-night, and I think you'll say my missus has done her best to make you comfortable. You're quite sure you won't have another glass of ale? Very well. Good night."

It was half-past eleven by the clock in the passage as they went upstairs to the bedroom, the window of which looked on to the wood at the back of the house.

Isaac locked the door, set his candle on the chest of drawers, and wearily got ready for bed. The bleak autumn wind was still blowing, and the solemn, monotonous surging, moan of it in the wood was dreary and awful to hear through the night-silence. Isaac felt strangely wakeful. He resolved, as he lay down in bed, to keep the candle alight until he began to grow sleepy, for there was something unendurably depressing in the bare idea of lying awake in the darkness, listening to the dismal, ceaseless moaning of the wind in the wood.

Sleep stole on him before he was aware of it. His eyes closed, and he fell off insensibly to rest without having so much as thought of extinguishing the candle.

The first sensation of which he was conscious after sinking into slumber was a strange shivering that ran through him suddenly from head to foot, and a dreadful sinking pain at the heart, such as he had never felt before. The shivering only disturbed his slumbers; the pain woke him instantly. In one moment he passed from a state of sleep to a state of wakefulness—his eyes wide open—his mental perceptions cleared on a sudden, as if by a miracle.

The candle had burnt down nearly to the last morsel of tallow, but the top of the unsnuffed wick had just fallen off, and the light in the little room was, for the moment, fair and full.

Between the foot of his bed and the closed door there stood a woman with a knife in her hand, looking at him.

He was stricken speechless with terror, but he did not lose the preternatural clearness of his faculties, and he never took his eyes off the woman. She said not a word as they stared each other in the face, but she began to move slowly towards the left-hand side of the bed.

His eyes followed her. She was a fair, fine woman, with yellowish flaxen hair and light grey eyes, with a droop in the left eyelid. He noticed those things and fixed them on his mind before she was round at the side of the bed. Speechless, with no expression in her face, with no noise following her footfall, she came closer and closer—stopped—and slowly raised the knife. He laid his right arm over his throat to save it; but, as he saw the knife coming down, threw his hand across the bed to the right side, and jerked his body over that way just as the knife descended on the mattress within an inch of his shoulder.

His eyes fixed on her arm and hand as she slowly drew her knife out of the bed: a white, well-shaped arm, with a pretty down lying lightly over the fair skin—a delicate lady's hand, with the crowning beauty of a pink flush under and round the finger nails.

She drew the knife out, and passed back again slowly to the foot of the bed; stopped there for a moment looking at him; then came on—still speechless, still with no expression on the blank beautiful face, still with no sound following the stealthy footfalls—came on to the right side of the bed, where he now lay.

As she approached she raised the knife again, and he drew himself away to the left side. She struck, as before, right into the mattress, with a deliberate perpendicularly-downward action of the arm. This time his eyes wandered from her to the knife. It was like the large clasp-knives which he had often seen labouring men use to cut their bread and bacon with. Her delicate little fingers did not conceal more than two thirds of the handle: he noticed that it was made of buck-horn, clean and shining as the blade was, and looking like new.

For the second time she drew the knife out, concealed it in the wide sleeve of her gown, then stopped by the bedside, watching him. For an instant he saw her standing in that position, then the wick of the spent candle fell over into the socket; the flame diminished to a little blue point, and the room grew dark.

A moment, or less, if possible, passed so, and then the wick flamed up, smokingly, for the last time. His eyes were still looking eagerly over the right-hand side of the bed when the final flash of light came, but they discerned nothing. The fair woman with the knife was gone.

The conviction that he was alone again weakened the hold of the terror that had struck him dumb up to this time. The preternatural sharpness which the very intensity of his panic had mysteriously imparted to his faculties left them suddenly. His brain grew confused—his heart beat wildly—his ears opened for the first time since the appearance of the woman to a sense of the woeful ceaseless moaning of the wind among the trees. With the dreadful conviction of the reality of what he had seen still strong within him, he leaped out of bed, and screaming "Murder! Wake up, there! wake up!" dashed headlong through the darkness to the door.

It was fast locked, exactly as he had left it on going to bed.

His cries on starting up had alarmed the house. He heard the terrified, confused exclamations of women; he saw the master of the house approaching along the passage with his burning rush candle in one hand and his gun in the other.

"What is it?" asked the landlord breathlessly.

Isaac could only answer in a whisper. "A woman, with a knife in her hand," he gasped out. "In my room—a fair, yellow-haired woman; she jobbed at me with the knife twice over."

The landlord's pale cheeks grew paler. He looked at Isaac eagerly by the flickering light of his candle, and his face began to get red again; his voice altered, too, as well as his complexion. "She seems to have missed you twice," he said.

"I dodged the knife as it came down," Isaac went on, in the same scared whisper. "It struck the bed each time."

The landlord took his candle into the bedroom immediately. In less than a minute he came out again into the passage in a violent passion.

"The devil fly away with you and your woman with the knife! There isn't a mark in the bedclothes anywhere. What do you mean by coming into a man's place, and frightening his family out of their wits about a dream?"

"I'll leave your house," said Isaac faintly. "Better out on the road, in rain and dark, on my road home, than back again in that room, after what I've seen in it. Lend me a light to get my clothes by, and tell me what I'm to pay."

"Pay!" cried the landlord, leading the way with his light sulkily into the bedroom. "You'll find your score on the slate when you go downstairs. I wouldn't have taken you in for all the money you've got about you if I'd known your dreaming, screeching ways beforehand. Look at the bed. Where's the cut of a knife in it? Look at the window—is the lock bursted? Look at the door (which I heard you fasten yourself)—is it broke in? A murdering woman with a knife in my house! You ought to be ashamed of yourself!"

Isaac answered not a word. He huddled on his clothes, and then they went downstairs together.

"Nigh on twenty minutes past two!" said the landlord, as they passed the clock. "A nice time in the morning to frighten honest people out of their wits!"

Isaac paid his bill, and the landlord let him out at the front door, asking, with a grin of contempt, as he undid the strong fastenings, whether "the murdering woman got in that way."

They parted without a word on either side. The rain had ceased, but the night was dark, and the wind bleaker than ever. Little did the darkness, or the cold, or the uncertainty about the way home matter to Isaac. If he had been turned out into a wilderness in a thunderstorm, it would have been a relief after what he had suffered in the bedroom of the inn.

What was the fair woman with the knife? The creature of a dream, or that other creature from the unknown world called among men by the name of ghost? He could make nothing of the mystery—had made nothing of it, even when it was midday on Wednesday, and when he stood, at last, after many times missing his road, once more on the doorstep of home.

Chapter Three

His mother came out eagerly to receive him. His face told her in a moment that something was wrong.

"I've lost the place; but that's my luck. I dreamed an ill dream last night, mother—or maybe I saw a ghost. Take it either way, it scared me out of my senses, and I'm not my own man again yet."

"Isaac, your face frightens me. Come in to the fire—come in, and tell mother all about it."

He was as anxious to tell as she was to hear; for it had been his hope all the way home, that his mother, with her quicker capacity and superior knowledge, might be able to throw some light on the mystery which he could not clear up for himself. His memory of the dream was still mechanically vivid, though his thoughts were entirely confused by it.

His mother's face grew paler and paler as he went on. She never interrupted him by so much as a single word; but when he had done, she moved her chair close to his, put her arm round his neck, and said to him,

"Isaac, you dreamed your ill dream on this Wednesday morning. What time was it when you saw the fair woman with the knife in her hand?"

Isaac reflected on what the landlord had said when they had passed by the clock on his leaving the inn; allowed as nearly as he could for the time that must have elapsed between the unlocking of his bedroom door and the paying of his bill just before going away, and answered,

"Somewhere about two o'clock in the morning."

His mother suddenly quitted her hold of his neck, and struck her hands together with a gesture of despair.

"This Wednesday is your birthday, Isaac, and two o'clock in the morning was the time when you were born."

Isaac's capacities were not quick enough to catch the infection of his mother's superstitious dread. He was amazed, and a little startled also, when she suddenly rose from her chair, opened her old writing-desk, took pen, ink, and paper and then said to him,

"Your memory is but a poor one, Isaac, and now I'm an old woman, mine's not much better. I want all about this dream of yours to be as well known to both of us, years hence, as it is now. Tell me over again all you told me a minute ago, when you spoke of what the woman with the knife looked like."

Isaac obeyed, and marvelled much as he saw his mother carefully set down on paper the very words that he was saying.

"Light grey eyes," she wrote, as they came to the descriptive part, "with a droop in the left eyelid; flaxen hair, with gold-yellow streak in it; white arms, with a down upon them; little lady's hand, with a reddish look about the finger-nails; clasp-knife with a buckhorn handle, that seemed as good as new." To these particulars Mrs. Scatchard added the year, month, day of the week, and time in the morning when the woman of the dream appeared to her son. She then locked up the paper carefully in her writing-desk.

Neither on that day nor on any day after could her son induce her to return to the matter of the dream. She obstinately kept her thoughts about it to herself, and even refused to refer again to the paper in her writing-desk. Ere long Isaac grew weary of attempting to make her break her resolute silence; and time, which sooner or later wears out all things, gradually wore out the impression produced on him by the dream. He began by thinking of it carelessly, and he ended by not thinking of it at all.

The result was the more easily brought about by the advent of some important changes for the better in his prospects which commenced not long after his terrible night's experience at the inn. He reaped at last the reward of his long and patient suffering under adversity by getting an excellent place, keeping it for seven years, and leaving it, on the death of his master, not only with an excellent character, but also with a comfortable annuity bequeathed to him as a reward for saving his mistress's life in a carriage accident. Thus it happened that Isaac Scatchard returned to his old mother, seven years after the time of the dream at the inn, with an annual sum of money at his disposal sufficient to keep them both in ease and independence for the rest of their lives.

The mother, whose health had been bad of late years, profited so much by the care bestowed on her and by freedom from money anxieties, that when Isaac's birthday came round she was able to sit up comfortably at table and dine with him.

On that day, as the evening drew on, Mrs. Scatchard discovered that a bottle of tonic medicine which she was accustomed to take, and in which she had fancied that a dose or more was still left, happened to be empty. Isaac immediately volunteered to go to the chemist's and get it filled again. It was as rainy and bleak an autumn night as on the memorable past occasion when he lost his way and slept at the road-side inn.

On going into the chemist's shop he was passed hurriedly by a poorly-dressed woman coming out of it. The glimpse he had of her face struck him, and he looked back after her as she descended the doorsteps.

"You're noticing that woman?" said the chemist's apprentice behind the counter. "It's my opinion there's something wrong with her. She's been asking for laudanum to put to a bad tooth. Master's out for half an hour, and I told her I wasn't allowed to sell poison to strangers in his absence. She laughed in a queer way, and said she would come back in half an hour. If she expects master to serve her, I think she'll be disappointed. It's a case of suicide, sir, if ever there was one yet."

These words added immeasurably to the sudden interest in the woman which Isaac had felt at the first sight of her face. After he had got the medicine-bottle filled, he looked about anxiously for her as soon as he was out in the street. She was walking slowly up and down on the opposite side of the road. With his heart, very much to his own surprise, beating fast, Isaac crossed over and spoke to her.

He asked if she was in any distress. She pointed to her torn shawl, her scanty dress, her crushed, dirty bonnet; then moved under a lamp so as to let the light fall on her stern, pale, but still most beautiful face.

"I look like a comfortable, happy woman, don't I?" she said, with a bitter laugh.

She spoke with a purity of intonation which Isaac had never heard before from other than ladies' lips. Her slightest actions seemed to have the easy, negligent grace of a thorough-bred woman. Her skin, for all its poverty-stricken paleness, was as delicate as if her life had been passed in the enjoyment of every social comfort that wealth can purchase. Even her small, finely-shaped hands, gloveless as they were, had not lost their whiteness.

Little by little, in answer to his questions, the sad story of the woman came out. There is no need to relate it here; it is told over and over again in police reports and paragraphs about attempted suicides.

"My name is Rebecca Murdoch," said the woman, as she ended. "I have ninepence left, and I thought of spending it at the chemist's over the way in securing a passage to the other world. Whatever it is, it can't be worse to me than this, so why should I stop here?"

Besides the natural compassion and sadness moved in his heart by what he heard, Isaac felt within him some mysterious influence at work all the time the woman was speaking which utterly confused his ideas and almost deprived him of his powers of speech. All that he could say in answer to her last reckless words was that he would prevent her from attempting her own life, if he followed her about all night to do it. His rough, trembling earnestness seemed to impress her.

"I won't occasion you that trouble," she answered, when he repeated his threat. "You have given me a fancy for living by speaking kindly to me. No need for the mockery of protestations and promises. You may believe me without them. Come to Fuller's Meadow to-morrow at twelve, and you will find me alive, to answer for myself—No!—no money. My ninepence will do to get me as good a night's lodging as I want."

She nodded and left him. He made no attempt to follow—he felt no suspicion that she was deceiving him.

"It's strange, but I can't help believing her," he said to himself, and walked away, bewildered, towards home.

On entering the house, his mind was still so completely absorbed by its new subject of interest that he took no notice of what his mother was doing when he came in with the bottle of medicine. She had opened her old writing-desk in his absence, and was now reading a paper attentively that lay inside it. On every birthday of Isaac's since she had written down the particulars of his dream from his own. lips, she had been accustomed to read that same paper, and ponder over it in private.

The next day he went to Fuller's Meadow.

He had done only right in believing her so implicitly. She was there, punctual to a minute, to answer for herself. The last-left faint defences in Isaac's heart against the fascination which a word or look from her began inscrutably to exercise over him sank down and vanished before her for ever on that memorable morning.

When a man previously insensible to the influence of women forms an attachment in middle life, the instances are rare indeed, let the warning circumstances be what they may, in which he is found capable of freeing himself from the tyranny of the new ruling passion. The charm of being spoken to familiarly, fondly, and gratefully by a woman whose language and manners still retained enough of their early refinement to hint at the high social station that she had lost, would have been a dangerous luxury to a man of Isaac's rank at the age of twenty. But it was far more than that—it was certain ruin to him—now that his heart was opening unworthily to a new influence at that middle time of life when strong feelings of all kinds, once implanted, strike root most stubbornly in a man's moral nature. A few more stolen interviews after that first morning in Fuller's Meadow completed his infatuation. In less than a month from the time when he first met her, Isaac Scatchard had consented to give Rebecca Murdoch a new interest in existence, and a chance of recovering the character she had lost by promising to make her his wife.

She had taken possession, not of his passions only, but of his faculties as well. All the mind he had he put into her keeping. She directed him on every point—even instructing him how to break the news of his approaching marriage in the safest manner to his mother.

"If you tell her how you met me and who I am at first," said the cunning woman, "she will move heaven and earth to prevent our marriage. Say I am the sister of one of your fellow-servants—ask her to see me before you go into any more particulars—and leave it to me to do the rest. I mean to make her love me next best to you, Isaac, before she knows anything of who I really am."

The motive of the deceit was sufficient to sanctify it to Isaac. The stratagem proposed relieved him of his one great anxiety, and quieted his uneasy conscience on the subject of his mother. Still, there was something wanting to perfect his happiness, something that he could not realize, something mysteriously untraceable, and yet something that perpetually made itself felt; not when he was absent from Rebecca Murdoch, but, strange to say, when he was actually in her presence! She was kindness itself with him. She never made him feel his inferior capacities and inferior manners. She showed the sweetest anxiety to please him in the smallest trifles; but, in spite of all these attractions, he never could feel quite at his ease with her. At their first meeting, there had mingled with his admiration, when he looked in her face, a faint, involuntary feeling of doubt whether that face was entirely strange to him. No after familiarity had the slightest effect on this inexplicable, wearisome uncertainty.

Concealing the truth as he had been directed, he announced his marriage engagement precipitately and confusedly to his mother on the day when he contracted it. Poor Mrs. Scatchard showed her perfect confidence in her son by flinging her arms round his neck, and giving him joy of having found at last, in the sister of one of his fellow-servants, a woman to comfort and care for him after his mother was gone. She was all eagerness to see the woman of her son's choice, and the next day was fixed for the introduction.

It was a bright sunny morning, and the little cottage parlour was full of light as Mrs. Scatchard, happy and expectant, dressed for the occasion in her Sunday gown, sat waiting for her son and her future daughter-in-law.

Punctual to the appointed time, Isaac hurriedly and nervously led his promised wife into the room. His mother rose to receive her—advanced a few steps, smiling—looked Rebecca full in the eyes, and suddenly stopped. Her face, which had been flushed the moment before, turned white in an instant; her eyes lost their expression of softness and kindness, and assumed a blank look of terror; her outstretched hands fell to her sides, and she staggered back a few steps with a low cry to her son.

"Isaac," she whispered, clutching him fast by the arm when he asked alarmedly if she was taken ill, "Isaac, does that woman's face remind you of nothing?"

Before he could answer—before he could look round to where Rebecca stood, astonished and angered by her reception, at the lower end of the room, his mother pointed impatiently to her writing-desk, and gave him the key.

"Open it," she said, in a quick, breathless whisper.

"What does this mean? Why am I treated as if I had no business here? Does your mother want to insult me?" asked Rebecca angrily.

"Open it, and give me the paper in the left-hand drawer. Quick! quick, for Heaven's sake!" said Mrs. Scatchard, shrinking farther back in terror.

Isaac gave her the paper. She looked it over eagerly for a moment, then followed Rebecca, who was now turning away haughtily to leave the room, and caught her by the shoulder—abruptly raised the long, loose sleeve of her gown, and glanced at her hand and arm. Something like fear began to steal over the angry expression of Rebecca's face as she shook herself free from the old woman's grasp. "Mad!" she said to herself; "and Isaac never told me." With these few words she left the room.

Isaac was hastening after her when his mother turned and stopped his farther progress. It wrung his heart to see the misery and terror in her face as she looked at him.

"Light grey eyes," she said, in low, mournful, awestruck tones, pointing towards the open door; "a droop in the left eyelid; flaxen hair, with a gold-yellow streak in it; white arms, with a down upon them; little lady's hand, with a reddish look under the finger-nails—*The Dream-Woman*, Isaac, the Dream-Woman!"

The faint cleaving doubt which he had never been able to shake off in Rebecca Murdoch's presence, was fatally set at rest for ever. He *had* seen her face, then, before—seven years before, on his birthday, in the bedroom of the lonely inn.

"Be warned! oh, my son, be warned! Isaac, Isaac, let her go, and do you stop with me!"

Something darkened the parlour window as those words were said. A sudden chill ran through him, and he glanced sidelong at the shadow. Rebecca Murdoch had come back. She was peering in curiously at them over the low window-blind.

"I have promised to marry, mother," he said, "and marry I must."

The tears came into his eyes as he spoke and dimmed his sight, but he could just discern the fatal face outside moving away again from the window.

His mother's head sank lower.

"Are you faint?" he whispered.

"Broken-hearted, Isaac."

He stooped down and kissed her. The shadow, as he did so, returned to the window, and the fatal face peered in curiously once more.

Chapter Four

Three weeks after that day Isaac and Rebecca were man and wife. All that was hopelessly dogged and stubborn in the man's moral nature seemed to have closed round his fatal passion, and to have fixed it unassailably in his heart.

After that first interview in the cottage parlour no consideration would induce Mrs. Scatchard to see her son's wife again, or even to talk of her when Isaac tried hard to plead her cause after their marriage.

This course of conduct was not in any degree occasioned by a discovery of the degradation in which Rebecca had lived. There was no question of that between mother and son. There was no question of anything but the fearfully-exact resemblance between the living, breathing woman, and the spectre-woman of Isaac's dream.

Rebecca, on her side, neither felt nor expressed the slightest sorrow at the estrangement between herself and her mother-in-law. Isaac, for the sake of peace, had never contradicted her first idea that age and long illness had affected Mrs. Scatchard's mind. He even allowed his wife to upbraid him for not having confessed this to her at the time of their marriage engagement, rather than risk anything by hinting at the truth. The sacrifice of his integrity before his one all-mastering delusion seemed but a small thing, and cost his conscience but little after the sacrifices he had already made.

The time of waking from this delusion—the cruel and the rueful time—was not far off. After some quiet months of married life, as the summer was ending, and the year was getting on towards the month of his birthday, Isaac found his wife altering towards him. She grew sullen and contemptuous; she formed acquaintances of the most dangerous kind in defiance of his objections, his entreaties, and his commands; and, worst of all, she learned, ere long, after every fresh difference with her husband, to seek the deadly self-oblivion of drink. Little by little, after the first miserable discovery that his wife was keeping company with drunkards, the shocking certainty forced itself on Isaac that she had grown to be a drunkard herself.

He had been in a sadly desponding state for some time before the occurrence of these domestic calamities. His mother's health, as he could but too plainly discern every time he went to see her at the cottage, was failing fast, and he upbraided himself in secret as the cause of the bodily and mental suffering she endured. When to his remorse on his mother's account was added the shame and misery occasioned by the discovery of his wife's degradation, he sank under the double trial—his face began to alter fast, and he looked what he was, a spirit-broken man.

His mother, still struggling bravely against the illness that was hurrying her to the grave, was the first to notice the sad alteration in him, and the first to hear of his last worst trouble with his wife. She could only weep bitterly on the day when he made his humiliating confession, but on the next occasion when he went to see her she had taken a resolution in reference to his domestic afflictions which astonished and even alarmed him. He found her dressed to go out, and on asking the reason received this answer:

"I am not long for this world, Isaac," she said, "and I shall not feel easy on my death-bed unless I have done my best to the last to make my son happy. I mean to put my own fears and my own feelings out of the question, and to go with you to your wife, and try what I can do to reclaim her. Give me your arm, Isaac, and let me do the last thing I can in this world to help my son before it is too late."

He could not disobey her, and they walked together slowly towards his miserable home.

It was only one o'clock in the afternoon when they reached the cottage where he lived. It was their dinner-hour, and Rebecca was in the kitchen. He was thus able to take his mother quietly into the parlour, and then prepare his wife for the interview. She had fortunately drunk but little at that early hour, and she was less sullen and capricious than usual.

He returned to his mother with his mind tolerably at ease. His wife soon followed him into the parlour, and the meeting between her and Mrs. Scatchard passed off better than he had ventured to anticipate, though he observed with secret apprehension that his mother, resolutely as she controlled herself in other respects, could not look his wife in the face when she spoke to her. It was a relief to him, therefore, when Rebecca began to lay the cloth.

She laid the cloth, brought in the bread-tray, and cut a slice from the loaf for her husband, then returned to the kitchen. At that moment, Isaac, still anxiously watching his mother, was startled by seeing the same ghastly change pass over her face which had altered it so awfully on the morning when Rebecca and she first met. Before he could say a word, she whispered, with a look of horror,

"Take me back—home, home again, Isaac. Come with me, and never go back again."

He was afraid to ask for an explanation; he could only sign to her to be silent, and help her quickly to the door. As they passed the bread-tray on the table she stopped and pointed to it. "Did you see what your wife cut your bread with?" she asked, in a low whisper.

"No, mother—I was not noticing—what was it?"

"Look!"

He did look. A new clasp-knife, with a buck-horn handle, lay with the loaf in the bread-tray. He stretched out his hand shudderingly to possess himself of it; but, at the same time, there was a noise in the kitchen, and his mother caught at his arm.

"The knife of the dream! Isaac, I'm faint with fear. Take me away before she comes back."

He was hardly able to support her. The visible, tangible reality of the knife struck him with a panic, and utterly destroyed any faint doubts that he might have entertained up to this time in relation to the mysterious dream-warning of nearly eight years before. By a last desperate effort, he summoned self-possession enough to help his mother out of the house—so quietly that the "Dream-woman" (he thought of her by that name now) did not hear them departing from the kitchen.

"Don't go back, Isaac—don't go back!" implored Mrs. Scatchard, as he turned to go away, after seeing her safely seated again in her own room.

"I must get the knife," he answered, under his breath. His mother tried to stop him again, but he hurried out without another word.

On his return he found that his wife had discovered their secret departure from the house. She had been drinking, and was in a fury of passion. The dinner in the kitchen was flung under the grate; the cloth was off the parlour table. Where was the knife?

Unwisely, he asked for it. She was only too glad of the opportunity of irritating him which the request afforded her. "He wanted the knife, did he? Could he give her a reason why? No! Then he should not have it—not if he went down on his knees to ask for it." Further recriminations elicited the fact that she had bought it a bargain, and that she considered it her own especial property. Isaac saw the uselessness of attempting to get the knife by fair means, and determined to search for it, later in the day, in secret. The search was unsuccessful. Night came on, and he left the house to walk about the streets. He was afraid now to sleep in the same room with her.

Three weeks passed. Still sullenly enraged with him, she would not give up the knife; and still that fear of sleeping in the same room with her possessed him. He walked about at night, or dozed in the parlour, or sat watching by his mother's bedside. Before the expiration of the first week in the new month his mother died. It wanted then but ten days of her son's birthday. She had longed to live till that anniversary. Isaac was present at her death, and her last words in this world were addressed to him:

"Don't go back, my son, don't go back!"

He was obliged to go back, if it were only to watch his wife. Exasperated to the last degree by his distrust of her, she had revengefully sought to add a sting to his grief, during the last days of his mother's illness, by declaring that she would assert her right to attend the funeral. In spite of all that he could do or say, she held with wicked pertinacity to her word, and on the day appointed for the burial forced herself—inflamed and shameless with drink—into her husband's presence, and declared that she would walk in the funeral procession to his mother's grave.

This last worst outrage, accompanied by all that was most insulting in word and look, maddened him for the moment. He struck her.

The instant the blow was dealt he repented it. She crouched down, silent, in a corner of the room, and eyed him steadily; it was a look that cooled his hot blood and made him tremble. But there was no time now to think of a means of making atonement. Nothing remained but to risk the worst till the funeral was over. There was but one way of making sure of her. He locked her into her bedroom.

When he came back some hours after, he found her sitting, very much altered in look and bearing, by the bedside, with a bundle on her lap. She rose, and faced him quietly, and spoke with a strange stillness in her voice, a strange repose in her eyes, a strange composure in her manner.

"No man has ever struck me twice," she said, "and my husband shall have no second opportunity. Set the door open and let me go. From this day forth we see each other no more."

Before he could answer she passed him and left the room. He saw her walk away up the street.

Would she return?

All that night he watched and waited, but no footstep came near the house. The next night, overpowered by fatigue, he lay down in bed in his clothes, with the door locked, the key on the table, and the candle burning. His slumber was not disturbed. The third night, the fourth, the fifth, the sixth passed, and nothing happened. He lay down on the seventh, still in his clothes, still with the door locked, the key on the table, and the candle burning, but easier in his mind.

Easier in his mind, and in perfect health of body when he fell off to sleep. But his rest was disturbed. He woke twice without any sensation of uneasiness. But the third time it was that never-to-be-forgotten shivering of the night at the lonely inn, that dreadful sinking pain at the heart, which once more aroused him in an instant.

His eyes opened towards the left-hand side of the bed, and there stood—

The Dream-Woman again? No! His wife; the living reality, with the dream-spectre's face, in the dream-spectre's attitude; the fair arm up, the knife clasped in the delicate white hand.

He sprang upon her almost at the instant of seeing her, and yet not quickly enough to prevent her from hiding the knife. Without a word from him—without a cry from her—he pinioned her in a chair. With one hand he felt up her sleeve, and there, where the Dream-Woman had hidden the knife, his wife had hidden it—the knife with the buck-horn handle, that looked like new.

In the despair of that fearful moment his brain was steady, his heart was calm. He looked at her fixedly with the knife in his hand, and said these last words:

"You told me we should see each other no more, and you have come back. It is my turn now to go, and to go for ever. I say that we shall see each other no more, and *my* word shall not be broken."

He left her, and set forth into the night. There was a bleak wind abroad, and the smell of recent rain was in the air. The distant church-clocks chimed the quarter as he walked rapidly beyond the last houses in the suburb. He asked the first policeman he met what hour that was of which the quarter past had just struck.

The man referred sleepily to his watch, and answered, "Two o'clock." Two in the morning. What day of the month was this day that had just begun? He reckoned it up from the date of his mother's funeral. The fatal parallel was complete: it was his birthday!

Had he escaped the mortal peril which his dream foretold? or had he only received a second warning?

As that ominous doubt forced itself on his mind, he stopped, reflected, and turned back again towards the city. He was still resolute to hold to his word, and never to let her see him more, but there was a thought now in his mind of having her watched and followed. The knife was in his possession; the world was before him; but a new distrust of her—a vague, unspeakable, superstitious dread had overcome him.

"I must know where she goes, now she thinks I have left her," he said to himself, as he stole back wearily to the precincts of his house.

It was still dark. He had left the candle burning in the bedchamber; but when he looked up to the window of the room now, there was no light in it. He crept cautiously to the house door. On going away, he remembered to have closed it; on trying it now, he found it open.

He waited outside, never losing sight of the house, till day-light. Then he ventured indoors—listened, and heard nothing—looked into kitchen, scullery, parlour, and found nothing; went up, at last, into the bedroom—it was empty. A picklock lay on the floor, betraying how she had gained entrance in the night, and that was the only trace of her.

Whither had she gone? That no mortal tongue could tell him. The darkness had covered her flight; and when the day broke, no man could say where the light found her.

Before leaving the house and the town for ever, he gave instructions to a friend and neighbour to sell his furniture for anything that it would fetch, and apply the proceeds to employing the police to trace her. The directions were honestly followed and the money was all spent, but the inquiries led to nothing. The picklock on the bedroom floor remained the one last useless trace of the Dream-Woman.

At this point of the narrative the landlord paused, and, turning towards the window of the room in which we were sitting, looked in the direction of the stableyard.

"So far," he said, "I tell you what was told to me. The little that remains to be added lies within my own experience. Between two and three months after the events I have just been relating, Isaac Scatchard came to me, withered and old-looking before his time, just as you saw him to-day. He had his testimonials to character with him, and he asked for employment here. Knowing that my wife and he were distantly related, I gave him a trial in consideration of that relationship, and liked him in spite of his queer habits. He is as sober, honest, and willing a man as there is in England. As for his restlessness at night, and his sleeping away his leisure time in the day, who can wonder at it after hearing his story? Besides, he never objects to being roused up when he's wanted, so there's not much inconvenience to complain of, after all."

"I suppose he is afraid of a return of that dreadful dream, and of waking out of it in the dark?" said I.

"No," returned the landlord. "The dream comes back to him so often that he has got to bear with it by this time resignedly enough. It's his wife keeps him waking at night, as he has often told me."

"What! Has she never been heard of yet?"

"Never. Isaac himself has the one perpetual thought about her, that she is alive and looking for him. I believe he wouldn't let himself drop off to sleep towards two in the morning for a king's ransom. Two in the morning, he says, is the time she will find him, one of these days. Two in the morning is the time all the year round when he likes to be most certain that he has got that clasp-knife safe about him. He does not mind being alone as long as he is awake, except on the night before his birthday, when he firmly believes himself to be in peril of his life. The birthday has only come round once since he has been here, and then he sat up along with the night-porter. "She's looking for me," is all he says when anybody speaks to him about the one anxiety of his life; "she's looking for me." He may be right. She *may* be looking for him. Who can tell?"

"Who can tell?" said I.

A Terribly Strange Bed

Shortly after my education at college was finished, I happened to be staying at Paris with an English friend. We were both young men then, and lived, I am afraid, rather a wild life, in the delightful city of our sojourn. One night we were idling about the neighbour-hood of the Palais Royal, doubtful to what amusement we should next betake ourselves. My friend proposed a visit to Frascati's; but his suggestion was not to my taste. I knew Frascati's, as the French saying is, by heart; had lost and won plenty of five-franc pieces there, merely for amusement's sake, until it was amusement no longer, and was thoroughly tired, in fact, of all the ghastly respect-abilities of such a social anomaly as a respectable gambling-house. "For Heaven's sake," said I to my friend, "let us go somewhere where we can see a little genuine, blackguard, poverty-stricken gaming with no false gingerbread glitter thrown over it all. Let us get away from fashionable Frascati's, to a house where they don't mind letting in a man with a ragged coat, or a man with no coat, ragged or otherwise." "Very well," said my friend, "we needn't go out of the Palais Royal to find the sort of company you want. Here's the place just before us; as blackguard a place, by all report, as you could possibly wish to see." In another minute we arrived at the door and entered the house.

When we got upstairs, and had left our hats and sticks with the doorkeeper, we were admitted into the chief gambling-room. We did not find many people assembled there. But, few as the men were who looked up at us on our entrance, they were all types—lamentably true types—of their respective classes.

We had come to see blackguards; but these men were something worse. There is a comic side, more or less appreciable, in all blackguardism—here there was nothing but tragedy—mute, weird tragedy. The quiet in the room was horrible. The thin, haggard, long-haired young man, whose sunken eyes fiercely watched the turning up of the cards, never spoke; the flabby, fat-faced, pimply player, who pricked his piece of pasteboard perseveringly, to register how often black won, and how often red—never spoke; the dirty, wrinkled old man, with the vulture eyes and the darned great-coat, who had lost his last *sou,* and still looked on desperately, after he could play no longer—never spoke. Even the voice of the croupier sounded as if it were strangely dulled and thickened in the atmosphere of the room. I had entered the place to laugh, but the spectacle before me was something to weep over. I soon found it necessary to take refuge in excitement from the depression of spirits which was fast stealing on me. Unfortunately I sought the nearest excitement, by going to the table and beginning to play. Still more unfortunately, as the event will show, I won—won prodigiously; won incredibly; won at such a rate that the regular players at the table crowded round me; and staring at my stakes with hungry, superstitious eyes, whispered to one another that the English stranger was going to break the bank.

The game was *Rouge et Noir.* I had played at it in every city in Europe, without, however, the care or the wish to study the Theory of Chances—that philosopher's stone of all gamblers! And a gambler, in the strict sense of the word, I had never been. I was heartwhole from the corroding passion for play. My gaming was a mere idle amusement. I never resorted to it by necessity, because I never knew what it was to want money. I never practised it so incessantly as to lose more than I could afford, or to gain more than I could coolly pocket without being thrown off my balance by my good luck. In short, I had hitherto frequented gambling-tables—just as I frequented ballrooms and opera-houses—because they amused me, and because I had nothing better to do with my leisure hours.

But on this occasion it was very different—now, for the first time in my life, I felt what the passion for play really was. My success first bewildered, and then, in the most literal meaning of the word, intoxicated me. Incredible as it may appear, it is nevertheless true, that I only lost when I attempted to estimate chances, and played according to previous calculation. If I left everything to luck, and staked without any care or consideration, I was sure to win—to win in the face of every recognized probability in favour of the bank. At first some of the men present ventured their money safely enough on my colour; but I speedily increased my stakes to sums which they dared not risk. One after another they left off playing, and breathlessly looked on at my game.

Still, time after time, I staked higher and higher, and still won. The excitement in the room rose to fever pitch. The silence was interrupted by a deep-muttered chorus of oaths and exclamations in different languages, every time the gold was shovelled across to my side of the table—even the imperturbable croupier dashed his rake on the floor in a (French) fury of astonishment at my success. But one man present preserved his self-possession, and that man was my friend. He came to my side, and whispering in English, begged me to leave the place, satisfied with what I had already gained. I must do him the justice to say that he repeated his warnings and entreaties several times, and only left me and went away after I had rejected his advice (I was to all intents and purposes gambling drunk) in terms which rendered it impossible for him to address me again that night.

Shortly after he had gone, a hoarse voice behind me cried: "Permit me, my dear sir—permit me to restore to their proper place two napoleons which you have dropped. Wonderful luck, sir! I pledge you my word of honour, as an old soldier, in the course of my long experience in this sort of thing, I never saw such luck as yours—never! Go on, sir—*Sacré mille bombes!* Go on boldly, and break the bank!"

I turned round and saw, nodding and smiling at me with inveterate civility, a tall man, dressed in a frogged and braided surtout.

If I had been in my senses, I should have considered him, personally, as being rather a suspicious specimen of an old soldier. He had goggling, blood-shot eyes, mangy moustaches, and a broken nose. His voice betrayed a barrack-room intonation of the worst order, and he had the dirtiest pair of hands I ever saw—even in France. These little personal peculiarities exercised, however, no repelling influence on me. In the mad excitement, the reckless triumph of that moment, I was ready to "fraternize" with anybody who encouraged me in my game. I accepted the old soldier's offered pinch of snuff; clapped him on the back, and swore he was the honestest fellow in the world —the most glorious relic of the Grand Army that I had ever met with. "Go on!" cried my military friend, snapping his fingers in ecstasy—"Go on, and win! Break the bank—*Mille tonnerres!* my gallant English comrade, break the bank!"

And I *did* go on—went on at such a rate, that in another quarter of an hour the croupier called out, "Gentlemen, the bank has discontinued for to-night." All the notes, and all the gold in that "bank," now lay in a heap under my hands; the whole floating capital of the gambling-house was waiting to pour into my pockets!

"Tie up the money in your pocket-handkerchief, my worthy sir," said the old soldier, as I wildly plunged my hands into my heap of gold. "Tie it up, as we used to tie up a bit of dinner in the Grand Army; your winnings are too heavy for any breeches-pockets that ever were sewed. There! that's it—shovel them in, notes and all! *Credié!* what luck! Stop! another napoleon on the floor! *Ah! sacré petit polison de Napoleon!* have I found thee at last? Now then, Sir—two tight double knots each way with your honourable permission, and the money's safe. Feel it! feel it, fortunate sir! hard and round as a cannon-ball—*Ah, bah!* if they had only fired such cannon-balls at us at Austerlitz—*nom d'une pipe!* if they only had! And now, as an ancient grenadier, as an ex-brave of the French army, what remains for me to do? I ask what? Simply this, to entreat my valued English friend to drink a bottle of champagne with me, and toast the goddess Fortune in foaming goblets before we part!"

Excellent ex-brave! Convivial ancient grenadier! Champagne by all means! An English cheer for an old soldier! Hurrah! hurrah! Another English cheer for the goddess Fortune! Hurrah! hurrah! hurrah!

"Bravo! the Englishman; the amiable, gracious Englishman, in whose veins circulates the vivacious blood of France! Another glass? *Ah, bah!*—the bottle is empty! Never mind! *Vive le vin!* I, the old soldier, order another bottle, and half a pound of *bonbons* with it!"

"No, no, ex-brave; never—ancient grenadier! *Your* bottle last time; *my* bottle this. Behold it! Toast away! The French Army! the great Napoleon! the present company! the croupier! the honest croupier's wife and daughters—if he has any! the Ladies generally! everybody in the world!"

By the time the second bottle of champagne was emptied, I felt as if I had been drinking liquid fire—my brain seemed all aflame. No excess in wine had ever had this effect on me before in my life. Was it the result of a stimulant acting upon my system when I was in a highly excited state? Was my stomach in a particularly disordered condition? Or was the champagne amazingly strong?

"Ex-brave of the French Army!" cried I, in a mad state of exhilaration, "*I* am on fire! how are *you?* You have set me on fire. Do you hear, my hero of Austerlitz? Let us have a third bottle of champagne to put the flame out!"

The old soldier wagged his head, rolled his goggle-eyes, until I expected to see them slip out of their sockets, placed his dirty forefinger by the side of his broken nose; solemnly ejaculated "Coffee!" and immediately ran off into an inner room.

The word pronounced by the eccentric veteran seemed to have a magical effect on the rest of the company present. With one accord they all rose to depart. Probably they had expected to profit by my intoxication; but finding that my new friend was benevolently bent on preventing me from getting dead drunk, had now abandoned all hope of thriving pleasantly on my winnings. Whatever their motive might be, at any rate they went away in a body. When the old soldier returned, and sat down again opposite to me at the table, we had the room to ourselves. I could see the croupier in a sort of vestibule which opened out of it, eating his supper in solitude. The silence was now deeper than ever.

A sudden change, too, had come over the "ex-brave." He assumed a portentously solemn look; and when he spoke to me again, his speech was ornamented by no oaths, enforced by no finger-snapping, enlivened by no apostrophes or exclamations.

"Listen, my dear sir," said he, in mysteriously confidential tones—"listen to an old soldier's advice. I have been to the mistress of the house (a very charming woman, with a genius for cookery!) to impress on her the necessity of making us some particularly strong and good coffee. You must drink this coffee in order to get rid of your little amiable exaltation of spirits before you think of going home—you *must,* my good and gracious friend! With all that money to take home to-night, it is a sacred duty to yourself to have your wits about you. You are known to be a winner to an enormous extent by several gentlemen present to-night, who, in a certain point of view, are very worthy and excellent fellows; but they are mortal men, my dear sir, and they have their amiable weaknesses. Need I say more? Ah, no, no! you understand me! Now, this is what you must do—send for a cabriolet when you feel quite well again—draw up all the windows when you get into it—and tell the driver to take you home only through the large and well-lighted thoroughfares. Do this; and you and your money will be safe. Do this; and to-morrow you will thank an old soldier for giving you a word of honest advice."

Just as the ex-brave ended his oration in very lachrymose tones, the coffee came in, ready poured out in two cups. My attentive friend handed me one of the cups with a bow. I was parched with thirst, and drank it off at a draught. Almost instantly afterward, I was seized with a fit of giddiness, and felt more completely intoxicated than ever. The room whirled round and round furiously; the old soldier seemed to be regularly bobbing up and down before me like the piston of a steam-engine. I was half deafened by a violent singing in my ears; a feeling of utter bewilderment, helplessness, idiocy, overcame me. I rose from my chair, holding on by the table to keep my balance; and stammered out that I felt dreadfully unwell—so unwell that I did not know how I was to get home.

"My dear friend," answered the old soldier—and even his voice seemed to be bobbing up and down as he spoke—"my dear friend, it would be madness to go home in *your* state; you would be sure to lose your money; you might be robbed and murdered with the greatest ease. *I* am going to sleep here; do *you* sleep here, too— they make up capital beds in this house —take one; sleep off the effects of the wine, and go home safely with your winnings to-morrow—to-morrow, in broad daylight."

I had but two ideas left: one, that I must never let go hold of my handkerchief full of money; the other, that I must lie down somewhere immediately, and fall off into a comfortable sleep. So I agreed to the·proposal about the bed, and took the offered arm of the old soldier, carrying my money with my disengaged hand. Preceded by the croupier, we passed along some passages and up a flight of stairs into the bedroom which I was to occupy. The ex-brave shook me warmly by the hand, proposed that we should breakfast together, and then, followed by the croupier, left me for the night.

I ran to the wash-hand stand; drank some of the water in my jug; poured the rest out, and plunged my face into it; then sat down in a chair and tried to compose myself. I soon felt better. The change for my lungs, from the fetid atmosphere of the gambling-room to the cool air of the apartment I now occupied, the almost equally refreshing change for my eyes, from the glaring gaslights of the "salon" to the dim, quiet flicker of one bedroom-candle, aided wonderfully the restorative effects of cold water. The giddiness left me, and I began to feel a little like a reasonable being again. My first thought was of the risk of sleeping all night in a gambling-house; my second, of the still greater risk of trying to get out after the house was closed, and of going home alone at night through the streets of Paris with a large sum of money about me. I had slept in worse places than this on my travels; so I determined to lock, bolt, and barricade my door, and take my chance till the next morning.

Accordingly, I secured myself against all intrusion; looked under the bed, and into the cupboard; tried the fastening of the window; and then, satisfied that I had taken every proper precaution, pulled off my upper clothing, put my light, which was a dim one, on the hearth among a feathery litter of wood-ashes, and got into bed, with the handkerchief full of money under my pillow.

I soon felt not only that I could not go to sleep, but that I could not even close my eyes. I was wide awake, and in a high fever. Every nerve in my body trembled—every one of my senses seemed to be preternaturally sharpened. I tossed and rolled, and tried every kind of position, and perseveringly sought out the cold corners of the bed, and all to no purpose. Now I thrust my arms over the clothes: now I poked them under the clothes; now I violently shot my legs straight out down to the bottom of the bed; now I convulsively coiled them up as near my chin as they would go; now I shook out my crumpled pillow, changed it to the cool side, patted it flat, and lay down quietly on my back; now I fiercely doubled it in two, set it up on end, thrust it against the board of the bed, and tried a sitting posture. Every effort was in vain; I groaned with vexation as I felt that I was in for a sleepless night.

What could I do? I had no book to read. And yet, unless I found out some method of diverting my mind, I felt certain that I was in the condition to imagine all sorts of horrors; to rack my brain with forebodings of every possible and impossible danger; in short, to pass the night in suffering all conceivable varieties of nervous terror.

I raised myself on my elbow, and looked about the room—which was brightened by a lovely moonlight pouring straight through the window—to see if it contained any pictures or ornaments that I could at all clearly distinguish. While my eyes wandered from wall to wall, a remembrance of Le Maistre's delightful little book, *Voyage autour de ma Chambre,* occurred to me. I resolved to imitate the French author, and find occupation and amusement enough to relieve the tedium of my wakefulness, by making a mental inventory of every article of furniture I could see, and by following up to their sources the multitude of associations which even a chair, a table, or a wash-hand stand may be made to call forth.

In the nervous unsettled state of my mind at that moment, I found it much easier to make my inventory than to make my reflections, and thereupon soon gave up all hope of thinking in Le Maistre's fanciful track—or, indeed, of thinking at all. I looked about the room at the different articles of furniture, and did nothing more.

There was, first, the bed I was lying in; a four-post bed, of all things in the world to meet with in Paris—yes, a thorough clumsy British four-poster, with a regular top lined with chintz —the regular fringed valance all round—the regular stifling, unwholesome curtains, which I remembered having mechanically drawn back against the posts without particularly noticing the bed when I first got into the room. Then there was the marble-topped, wash-hand stand, from which the water I had spilled, in my hurry to pour it out, was still dripping, slowly and more slowly, on to the brick floor. Then two small chairs, with my coat, waistcoat, and trousers flung on them. Then a large elbow-chair covered with dirty-white dimity, and my cravat and shirt collar thrown over the back. Then a chest of drawers with two of the brass handles off, and a tawdry, broken china inkstand placed on it by way of ornament for the top. Then the dressing-table, adorned by a very small looking-glass, and a very large pincushion. Then the window—an unusually large window. Then a dark old picture, which the feeble candle dimly showed me. It was a picture of a fellow in high Spanish hat, crowned with a plume of towering feathers. A swarthy, sinister ruffian, looking upward, shading his eyes with his hand, and looking intently upward—it might be at some tall gallows at which he was going to be hanged. At any rate, he had the appearance of thoroughly deserving it.

This picture put a kind of constraint upon me to look upward too—at the top of the bed. It was a gloomy and not an interesting object, and I looked back at the picture. I counted the feathers in the man's hat—they stood out in relief—three white, two green. I observed the crown of his hat, which was of conical shape, according to the fashion supposed to have been favoured by Guido Fawkes. I wondered what he was looking up at. It couldn't be at the stars; such a desperado was neither astrologer nor astronomer. It must be at the high gallows, and he was going to be hanged presently. Would the executioner come into possession of his conical crowned hat and plume of feathers? I counted the feathers again—three white, two green.

While I still lingered over this very improving and intellectual employment, my thoughts insensibly began to wander. The moonlight shining into the room reminded me of a certain moonlight night in England—the night after a picnic party in a Welsh valley. Every incident of the drive homeward, through lovely scenery, which the moonlight made lovelier than ever, came back to my remembrance, though I had never given the picnic a thought for years; though, if I had *tried* to recollect it, I could certainly have recalled little or nothing of that scene long past. Of all the wonderful faculties that help to tell us we are immortal, which speaks the sublime truth more eloquently than memory? Here was I, in a strange house of the most suspicious character, in a situation of uncertainty, and even of peril, which might seem to make the cool exercise of my recollection almost out of the question; nevertheless, remembering, quite involuntarily, places, people, conversations, minute circumstances of every kind, which I had thought forgotten for ever; which I could not possibly have recalled at will, even under the most favourable auspices. And what cause had produced in a moment the whole of this strange, complicated, mysterious effect? Nothing but some rays of moonlight shining in at my bedroom window.

I was still thinking of the picnic—of our merriment on the drive home—of the sentimental young lady who *would* quote "Childe Harold" because it was moonlight. I was absorbed by these past scenes and past amusements, when, in an instant, the thread on which my memories hung snapped asunder; my attention immediately came back to present things more vividly than ever, and I found myself, I neither knew why nor wherefore, looking hard at the picture again.

Looking for what?

Good God! the man had pulled his hat down on his brows! No!

the hat itself was gone! Where was the conical crown? Where the feathers—three white, two green? Not there! In place of the hat and feathers, what dusky object was it that now hid his forehead, his eyes, his shading hand?

Was the bed moving?

I turned on my back and looked up. Was I mad? drunk? dreaming? giddy again? or was the top of the bed really moving down—sinking slowly, regularly, silently, horribly, right down throughout the whole of its length and breadth—right down upon me, as I lay underneath?

My blood seemed to stand still. A deadly paralysing coldness stole all over me as I turned my head round on the pillow and determined to test whether the bed-top was really moving or not, by keeping my eye on the man in the picture.

The next look in that direction was enough. The dull, black, frowzy outline of the valance above me was within an inch of being parallel with his waist. I still looked breathlessly. And steadily and slowly—very slowly—I saw the figure, and the line of frame below the figure, vanish, as the valance moved down before it.

I am, constitutionally, anything but timid. I have been on more than one occasion in peril of my life, and have not lost my self-possession for an instant; but when the conviction first settled on my mind that the bed-top was really moving, was steadily and continuously sinking down upon me, I looked up shuddering, helpless, panic-stricken, beneath the hideous machinery for murder, which was advancing closer and closer to suffocate me where I lay.

I looked up, motionless, speechless, breathless. The candle, fully spent, went out; but the moonlight still brightened the room. Down and down, without pausing and without sounding, came the bed-top, and still my panic terror seemed to bind me faster and faster to the mattress on which I lay—down and down it sank, till the dusty odour from the lining of the canopy came stealing into my nostrils.

At that final moment the instinct of self-preservation startled me out of my trance, and I moved at last. There was just room for me to roll myself sidewise off the bed. As I dropped noiselessly to the floor, the edge of the murderous canopy touched me on the shoulder.

Without stopping to draw my breath, without wiping the cold sweat from my face, I rose instantly on my knees to watch the bed-top. I was literally spellbound by it. If I had heard footsteps behind me, I could not have turned round; if a means of escape had been miraculously provided for me, I could not have moved to take advantage of it. The whole life in me was, at that moment, concentrated in my eyes.

It descended—the whole canopy, with the fringe round it, came down—down—close down; so close that there was not room now to squeeze my finger between the bed-top and the bed. I felt at the sides, and discovered that what had appeared to me from beneath to be the ordinary light canopy of a four-post bed was in reality a thick, broad mattress, the substance of which was concealed by the valance and its fringe. I looked up and saw the four posts rising hideously bare. In the middle of the bed-top was a huge wooden screw that had evidently worked it down through a hole in the ceiling, just as ordinary presses are worked down on the substance selected for compression. The frightful apparatus moved without making the faintest noise. There had been no creaking as it came down; there was now not the faintest sound from the room above. Amid a dead and awful silence I beheld before me—in the nineteenth century, and in the civilized capital of France—such a machine for secret murder by suffocation as might have existed in the worst days of the Inquisition, in the lonely inns among the Hartz Mountains, in the mysterious tribunals of Westphalia! Still, as I looked on it, I could not move, I could hardly breathe, but I began to recover the power of thinking, and in a moment I discovered the murderous conspiracy framed against me in all its horror.

My cup of coffee had been drugged, and drugged too strongly. I had been saved from being smothered by having taken an overdose of some narcotic. How I had chafed and fretted at the fever fit which had preserved my life by keeping me awake! How recklessly I had confided myself to the two wretches who had led me into this room, determined, for the sake of my winnings, to kill me in my sleep by the surest and most horrible contrivance for secretly accomplishing my destruction! How many men, winners like me, had slept, as I had proposed to sleep, in that bed, and had never been seen or heard of more! I shuddered at the bare idea of it.

But ere long all thought was again suspended by the sight of the murderous canopy moving once more. After it had remained on the bed—as nearly as I could guess—about ten minutes, it began to move up again. The villains who worked it from above evidently believed that their purpose was now accomplished. Slowly and silently, as it had descended, that horrible bed-top rose towards its former place. When it reached the upper extremities of the four posts, it reached the ceiling, too. Neither hole nor screw could be seen; the bed became in appearance an ordinary bed again—the canopy an ordinary canopy—even to the most suspicious eyes.

Now, for the first time, I was able to move—to rise from my knees—to dress myself in my upper clothing—and to consider of how I should escape. If I betrayed by the smallest noise that the attempt to suffocate me had failed, I was certain to be murdered. Had I made any noise already? I listened intently, looking towards the door.

No! no footsteps in the passage outside—no sound of a tread, light or heavy, in the room above—absolute silence everywhere. Besides locking and bolting my door, I had moved an only wooden chest against it, which I had found under the bed. To remove this chest (my blood ran cold as I though of what its contents *might* be!) without making some disturbance was impossible; and, moreover, to think of escaping through the house, now barred up for the night, was sheer insanity. Only one chance was left me—the window. I stole to it on tiptoe.

My bedroom was on the first floor, above an *entresol*, and looked into a back street. I raised my hand to open the window, knowing that on that action hung, by the merest hair-breadth, my chance of safety. They keep vigilant watch in a House of Murder. If any part of the frame cracked, if the hinge creaked, I was a lost man! It must have occupied me at least five minutes, reckoning by time—five *hours*, reckoning by suspense—to open that window. I succeeded in doing it silently—in doing it with all the dexterity of a house-breaker—and then looked down into the street. To leap the distance beneath me would be almost certain destruction! Next, I looked round at the sides of the house. Down the left side ran a thick water pipe—it passed close by the outer edge of the window. The moment I saw the pipe I knew I was saved. My breath came and went freely for the first time since I had seen the canopy of the bed moving down upon me!

To some men the means of escape which I had discovered might have seemed difficult and dangerous enough—to *me* the prospect of slipping down the pipe into the street did not suggest even a thought of peril. I had always been accustomed, by the practice of gymnastics, to keep up my schoolboy powers as a daring and expert climber; and knew that my head, hands, and feet would serve me faithfully in any hazards of ascent or descent. I had already got one leg over the window-sill, when I remembered the handkerchief filled with money under my pillow. I could well have afforded to leave it behind me, but I was revengefully determined that the miscreants of the gambling house should miss their plunder as well as their victim. So I went back to the bed and tied the heavy handkerchief at my back by my cravat.

Just as I had made it tight and fixed it in a comfortable place, I thought I heard a sound of breathing outside the door. The chill feeling of horror ran through me again as I listened. No! dead silence still in the passage—I had only heard the night air blowing softly into the room. The next moment I was on the window-sill— and the next I had a firm grip on the water-pipe with my hands and knees.

I slid down into the street easily and quietly, as I thought I should, and immediately set off at the top of my speed to a branch Prefecture of Police, which I knew was situated in the immediate neighbourhood. A Sub-prefect, and several picked men among his subordinates, happened to be up, maturing, I believe, some scheme for discovering the perpetrator of a mysterious murder which all Paris was talking of just then. When I began my story, in a breathless hurry and in very bad French, I could see that the Sub-prefect suspected me of being a drunken Englishman who had robbed somebody; but he soon altered his opinion as I went on, and before I had anything like concluded, he shoved all the papers before him into a drawer, put on his hat, supplied me with another (for I was bare-headed), ordered a file of soldiers, desired his expert followers to get ready all sorts of tools for breaking open doors and ripping up brick flooring, and took my arm, in the most friendly and familiar manner possible, to lead me with him out of the house. I will venture to say that when the Sub-prefect was a little boy, and was taken for the first time to the play, he was not half as much pleased as he was now at the job in prospect for him at the gambling-house!

Away we went through the streets, the Sub-prefect cross-examining and congratulating me in the same breath as we marched at the head of our formidable *posse comitatus*. Sentinels were placed at the back and front of the house the moment we got to it; a tremendous battery of knocks was directed against the door; a light appeared at a window; I was told to conceal myself behind the police—then came more knocks and a cry of "Open in the name of the law!" At that terrible summons bolts and locks gave way before an invisible hand, and the moment after the Sub-prefect was in the passage, confronting a waiter half-dressed and ghastly pale. This was the short dialogue which immediately took place:

"We want to see the Englishman who is sleeping in this house."

"He went away hours ago."

"He did no such thing. His friend went away; *he* remained. Show us to his bedroom!"

"I swear to you, Monsieur le Sous-prefect, he is not here! he——"

"I swear to you, Monsieur le Garçon, he is. He slept here—he didn't find your bed comfortable—he came to us to complain of it—here he is among my men—and here am I ready to look for a flea or two in his bedstead. Renaudin!"—calling to one of the subordinates, and pointing to the waiter—"collar that man and tie his hands behind him. Now, then, gentlemen, let us walk upstairs!"

Every man and woman in the house was secured—the "Old Soldier" the first. Then I identified the bed in which I had slept, and then we went into the room above.

No object that was at all extraordinary appeared in any part of it. The Sub-prefect looked round the place, commanded everybody to be silent, stamped twice on the floor, called for a candle, looked attentively at the spot he had stamped on, and ordered the flooring there to be carefully taken up. This was done in no time. Lights were produced, and we saw a deep raftered cavity between the floor of this room and the ceiling of the room beneath. Through this cavity there ran perpendicularly a sort of case of iron thickly greased; and inside the case appeared the screw, which communicated with the bed-top below. Extra lengths of screw, freshly oiled; levers covered with felt; all the complete upper works of a heavy press—constructed with infernal ingenuity so as to join the fixtures below, and when taken to pieces again, to go into the smallest possible compass—were next discovered and pulled out on the floor. After some little difficulty the Sub-prefect succeeded in putting the machinery together, and, leaving his men to work it, descended with me to the bedroom. The smothering canopy was then lowered, but not so noiselessly as I had seen it lowered. When I mentioned this to the Sub-prefect, his answer, simple as it was, had a terrible significance. "My men," said he, "are working down the bed-top for the first time—the men whose money you won were in better practice."

We left the house in the sole possession of two police agents—every one of the inmates being removed to prison on the spot. The Sub-prefect, after taking down my *procès verbal* in his office, returned with me to my hotel to get my passport. "Do you think," I asked, as I gave it to him, "that any men have really been smothered in that bed, as they tried to smother *me?*"

"I have seen dozens of drowned men laid out at the Morgue," answered the Sub-prefect, "in whose pocketbooks were found letters stating that they had committed suicide in the Seine, because they had lost everything at the gaming table. Do I know how many of those men entered the same gambling-house that *you* entered? won as *you* won? took that bed as *you* took it? slept in it? were smothered in it? and were privately thrown into the river, with a letter of explanation written by the murderers and placed in their pocketbooks? No man can say how many or how few have suffered the fate from which you have escaped. The people of the gambling-house kept their bedstead machinery a secret from *us*—even from the police! The dead kept the rest of the secret for them. Good night, or rather good morning, Monsieur Faulkner! Be at my office again at nine o'clock—in the meantime, *au revoir!*"

The rest of my story is soon told. I was examined and re-examined; the gambling-house was strictly searched all through from top to bottom; the prisoners were separately interrogated; and two of the less guilty among them made a confession. I discovered that the Old Soldier was the master of the gambling-house—*justice* discovered that he had been drummed out of the army as a vagabond years ago; that he had been guilty of all sorts of villainies since; that he was in possession of stolen property, which the owners identified; and that he, the croupier, another accomplice, and the woman who had made my cup of coffee, were all in the secret of the bedstead. There appeared some reason to doubt whether the inferior persons attached to the house knew anything of the suffocating machinery; and they received the benefit of that doubt, by being treated simply as thieves and vagabonds. As for the Old Soldier and his two head myrmidons, they went to the galleys; the woman who had drugged my coffee was imprisoned for I forget how many years; the regular attendants at the gambling-house were considered "suspicious" and placed under "surveillance"; and I became, for one whole week (which is a long time) the head "lion" in Parisian society. My adventure was dramatized by three illustrious playmakers, but never saw theatrical daylight; for the censorship forbade the introduction on the stage of a correct copy of the gambling-house bedstead.

One good result was produced by my adventure, which any censorship must have approved: it cured me of ever again trying *Rouge et Noir* as an amusement. The sight of a green cloth, with packs of cards and heaps of money on it, will henceforth be for ever associated in my mind with the sight of a bed canopy descending to suffocate me in the silence and darkness of the night.

The Dead Hand

When this present nineteenth century was younger by a good many years than it is now, a certain friend of mine, named Arthur Holliday, happened to arrive in the town of Doncaster exactly in the middle of the race-week, or, in other words, in the middle of the month of September.

He was one of those reckless, rattle-pated, open-hearted, and open-mouthed young gentlemen who possess the gift of familiarity in its highest perfection, and who scramble carelessly along the journey of life, making friends, as the phrase is, wherever they go. His father was a rich manufacturer, and had bought landed property enough in one of the midland counties to make all the born squires in his neighbourhood thoroughly envious of him. Arthur was his only son, possessor in prospect of the great estate and the great business after his father's death; well supplied with money, and not too rigidly looked after during his father's lifetime. Report, or scandal, whichever you please, said that the old gentleman had been rather wild in his youthful days, and that, unlike most parents, he was not disposed to be violently indignant when he found that his son took after him. This may be true or not. I myself only knew the elder Mr. Holliday when he was getting on in years, and then he was as quiet and respectable a gentleman as ever I met with.

Well, one September, as I told you, young Arthur comes to Doncaster, having decided all of a sudden, in his hare-brained way, that he would go to the races. He did not reach the town till towards the close of evening, and he went at once to see about his dinner and bed at the principal hotel. Dinner they were ready enough to give him, but as for a bed, they laughed when he mentioned it. In the race-week at Doncaster it is no uncommon thing for visitors who have not bespoken apartments to pass the night in their carriages at the inn doors. As for the lower sort of strangers, I myself have often seen them, at that full time, sleeping out on the door-steps for want of a covered place to creep under. Rich as he was, Arthur's chance of getting a night's lodging (seeing that he had not written beforehand to secure one) was more than doubtful. He tried the second hotel, and the third hotel, and two of the inferior inns after that, and was met everywhere with the same form of answer. No accommodation for the night of any sort was left. All the bright golden sovereigns in his pocket would not buy him a bed at Doncaster in the race-week.

To a young fellow of Arthur's temperament, the novelty of being turned away into the street like a penniless vagabond, at every house where he asked for a lodging, presented itself in the light of a new and highly amusing piece of experience. He went on with his carpet-bag in his hand, applying for a bed at every place of entertainment for travellers that he could find in Doncaster, until he wandered into the outskirts of the town.

By this time the last glimmer of twilight had faded out, the moon was rising dimly in a mist, the wind was getting cold, the clouds were gathering heavily, and there was every prospect that it was soon going to rain!

The look of the night had rather a lowering effect on young Holliday's good spirits. He began to contemplate the houseless situation in which he was placed from the serious rather than the humorous point of view, and he looked about him for another public house to inquire at with something very like downright anxiety in his mind on the subject of a lodging for the night.

The suburban part of the town towards which he had now strayed was hardly lighted at all, and he could see nothing of the houses as he passed them, except that they got progressively smaller and dirtier the farther he went. Down the winding road before him shone the dull gleam of an oil lamp, the one faint lonely light that struggled ineffectually with the foggy darkness all round him. He resolved to go on as far as this lamp, and then, if it showed him nothing in the shape of an inn, to return to the central part of the town, and to try if he could not at least secure a chair to sit down on through the night at one of the principal hotels.

As he got near the lamp he heard voices, and, walking close under it, found that it lighted the entrance to a narrow court, on the wall of which was painted a long hand in faded flesh-colour, pointing with a lean forefinger, to this inscription:

THE TWO ROBINS

Arthur turned into the court without hesitation to see what The Two Robins could do for him. Four or five men were standing together round the door of the house, which was at the bottom of the court, facing the entrance from the street. The men were all listening to one other man, better dressed than the rest, who was telling his audience something, in a low voice, in which they were apparently very much interested.

On entering the passage, Arthur was passed by a stranger with a knapsack in his hand, who was evidently leaving the house.

"No," said the traveller with the knapsack, turning round and addressing himself cheerfully to a fat, sly-looking bald-headed man, with a dirty white apron on, who had followed him down the passage, "no, Mr. Landlord, I am not easily scared by trifles; but I don't mind confessing that I can't quite stand *that.*"

It occurred to young Holliday, the moment he heard these words, that the stranger had been asked an exorbitant price for a bed at The Two Robins, and that he was unable or unwilling to pay it. The moment his back was turned, Arthur, comfortably conscious of his own well-filled pockets, addressed himself in a great hurry, for fear any other benighted traveller should slip in and forestall him, to the sly-looking landlord with the dirty apron and the bald head.

"If you have got a bed to let," he said, "and if that gentleman who has just gone out won't pay your price for it, I will."

The sly landlord looked hard at Arthur.

"Will you, sir?" he asked, in a meditative, doubtful way.

"Name your price," said young Holliday, thinking that the landlord's hesitation sprang from some boorish distrust of him. "Name your price, and I'll give you the money at once, if you like."

"Are you game for five shillings?" inquired the landlord, rubbing his stubbly double chin, and looking up thoughtfully at the ceiling above him.

Arthur nearly laughed in the man's face; but, thinking it prudent to control himself, offered the five shillings as seriously as he could. The sly landlord held out his hand, then suddenly drew it back again.

"You're acting all fair and aboveboard by me," he said, "and, before I take your money, I'll do the same by you. Look here; this is how it stands. You can have a bed all to yourself for five shillings, but you can't have more than a half share of the room it stands in. Do you see what I mean, young gentleman?"

"Of course I do," returned Arthur, a little irritably. "You mean that it is a double-bedded room, and that one of the beds is occupied?"

The landlord nodded his head, and rubbed his double chin harder than ever. Arthur hesitated, and mechanically moved back a step or two towards the door. The idea of sleeping in the same room with a total stranger did not present an attractive prospect to him. He felt more than half inclined to drop his five shillings into his pocket, and to go out into the street once more.

"Is it yes or no?" asked the landlord. "Settle it as quick as you can, because there's lots of people wanting a bed at Doncaster to-night besides you."

Arthur looked towards the court, and heard the rain falling heavily in the street outside. He thought he would ask a question or two before he rashly decided on leaving the shelter of The Two Robins.

"What sort of man is it who has got the other bed?" he inquired. "Is he a gentleman? I mean, is he a quiet, well-behaved person?"

"The quietest man I ever came across," said the landlord, rubbing his fat hands stealthily one over the other. "As sober as a judge, and as regular as clock-work in his habits. It hasn't struck nine not ten minutes ago, and he's in his bed already. I don't know whether that comes up to your notion of a quiet man: it goes a long way ahead of mine, I can tell you."

"Is he asleep, do you think?" asked Arthur.

"I know he's asleep," returned the landlord; "and what's more, he's gone off so fast that I'll warrant you don't wake him. This way, sir," said the landlord, speaking over young Holliday's shoulder, as if he was addressing some new guest who was approaching the house.

"Here you are," said Arthur, determined to be beforehand with the stranger, whoever he might be. "I'll take the bed." And he handed the five shillings to the landlord, who nodded, dropped the money carelessly into his waistcoat pocket, and lighted a candle.

"Come up and see the room," said the host of The Two Robins, leading the way to the staircase quite briskly, considering how fat he was.

They mounted to the second floor of the house. The landlord half opened a door fronting the landing, then stopped, and turned round to Arthur.

"It's a fair bargain, mind, on my side as well as on yours," he said. "You give me five shillings, and I give you in return a clean, comfortable bed; and I warrant, beforehand, that you won't be interfered with, or annoyed in any way, by the man who sleeps in the same room with you." Saying those words, he looked hard, for a moment, in young Holliday's face, and then led the way into the room.

It was larger and cleaner than Arthur had expected it would be. The two beds stood parallel with each other, a space of about six feet intervening between them. They were both of the same medium size, and both had the same plain white curtains, made to draw, if necessary, all round them.

The occupied bed was the bed nearest the window. The curtains were all drawn round it except the half curtain at the bottom, on the side of the bed farthest from the window. Arthur saw the feet of the sleeping man raising the scanty clothes into a sharp little eminence, as if he was lying flat on his back. He took the candle, and advanced softly to draw the curtain—stopped half-way, and listened for a moment—then turned to the landlord.

"He is a very quiet sleeper," said Arthur.

"Yes," said the landlord, "very quiet."

Young Holliday advanced with the candle, and looked in at the man cautiously.

"How pale he is," said Arthur.

"Yes," returned the landlord, "pale enough, isn't he?"

Arthur looked closer at the man. The bed-clothes were drawn up to his chin, and they lay perfectly still over the region of his chest. Surprised and vaguely startled as he noticed this, Arthur stooped down closer over the stranger, looked at his ashy, parted lips, listened breathlessly for an instant, looked again at the strangely still face, and the motionless lips and chest, and turned round suddenly on the landlord with his own cheeks as pale for the moment as the hollow cheeks of the man on the bed.

"Come here," he whispered, under his breath. "Come here, for God's sake! The man's not asleep—he is dead."

"You have found that out sooner than I thought you would," said the landlord, composedly. "Yes, he's dead, sure enough. He died at five o'clock to-day."

"How did he die? Who is he?" asked Arthur, staggered for the moment by the audacious coolness of the answer.

"As to who is he," rejoined the landlord, "I know no more about him than you do. There are his books, and letters, and things all sealed up in that brown paper parcel for the coroner's inquest to open to-morrow or next day. He's been here a week, paying his way fairly enough, and stopping indoors, for the most part, as if he was ailing. My girl brought him up his tea at five to-day, and as he was pouring of it out, he fell down in a faint, or a fit, or a compound of both, for anything I know. We couldn't bring him to, and I said he was dead. And the doctor couldn't bring him to, and the doctor said he was dead. And there he is. And the coroner's inquest's coming as soon as it can. And that's as much as I know about it."

Arthur held the candle close to the man's lips. The flame still burned straight up as steadily as ever. There was a moment of silence, and the rain pattered drearily through it against the panes of the window.

"If you haven't got nothing more to say to me," continued the landlord, "I suppose I may go. You don't expect your five shillings back, do you? There's the bed I promised you, clean and comfortable. There's the man I warranted not to disturb you, quiet in this world forever. If you're frightened to stop alone with him, that's not my lookout. I've kept my part of the bargain and I mean to keep the money. I'm not Yorkshire myself, young gentleman, but I've lived long enough in these parts to have my wits sharpened, and I shouldn't wonder if you found out the way to brighten up yours next time you come among us."

With these words the landlord turned towards the door, and laughed to himself softly, in high satisfaction at his own sharpness.

Startled and shocked as he was, Arthur had by this time sufficiently recovered himself to feel indignant at the trick that had been played on him, and at the insolent manner in which the landlord exulted in it.

"Don't laugh," he said, sharply, "till you are quite sure you have got the laugh against me. You shan't have the five shillings for nothing, my man. I'll keep the bed."

"Will you?" said the landlord. "Then I wish you a good night's rest." With that brief farewell he went out and shut the door after him.

A good night's rest! The words had hardly been spoken, the door had hardly been closed, before Arthur half repented the hasty words that had just escaped him. Though not naturally over-sensitive, and not wanting in courage of the moral as well as the physical sort, the presence of the dead man had an instantaneously chilling effect on his mind when he found himself alone in the room—alone, and bound by his own rash words to stay there till the next morning. An older man would have thought nothing of those words, and would have acted, without reference to them, as his calmer sense suggested. But Arthur was too young to treat the ridicule even of his inferiors with contempt—too young not to fear the momentary humiliation of falsifying his own foolish boast more than he feared the trial of watching out the long night in the same chamber with the dead.

"It is but a few hours," he thought to himself, "and I can get away the first thing in the morning."

He was looking towards the occupied bed as that idea passed through his mind, and the sharp angular eminence made in the clothes by the dead man's upturned feet again caught his eye. He advanced and drew the curtains, purposely abstaining, as he did so, from looking at the face of the corpse, lest he might unnerve himself at the outset by fastening some ghastly impression of it on his mind. He drew the curtain very gently, and sighed involuntarily as he closed it.

"Poor fellow," he said, almost as sadly as if he had known the man. "Ah! poor fellow!"

He went next to the window. The night was black, and he could see nothing from it. The rain still pattered heavily against the glass. He inferred, from hearing it, that the window was at the back of the house, remembering that the front was sheltered from the weather by the court and the buildings over it.

While he was still standing at the window—for even the dreary rain was a relief, because of the sound it made; a relief, also, because it moved, and had some faint suggestion, in consequence, of life and companionship in it—while he was standing at the window, and looking vacantly into the black darkness outside, he heard a distant church clock strike ten. Only ten! How was he to pass the time till the house was astir the next morning?

Under any other circumstances he would have gone down to the public-house parlour, would have called for his grog, and would have laughed and talked with the company, assembled as familiarly as if he had known them all his life. But the very thought of whiling away the time in this manner was now distasteful to him. The new situation in which he was placed seemed to have altered him to himself already. Thus far his life had been the common, trifling, prosaic, surface-life of a prosperous young man, with no troubles to conquer and no trials to face. He had lost no relation whom he loved, no friend whom he treasured. Till this night, what share he had of the immortal inheritance that is divided among us all had lain dormant within him. Till this night, Death and he had not once met, even in thought.

He took a few turns up and down the room, then stopped. The noise made by his boots on the poorly-carpeted floor jarred on his ear. He hesitated a little, and ended by taking the boots off, and walking backwards and forwards noiselessly.

All desire to sleep or to rest had left him. The bare thought of lying down on the unoccupied bed instantly drew the picture on his mind of a dreadful mimicry of the position of the dead man. Who was he? What was the story of his past life? Poor he must have been, or he would not have stopped at such a place as the Two Robins Inn; and weakened, probably, by long illness, or he could hardly have died in the manner which the landlord had described. Poor, ill, lonely—dead in a strange place—dead, with nobody but a stranger to pity him. A sad story; truly, on the mere face of it, a very sad story.

While these thoughts were passing through his mind, he had stopped insensibly at the window, close to which stood the foot of the bed with the closed curtains. At first he looked at it absently; then he became conscious that his eyes were fixed on it; and then a perverse desire took possession of him to do the very thing which he had resolved not to do up to this time—to look at the dead man.

He stretched out his hand towards the curtains, but checked himself in the very act of undrawing them, turned his back sharply on the bed, and walked towards the chimney-piece, to see what things were placed on it, and to try if he could keep the dead man out of his mind in that way.

There was a pewter inkstand on the chimney-piece, with some mildewed remains of ink in the bottle. There were two coarse china ornaments of the commonest kind; and there was a square of embossed card, dirty and fly-blown, with a collection of wretched riddles printed on it, in all sorts of zigzag directions, and in variously coloured inks. He took the card, and went away to read it at the table on which the candle was placed, sitting down with his back resolutely turned to the curtained bed.

He read the first riddle, the second, the third, all in one corner of the card, then turned it round impatiently to look at another. Before he could begin reading the riddles printed here the sound of the church clock stopped him.

Eleven.

He had got through an hour of the time in the room with the dead man.

Once more he looked at the card. It was not easy to make out the letters printed on it in consequence of the dimness of the light which the landlord had left him—a common tallow candle, furnished with a pair of heavy old-fashioned steel snuffers. Up to this time his mind had been too much occupied to think of the light. He had left the wick of the candle unsnuffed till it had risen higher than the flame, and had burned into an odd penthouse shape at the top, from which morsels of the charred cotton fell off from time to time in little flakes. He took up the snuffers now and trimmed the wick. The light brightened directly, and the room became less dismal.

Again he turned to the riddles, reading them doggedly and resolutely, now in one corner of the card, now in another. All his efforts, however, could not fix his attention on them. He pursued his occupation mechanically, deriving no sort of impression from what he was reading. It was as if a shadow from the curtained bed had got between his mind and the gaily-printed letters—a shadow that nothing could dispel. At last he gave up the struggle, threw the card from him impatiently, and took to walking softly up and down the room again.

The dead man, the dead man, the *hidden* dead man on the bed!

There was the one persistent idea still haunting him. Hidden! Was it only the body being there, or was it the body being there, *concealed,* that was preying on his mind? He stopped at the window with that doubt in him, once more listening to the pattering rain, once more looking out into the black darkness.

Still the dead man!

The darkness forced his mind back upon itself, and set his memory at work, reviving with a painfully-vivid distinctness the momentary impression it had received from his first sight of the corpse. Before long the face seemed to be hovering out in the middle of the darkness, confronting him through the window, with the paleness whiter—with the dreadful dull line of light between the imperfectly-closed eyelids broader than he had seen it—with the parted lips slowly dropping farther and farther away from each other—with the features growing larger and moving closer, till they seemed to fill the window, and to silence the rain, and to shut out the night.

The sound of a voice shouting below stairs woke him suddenly from the dream of his own distempered fancy. He recognized it as the voice of the landlord.

"Shut up at twelve, Ben," he heard it say. "I'm off to bed."

He wiped away the damp that had gathered on his forehead, reasoned with himself for a little while, and resolved to shake his mind free of the ghastly counterfeit which still clung to it by forcing himself to confront, if it was only for a moment, the solemn reality. Without allowing himself an instant to hesitate, he parted the curtains at the foot of the bed, and looked through.

There was the sad, peaceful, white face, with the awful mystery of stillness on it, laid back upon the pillow. No stir, no change there! He only looked at it for a moment before he closed the curtains again, but that moment steadied him, calmed him, restored him—mind and body—to himself. He returned to his old occupation of walking up and down the room, persevering in it this time till the clock struck again.

Twelve.

As the sound of the clock-bell died away, it was succeeded by the confused noise downstairs of the drinkers in the tap-room leaving the house. The next sound, after an interval of silence, was caused by the barring of the door and the closing of the shutters at the back of the inn. Then the silence followed again, and was disturbed no more.

He was alone now—absolutely, hopelessly alone with the dead man till the next morning.

The wick of the candle wanted trimming again. He took up the snuffers, but paused suddenly on the very point of using them, and looked attentively at the candle—then back, over his shoulder, at the curtained bed—then again at the candle. It had been lighted for the first time to show him the way upstairs, and three parts of it, at least, were already consumed. In another hour it would be burned out. In another hour, unless he called at once to the man who had shut up the inn for a fresh candle, he would be left in the dark.

Strongly as his mind had been affected since he had entered the room, his unreasonable dread of encountering ridicule and of exposing his courage to suspicion had not altogether lost its influence over him even yet.

He lingered irresolutely by the table, waiting till he could prevail on himself to open the door, and call from the landing to the man who had shut up the inn. In his present hesitating frame of mind, it was a kind of relief to gain a few moments only by engaging in the trifling occupation of snuffing the candle. His hand trembled a little, and the snuffers were heavy and awkward to use. When he closed them on the wick, he closed them a hair's breadth too low. In an instant the candle was out, and the room was plunged in pitch darkness.

The one impression which the absence of light immediately produced on his mind was distrust of the curtained bed—distrust which shaped itself into no distinct idea, but which was powerful enough, in its very vagueness, to bind him down to his chair, to make his heart beat fast, and to set him listening intently. No sound stirred in the room, but the familiar sound of the rain against the window, louder and sharper now than he had heard it yet.

Still the vague distrust, the inexpressible dread possessed him, and kept him in his chair. He had put his carpet-bag on the table when he first entered the room, and he now took the key from his pocket, reached out his hand softly, opened the bag, and groped in it for his travelling writing-case, in which he knew that there was a small store of matches. When he had got one of the matches, he waited before he struck it on the coarse wooden table, and listened intently again without knowing why. Still there was no sound in the room but the steady, ceaseless rattling sound of the rain.

He lighted the candle again without another moment of delay, and, on the instant of its burning up, the first object in the room that his eyes sought for was the curtained bed.

Just before the light had been put out he had looked in that direction, and had seen no change, no disarrangement of any sort in the folds of the closely-drawn curtains.

When he looked at the bed now, he saw hanging over the side of it a long white hand.

It lay perfectly motionless midway on the side of the bed, where the curtain at the head and the curtain at the foot met. Nothing more was visible. The clinging curtains hid everything but the long white hand.

He stood looking at it, unable to stir, unable to call out—feeling nothing, knowing nothing—every faculty he possessed gathered up and lost in the one seeing faculty. How long that first panic held him he never could tell afterwards. It might have been only for a moment—it might have been for many minutes together. How he got to the bed—whether he ran to it headlong, or whether he approached it slowly—how he wrought himself up to unclose the curtains and look in, he never has remembered, and never will remember to his dying day. It is enough that he did go to the bed, and that he did look inside the curtains.

The man had moved. One of his arms was outside the clothes; his face was turned a little on the pillow; his eyelids were wide open. Changed as to position and as to one of the features, the face was otherwise fearfully and wonderfully unaltered. The dead paleness and the dead quiet were on it still.

One glance showed Arthur this—one glance before he flew breathlessly to the door and alarmed the house.

The man whom the landlord called "Ben" was the first to appear on the stairs. In three words Arthur told him what had happened, and sent him for the nearest doctor.

I, who tell you this story, was then staying with a medical friend of mine, in practice at Doncaster, taking care of his patients for him during his absence in London; and I, for the time being, was the nearest doctor. They had sent for me from the inn when the stranger was taken ill in the afternoon, but I was not at home, and medical assistance was sought for elsewhere. When the man from

The Two Robins rang the night-bell, I was just thinking of going to bed. Naturally enough, I did not believe a word of his story about "a dead man who had come to life again." However, I put on my hat, armed myself with one or two bottles of restorative medicine, and ran to the inn, expecting to find nothing more remarkable, when I got there, than a patient in a fit.

My surprise at finding that the man had spoken the literal truth was almost, if not quite, equalled by my astonishment at finding myself face to face with Arthur Holliday as soon as I entered the bedroom. It was no time then for giving or seeking explanations. We just shook hands amazedly, and then I ordered everybody but Arthur out of the room, and hurried to the man on the bed.

The kitchen fire had not been long out. There was plenty of hot water in the boiler, and plenty of flannel to be had. With these, with my medicines, and with such help as Arthur could render under my direction, I dragged the man literally out of the jaws of death. In less than an hour from the time when I had been called in, he was alive and talking in the bed on which he had been laid out to wait for the coroner's inquest.

You will naturally ask me what had been the matter with him, and I might treat you, in reply, to a long theory, plentifully sprinkled with what the children call hard words. I prefer telling you that, in this case, cause and effect could not be satisfactorily joined together by any theory whatever. There are mysteries in life and the conditions of it which human science has not fathomed yet; and I candidly confess to you that, in bringing that man back to existence, I was, morally speaking, groping haphazard in the dark. I know (from the testimony of the doctor who attended him in the afternoon) that the vital machinery, so far as its action is appreciable by our senses, had, in this case, unquestionably stopped, and I am equally certain (seeing that I recovered him) that the vital principal was not extinct. When I add that he had suffered from a long and complicated illness, and that his whole nervous system was utterly deranged, I have told you all I really know of the physical condition of my dead-alive patient at The Two Robins inn.

When he "came to," as the phrase goes, he was a startling object to look at, with his colourless face, his sunken cheeks, his wild black eyes, and his long black hair. The first question he asked me about himself when he could speak made me suspect that I had been called in to a man in my own profession. I mentioned to him my surmise, and he told me that I was right.

He said he had come last from Paris, where he had been attached to a hospital; that he had lately returned to England, on his way to Edinburgh, to continue his studies; that he had been taken ill on the journey; and that he had stopped to rest and recover himself at Doncaster. He did not add a word about his name, or who he was, and of course I did not question him on the subject. All I inquired when he ceased speaking was what branch of the profession he intended to follow.

"Any branch," he said, bitterly, "which will put bread into the mouth of a poor man."

At this, Arthur, who had been hitherto watching him in silent curiosity, burst out impetuously in his usual good-humoured way.

"My dear fellow" (everybody was "my dear fellow" with Arthur), "now you have come to life again, don't begin by being downhearted about your prospects. I'll answer for it I can help you to some capital thing in the medical line, or, if I can't, I know my father can."

The medical student looked at him steadily.

"Thank you," he said, coldly; then added, "May I ask who your father is?"

"He's well enough known all about this part of the country," replied Arthur. "He is a great manufacturer, and his name is Holliday."

My hand was on the man's wrist during this brief conversation. The instant the name of Holliday was pronounced I felt the pulse under my fingers flutter, stop, go on suddenly with a bound, and beat afterwards for a minute or two at the fever rate.

"How did you come here?" asked the stranger, quickly, excitably, passionately almost.

Arthur related briefly what had happened from the time of his first taking the bed at the inn.

"I am indebted to Mr. Holliday's son, then, for the help that has saved my life," said the medical student, speaking to himself, with a singular sarcasm in his voice. "Come here!"

He held out, as he spoke, his long, white, bony right hand.

"With all my heart," said Arthur, taking his hand cordially.

"I may confess it now," he continued, laughing, "upon my honour, you almost frightened me out of my wits."

The stranger did not seem to listen. His wild black eyes were fixed with a look of eager interest on Arthur's face, and his long bony fingers kept tight hold of Arthur's hand. Young Holliday, on his side, returned the gaze, amazed and puzzled by the medical student's odd language and manners. The two faces were close together; I looked at them, and, to my amazement, I was suddenly impressed by the sense of a likeness between them—not in features or complexion, but solely in expression. It must have been a strong likeness, or I should certainly not have found it out, for I am naturally slow at detecting resemblances between faces.

"You have saved my life," said the strange man, still looking hard in Arthur's face, still holding tightly by his hand. "If you had been my own brother, you could not have done more for me than that."

He laid a singularly strong emphasis on those three words "my own brother," and a change passed over his face as he pronounced them—a change that no language of mine is competent to describe.

"I hope I have not done being of service to you yet," said Arthur. "I'll speak to my father as soon as I get home."

"You seem to be fond and proud of your father," said the medical student. "I suppose, in return, he is fond and proud of you?"

"Of course he is," answered Arthur, laughing. "Is there anything wonderful in that? Isn't *your* father fond——"

The stranger suddenly dropped young Holliday's hand and turned his face away.

"I beg your pardon," said Arthur. "I hope I have not unintentionally pained you. I hope you have not lost your father?"

"I can't well lose what I have never had," retorted the medical student, with a harsh mocking laugh.

"What you have never had!"

The strange man suddenly caught Arthur's hand again, suddenly looked once more hard in his face.

"Yes," he said, with a repetition of the bitter laugh. "You have brought a poor devil back into the world who has no business there. Do I astonish you? Well, I have a fancy of my own for telling you what men in my situation generally keep a secret. I have no name and no father. The merciful law of society tells me I am nobody's son! Ask your father if he will be my father too, and help me on in life with the family name."

Arthur looked at me more puzzled than ever.

I signed to him to say nothing, and then laid my fingers again on the man's wrist. No. In spite of the extraordinary speech that he had just made, he was not, as I had been disposed to suspect, beginning to get light-headed. His pulse, by this time, had fallen back to a quiet, slow beat, and his skin was moist and cool. Not a symptom of fever or agitation about him.

Finding that neither of us answered him, he turned to me, and began talking of the extraordinary nature of his case, and asking my advice about the future course of medical treatment to which he ought to subject himself. I said the matter required careful thinking over, and suggested that I should send him a prescription a little later. He told me to write it at once, as he would most likely be leaving Doncaster in the morning before I was up. It was quite useless to represent to him the folly and danger of such a proceeding as this. He heard me politely and patiently, but held to his resolution, without offering any reasons or explanations, and repeated to me that, if I wished to give him a chance of seeing my prescription, I must write it at once.

Hearing this, Arthur volunteered the loan of a travelling writing-case which he said he had with him, and, bringing it to the bed, shook the note-paper out of the pocket of the case forthwith in his usual careless way. With the paper there fell out on the counterpane of the bed a small packet of sticking-plaster, and a little water-colour drawing of a landscape.

The medical student took up the drawing and looked at it. His eye fell on some initials neatly written in cipher in one corner. He started and trembled; his pale face grew whiter than ever; his wild black eyes turned on Arthur, and looked through and through him.

"A pretty drawing," he said, in a remarkably quiet tone of voice.

"Ah! and done by such a pretty girl," said Arthur. "Oh, such a pretty girl! I wish it was not a landscape—I wish it was a portrait of her!"

"You admire her very much?"

Arthur, half in jest, half in earnest, kissed his hand for answer.

"Love at first sight," said young Holliday, putting the drawing away again. "But the course of it doesn't run smooth. It's the old story. She's monopolized, as usual; trammelled by a rash engagement to some poor man who is never likely to get money enough to marry her. It was lucky I heard of it in time, or I should certainly have risked a declaration when she gave me that drawing. Here, doctor, here is pen, ink, and paper all ready for you."

"When she gave you that drawing? Gave it? gave it?"

He repeated the words slowly to himself, and suddenly closed his eyes. A momentary distortion passed across his face, and I saw one of his hands clutch up the bedclothes and squeeze them hard. I thought he was going to be ill again, and begged that there might be no more talking. He opened his eyes when I spoke, fixed them once more searchingly on Arthur, and said, slowly and distinctly,

"You like her, and she likes you. The poor man may die out of your way. Who can tell that she may not give you herself as well as her drawing, after all?"

Before young Holliday could answer, he turned to me, and said in a whisper, "Now for the prescription." From that time, though he spoke to Arthur again, he never looked at him more.

When I had written the prescription, he examined it, approved of it, and then astonished us both by abruptly wishing us good night. I offered to sit up with him, and he shook his head. Arthur offered to sit up with him, and he said, shortly, with his face turned away, "No." I insisted on having somebody left to watch him. He gave way when he found I was determined, and said he would accept the services of the waiter at the inn.

"Thank you both," he said, as we rose to go. "I have one last favour to ask—not of you, doctor, for I leave you to exercise your professional discretion, but of Mr. Holliday." His eyes, while he spoke, still rested steadily on me, and never once turned towards Arthur. "I beg that Mr. Holliday will not mention to anyone, least of all to his father, the events that have occurred and the words that have passed in this room. I entreat him to bury me in his memory as, but for him, I might have been buried in my grave. I cannot give my reasons for making this strange request. I can only implore him to grant it."

His voice faltered for the first time, and he hid his face on the pillow. Arthur, completely bewildered, gave the required pledge. I took young Holliday away with me immediately afterwards to the house of my friend, determining to go back to the inn and to see the medical student again before he had left in the morning.

I returned to the inn at eight o'clock, purposely abstaining from waking Arthur, who was sleeping off the past night's excitement on one of my friend's sofas. A suspicion had occurred to me, as soon as I was alone in my bedroom, which made me resolve that Holliday and the stranger whose life he had saved should not meet again, if I could prevent it.

I have already alluded to certain reports or scandals which I knew of relating to the early life of Arthur's father. While I was thinking, in my bed, of what had passed at the inn; of the change in the student's pulse when he heard the name of Holliday; of the resemblance of expression that I had discovered between his face and Arthur's; of the emphasis he had laid on those three words, "my own brother"; and of his incomprehensible acknowledgement of his own illegitimacy—while I was thinking of these things, the reports I have mentioned suddenly flew into my mind, and linked themselves fast to the chain of my previous reflections. Something within me whispered, "It is best that those two young men should not meet again." I felt it before I slept; I felt it when I woke; and I went, as I told you, alone to the inn the next morning.

I had missed my only opportunity of seeing my nameless patient again. He had been gone nearly an hour when I inquired for him.

I have now told you everything that I know for certain in relation to the man whom I brought back to life in the double-bedded room of the inn at Doncaster. What I have next to add is matter for inference and surmise, and is not, strictly speaking, matter of fact.

I have to tell you, first, that the medical student turned out to be strangely and unaccountably right in assuming it as more than probable that Arthur Holliday would marry the young lady who had given him the water-colour drawing of the landscape. That marriage took place a little more than a year after the events occurred which I have just been relating.

The young couple came to live in the neighbourhood in which I was then established in practice. I was present at the wedding, and was rather surprised to find that Arthur was singularly reserved with me, both before and after his marriage, on the subject of the young lady's prior engagement. He only referred to it once when we were alone, merely telling me, on that occasion, that his wife had done all that honour and duty required of her in the matter, and that the engagement had been broken off with the full approval of her parents. I never heard more from him than this. For three years he and his wife lived together happily. At the expiration of that time the symptoms of a serious illness first declared themselves in Mrs. Arthur Holliday. It turned out to be a long, lingering, hopeless malady. I attended her throughout. We had been great friends when she was well, and we became more attached to each other than ever when she was ill. I had many long and interesting conversations with her in the intervals when she suffered least. The result of one of those conversations I may briefly relate, leaving you to draw any inferences from it that you please.

The interview to which I refer occurred shortly before her death.

I called one evening as usual, and found her alone, with a look in her eyes which told me she had been crying. She only informed me at first that she had been depressed in spirits, but by little and little she became more communicative, and confessed to me that she had been looking over some old letters which had been addressed to her, before she had seen Arthur, by a man to whom she had been engaged to be married. I asked her how the engagement came to be broken off. She replied that it had not been broken off, but that it had died out in a very mysterious way. The person to whom she was engaged—her first love, she called him—was very poor, and there was no immediate prospect of their being married. He followed my profession, and went abroad to study. They had corresponded regularly until the time when, as she believed, he had returned to England. From that period she heard no more of him. He was of a fretful, sensitive temperament, and she feared that she might have inadvertently done or said something to offend him. However that might be, he had never written to her again, and after waiting a year she had married Arthur. I asked when the first estrangement had begun, and found that the time at which she ceased to hear anything of her first lover exactly corresponded with the time at which I had been called in to my mysterious patient at The Two Robins Inn.

A fortnight after that conversation she died. In course of time Arthur married again. Of late years he has lived principally in London, and I have seen little or nothing of him.

I have some years to pass over before I can approach to anything like a conclusion of this fragmentary narrative. And even when that later period is reached, the little that I have to say will not occupy your attention for more than a few minutes.

One rainy autumn evening, while I was still practising as a country doctor, I was sitting alone, thinking over a case then under my charge, which sorely perplexed me, when I heard a low knock at the door of my room.

"Come in," I cried, looking up curiously to see who wanted me.

After a momentary delay, the lock moved, and a long, white, bony hand stole round the door as it opened, gently pushing it over a fold in the carpet which hindered it from working freely on the hinges. The hand was followed by a man whose face instantly struck me with a very strange sensation. There was something familiar to me in the look of him, and yet it was also something that suggested the idea of change.

He quietly introduced himself as "Mr. Lorn," presented to me some excellent professional recommendations, and proposed to fill the place, then vacant, of my assistant. While he was speaking I noticed it as singular that we did not appear to be meeting each other like strangers, and that, while I was certainly startled at seeing him, he did not appear to be at all startled at seeing me.

It was on the tip of my tongue to say that I thought I had met with him before. But there was something in his face, and something in my own recollections—I can hardly say what—which unaccountably restrained me from speaking, and which as unaccountably attracted me to him at once, and made me feel ready and glad to accept his proposal.

He took his assistant's place on that very day. We got on together as if we had been old friends from the first; but, throughout the whole time of his residence in my house, he never volunteered any confidences on the subject of his past life, and I never approached the forbidden topic except by hints, which he resolutely refused to understand.

I had long had a notion that my patient at the inn might have been a natural son of the elder Mr. Holliday's, and that he might also have been the man who was engaged to Arthur's first wife. And now another idea occurred to me, that Mr. Lorn was the only person in existence who could, if he chose, enlighten me on both those doubtful points. But he never did choose, and I was never enlightened. He remained with me till I removed to London to try my fortune there as a physician for the second time, and then he went his way and I went mine, and we have never seen one another since.

I can add no more. I may have been right in my suspicion, or I may have been wrong. All I know is that, in those days of my country practice, when I came home late, and found my assistant asleep, and woke him, he used to look, in coming to, wonderfully like the stranger at Doncaster as he raised himself in the bed on that memorable night.

"Blow Up with the Brig!"

I have got an alarming confession to make. I am haunted by a
Ghost.

If you were to guess for a hundred years, you would never guess
what my ghost is. I shall make you laugh to begin with—and
afterwards I shall make your flesh creep. My Ghost is the ghost of
a Bedroom Candlestick.

Yes, a bedroom candlestick and candle or a flat candlestick and
candle—put it which way you like—that is what haunts me. I wish
it was something pleasanter and more out of the common way; a
beautiful lady, or a mine of gold and silver, or a cellar of wine and
a coach and horses, and such-like. But, being what it is, I must
take it for what it is, and make the best of it—and I shall thank
you kindly if you will help me out by doing the same.

I am not a scholar myself; but I make bold to believe that the
haunting of any man with anything under the sun, begins with the
frightening of him. At any rate, the haunting of me with a bedroom candlestick and candle began with the frightening of me with
a bedroom candlestick and candle—the frightening of me half out
of my life; and, for the time being, the frightening of me altogether
out of my wits. That is not a very pleasant thing to confess, before
stating the particulars; but perhaps you will be the readier to
believe that I am not a downright coward, because you find me
bold enough to make a clean breast of it already, to my own great
disadvantage, so far.

Here are the particulars, as well as I can put them:

I was apprenticed to the sea when I was about as tall as my own
walking-stick; and I made good enough use of my time to be fit for
a mate's berth at the age of twenty-five years.

It was in the year eighteen hundred and eighteen, or nineteen, I
am not quite certain which, that I reached the before-mentioned
age of twenty-five. You will please to excuse my memory not being

very good for dates, names, numbers, places, and such-like. No fear, though, about the particulars I have undertaken to tell you of; I have got them all ship-shape in my recollection; I can see them, at this moment, as clear as noonday in my own mind. But there is a mist over what went before, and, for the matter of that, a mist likewise over much that came after—and it's not very likely to lift at my time of life, is it?

Well, in eighteen hundred and eighteen, or nineteen, when there was peace in our part of the world—and not before it was wanted, you will say—there was fighting, of a certain scampering, scrambling kind, going on in that old battlefield, which we seafaring men know by the name of the Spanish Main.

The possessions that belonged to the Spaniards in South America had broken into open mutiny and declared for themselves years before. There was plenty of bloodshed between the new government and the old; but the new had got the best of it, for the most part, under one General Bolivar—a famous man in his time, though he seems to have dropped out of people's memories now. Englishmen and Irishmen with a turn for fighting, and nothing particular to do at home, joined the General as volunteers; and some of our merchants here found it a good venture to send supplies across the ocean to the popular side. There was risk enough, of course, in doing this; but where one speculation of the kind succeeded, it made up for two, at the least, that failed. And that's the true principle of trade, wherever I have met with it, all the world over.

Among the Englishmen who were concerned in this Spanish-American business, I, your humble servant, happened in a small way to be one.

I was then mate of a brig belonging to a certain firm in the City, which drove a sort of general trade, mostly in queer out-of-the-way places, as far from home as possible; and which freighted the brig, in the year I am speaking of, with a cargo of gunpowder for General Bolivar and his volunteers. Nobody knew anything about our instructions, when we sailed, except the captain; and he didn't half seem to like them. I can't rightly say how many barrels of powder we had on board, or how much each barrel held—I only know we had no other cargo. The name of the brig was the *Good Intent*—a queer name enough, you will tell me, for a vessel laden with gunpowder, and sent to help a revolution. And as far as this particular voyage was concerned, so it was. I mean that for a joke, and I hope you will encourage me by laughing at it.

The *Good Intent* was the craziest old tub of a vessel I ever went to sea in, and the worst found in all respects. She was two hundred and thirty, or two hundred and eighty tons burden, I forget which; and she had a crew of eight, all told—nothing like as many as we ought by rights to have had to work the brig. However, we were well and honestly paid our wages; and we had to set that against the chance of foundering at sea, and, on this occasion, likewise, the chance of being blown up into the bargain.

In consideration of the nature of our cargo, we were harassed with new regulations which we didn't at all like, relative to smoking our pipes and lighting our lanterns; and, as usual in such cases, the captain who made the regulations, preached what he didn't practice. Not a man of us was allowed to have a bit of lighted candle in his hand when he went below—except the skipper; and he used his light, when he turned in, or when he looked over his charts on the cabin table, just as usual.

This light was a common kitchen candle or "dip," and it stood in an old battered flat candlestick, with all the japan worn and melted off, and all the tin showing through. It would have been more seamanlike and suitable in every respect if he had had a lamp or a lantern; but he stuck to his old candlestick; and that same old candlestick has ever afterwards stuck to *me*. That's another joke, if you please, and a better one than the first, in my opinion.

Well (I said "well" before, but it's a word that helps a man on like), we sailed in the brig, and shaped our course, first, for the Virgin Islands, in the West Indies; and, after sighting them, we made for the Leeward Islands next; and then stood on due south; till the look-out at the mast-head hailed the deck, and said he saw land. That land was the coast of South America. We had had a wonderful voyage so far. We had lost none of our spars or sails, and not a man of us had been harassed to death at the pumps. It wasn't often the *Good Intent* made such a voyage as that, I can tell you.

I was sent aloft to make sure about the land, and I did make sure of it.

When I reported the same to the skipper, he went below, and had a look at his letter of instructions and the chart. When he came on deck again, he altered our course a trifle to the eastward—I forget the point on the compass, but that don't matter. What I do remember is, that it was dark before we closed in with the land. We kept the lead going, and hove the brig to in from four to five fathoms water, or it might be six—I can't say for certain. I kept a sharp eye to the drift of the vessel, none of us knowing how the currents ran on that coast. We all wondered why the skipper didn't anchor; but he said, No, he must first show a light at the foretop mast-head, and wait for an answering light on shore. We did wait, and nothing of the sort appeared. It was starlight and calm. What little wind there was came in puffs off the land. I suppose we waited, drifting a little to the westward, as I made it out, best part of an hour before anything happened—and then, instead of seeing the light on shore, we saw a boat coming towards us, rowed by two men only.

We hailed them, and they answered "Friends!" and hailed us by our name. They came on board. One of them was an Irishman, and the other was a coffee-coloured native pilot, who jabbered a little English.

The Irishman handed a note to our skipper, who showed it to me. It informed us that the part of the coast we were off was not over safe for discharging our cargo, seeing that spies of the enemy (that is to say, of the old government) had been taken and shot in the neighbourhood the day before. We might trust the brig to the native pilot; and he had his instructions to take us to another part of the coast. The note was signed by the proper parties; so we let the Irishman go back alone in the boat, and allowed the pilot to exercise his lawful authority over the brig. He kept us stretching off from the land till noon the next day—his instructions, seemingly, ordering him to keep us well out of sight of the shore. We only altered our course, in the afternoon, so as to close in with the land again a little before midnight.

This same pilot was about as ill-looking a vagabond as ever I saw; a skinny, cowardly, quarrelsome mongrel, who swore at the men, in the vilest broken English, till they were every one of them ready to pitch him overboard. The skipper kept them quiet, and I kept them quiet, for the pilot being given us by our instructions, we were bound to make the best of him. Near nightfall, however, with the best will in the world to avoid it, I was unlucky enough to quarrel with him.

He wanted to go below with his pipe, and I stopped him, of

course, because it was contrary to orders. Upon that, he tried to hustle by me, and I put him away with my hand. I never meant to push him down; but, somehow, I did. He picked himself up as quick as lightning, and pulled out his knife. I snatched it out of his hand, slapped his murderous face for him, and threw his weapon overboard. He gave me one ugly look, and walked aft. I didn't think much of the look then; but I remembered it a little too well afterwards.

We were close in with the land again, just as the wind failed us, between eleven and twelve that night; and dropped our anchor by the pilot's directions.

It was pitch dark, and a dead airless calm. The skipper was on deck with two of our best men for watch. The rest were below, except the pilot, who coiled himself up, more like a snake than a man, on the forecastle. It was not my watch till four in the morning. But I didn't like the look of the night, or the pilot, or the state of things generally, and I shook myself down on deck to get my nap there, and be ready for anything at a moment's notice. The last I remember was the skipper whispering to me that he didn't like the look of things either, and that he would go below and consult his instructions again. That is the last I remember, before the slow, heavy, regular roll of the old brig on the ground swell rocked me off to sleep.

I was awoke by a scuffle on the forecastle, and a gag in my mouth. There was a man on my breast, and a man on my legs; and I was bound hand and foot in half a minute.

The brig was in the hands of the Spaniards. They were swarming all over her. I heard six heavy splashes in the water, one after another. I saw the captain stabbed to the heart as he came running up the companion—and I heard a seventh spash in the water. Except myself, every soul of us on board had been murdered and thrown into the sea. Why I was left, I couldn't think, till I saw the pilot stoop over me with a lantern, and look, to make sure of who I was. There was a devilish grin on his face, and he nodded his head at me, as much as to say, *You* were the man who hustled me down and slapped my face, and I mean to play the game of cat and mouse with you in return for it!

I could neither move nor speak; but I could see the Spaniards take off the main hatch and rig the purchases for getting up the cargo. A quarter of an hour afterwards, I heard the sweeps of a schooner, or other small vessel, in the water. The strange craft was laid alongside of us; and the Spaniards set to work to discharge our cargo into her. They all worked hard except the pilot; and he came, from time to time, with his lantern, to have another look at me, and to grin and nod always in the same devilish way. I am old enough now not to be ashamed of confessing the truth; and I don't mind acknowledging that the pilot frightened me.

The fright, and the bonds, and the gag, and the not being able to stir hand or foot, had pretty nigh worn me out, by the time the Spaniards gave over work. This was just as the dawn broke. They had shifted a good part of our cargo on board their vessel, but nothing like all of it; and they were sharp enough to be off with what they had got, before daylight.

I need hardly say that I had made up my mind, by this time, to the worst I could think of. The pilot, it was clear enough, was one of the spies of the enemy, who had wormed himself into the confidence of our consignees without being suspected. He, or more likely his employers, had got knowledge enough of us to suspect what our cargo was; we had been anchored for the night in the safest berth for them to suprise us in; and we had paid the penalty of having a small crew, and consequently an insufficient watch. All this was clear enough—but what did the pilot mean to do with *me*?

On the word of a man, it makes my flesh creep, now, only to tell you what he did with me.

After all the rest of them were out of the brig, except the pilot and two Spanish seamen, these last took me up, bound and gag-ged, as I was, lowered me into the hold of the vessel, and laid me along on the floor; lashing me to it with ropes' ends, so that I could just turn from one side to the other, but could not roll myself fairly over, so as to change my place. They then left me. Both of them were the worse for liquor: but the devil of a pilot was sober—mind that!—as sober as I am at the present moment.

I lay in the dark for a little while, with my heart thumping as if it was going to jump out of me. I lay about five minutes or so, when the pilot came down into the hold, alone.

He had the captain's cursed flat candlestick and a carpenter's awl in one hand, and a long thin twist of cotton yarn, well oiled, in the other. He put the candlestick, with a new "dip" candle lighted in it, down on the floor, about two feet from my face, and close against the side of the vessel. The light was feeble enough; but it was sufficient to show a dozen barrels of gunpowder or more, left all round me in the hold of the brig. I began to suspect what he was after, the moment I noticed the barrels. The horrors laid hold of me from head to foot; and the sweat poured off my face like water.

I saw him go, next, to one of the barrels of powder standing against the side of the vessel, in a line with the candle, and about three feet, or rather better, away from it. He bored a hole in the side of the barrel with his awl; and the horrid powder came trickling out, as black as hell, and dripped into the hollow of his hand, which he held to catch it. When he had got a good handful, he stopped up the hole by jamming one end of his oiled twist of cotton-yarn fast into it; and he then rubbed the powder into the whole length of the yarn, till he had blackened every hairsbreadth of it.

The next thing he did—as true as I sit here, as true as the heaven above us all—the next thing he did was to carry the free end of his long, lean, black, frightful slow-match to the lighted candle along-side my face. He tied it (the bloddy-minded villain!) in several folds, round the tallow dip, about a third of the distance down, measuring from the flame of the wick to the lip of the candlestick. He did that; he looked to see that my lashings were all safe; and then he put his face down close to mine, and whispered in my ear, "Blow up with the brig!"

He was on deck again the moment after; and he and the two others shoved the hatch on over me. At the farthest end from where I lay, they had not fitted it down quite true, and I saw a blink of daylight glimmering in when I looked in that direction. I heard the sweeps of the schooner fall into the water—splash! splash! fainter and fainter, as they swept the vessel out in the dead calm, to be ready for the wind in the offing. Fainter and fainter, splash! splash! for a quarter of an hour or more.

While those sounds were in my ears, my eyes were fixed on the candle.

It had been freshly lit—if left to itself it would burn for between six and seven hours. The slow-match was twisted round it about a third of the way down; and therefore the flame would be about two hours reaching it. There I lay, gagged, bound, lashed to the floor; seeing my own life burning down with the candle by my side—there I lay, alone on the sea, doomed to be blown to atoms, and to see that doom drawing on, nearer and nearer with every fresh second of time, through nigh on two hours to come; powerless to help myself and speechless to call for help to others. The wonder to me is that I didn't cheat the flame, the slow-match, and the powder, and die of the horror of my situation before my first half-hour was out in the hold of the brig.

I can't exactly say how long I kept the command of my senses after I had ceased to hear the splash of the schooner's sweeps in the water. I can trace back everything I did and everything I thought, up to a certain point; but, once past that, I get all abroad, and lose myself in my memory now, much as I lost myself in my own feelings at the time.

The moment the hatch was covered over me, I began, as every other man would have begun in my place, with a frantic effort to free my hands. In the mad panic I was in, I cut my flesh with the lashings as if they had been knife-blades; but I never stirred them. There was less chance still of freeing my legs, or of tearing myself from the fastenings that held me to the floor. I gave in, when I was all but suffocated for want of breath. The gag, you will please to remember, was a terrible enemy to me; I could only breathe freely through my nose—and that is but a poor vent when a man is straining his strength as far as ever it will go.

I gave in, and lay quiet, and got my breath again; my eyes glaring and straining at the candle all the time.

While I was staring at it, the notion struck me of trying to blow out the flame by pumping a long breath at it suddenly through my nostrils. It was too high above me, and too far away from me, to be reached in that fashion. I tried, and tried, and tried—and then I gave in again and lay quiet again; always with my eyes glaring at the candle, and the candle glaring at *me*. The splash of the schooner's sweeps was very faint by this time. I could only just hear them in the morning stillness. Splash! splash!—fainter and fainter—splash! splash!

Without exactly feeling my mind going, I began to feel it getting queer, as early as this. The snuff of the candle was growing taller and taller, and the length of tallow between the flame and the slow-match, which was the length of my life, was getting shorter and shorter. I calculated that I had rather less than an hour and a half to live.

An hour and a half! Was there a chance, in that time, of a boat pulling off to the brig from shore? Whether the land near which the vessel was anchored was in possession of our side, or in possession of the enemy's side, I made out that they must, sooner or later, send to hail the brig, merely because she was a stranger in those parts. The question for *me* was, how soon? The sun had not risen yet, as I could tell by looking through the chink in the hatch. There was no coast village near us, as we all knew, before the brig was seized, by seeing no lights on shore. There was no wind, as I could tell by listening, to bring any strange vessel near. If I had had six hours to live, there might have been a chance for me, reckoning from sunrise to noon. But with an hour and a half, which had dwindled to an hour and a quarter by this time—or, in other words, with the earliness of the morning, the uninhabited coast, and the dead calm all against me—there was not the ghost of a chance. As I felt that, I had another struggle—the last—with my bonds; and only cut myself the deeper for my pains.

I gave in once more, and lay quiet, and listened for the splash of the sweeps.

Gone! Not a sound could I hear but the blowing of a fish, now and then, on the surface of the sea, and the creak of the brig's crazy old spars, as she rolled gently from side to side with the little swell there was on the quiet water.

An hour and a quarter. The wick grew terribly, as the quarter slipped away; and the charred top of it began to thicken and spread out mushroom-shape. It would fall off soon. Would it fall off red-hot, and would the swing of the brig cant it over the side of the candle, and let it down on the slow-match? If it would, I had about ten minutes to live instead of an hour.

This discovery set my mind for a minute on a new tack altogether. I began to ponder with myself what sort of a death blowing-up might be. Painful? Well, it would be, surely, too sudden for that. Perhaps just one crash, inside me, or outside me, or both, and nothing more? Perhaps not even a crash; that and death and the scattering of this living body of mine into millions of fiery sparks, might all happen in the same instant? I couldn't make it out; I couldn't settle how it would be. The minute of calmness in my mind left it, before I had half done thinking; and I got all abroad again.

When I came back to my thoughts, or when they came back to me (I can't say which), the wick was awfully tall, the flame was burning with a smoke above it, the charred top was broad and red, and heavily spreading out to its fall.

My despair and horror at seeing it, took me in a new way, which was good and right, at any rate, for my poor soul. I tried to pray; in my own heart, you will understand, for the gag put all lip-praying out of my power. I tried, but the candle seemed to burn it up in me. I struggled hard to force my eyes from the slow, murdering flame, and to look up through the chink in the hatch at the blessed daylight. I tried once, tried twice; and gave it up. I tried next only to shut my eyes, and keep them shut—once—twice—and the second time I did it. "God bless old mother, and sister Lizzie; God keep them both, and forgive *me.*" That was all I had time to say, in my own heart, before my eyes opened again, in spite of me, and the flame of the candle flew into them, flew all over me, and burnt up the rest of my thoughts in an instant.

I couldn't hear the fish blowing now; I couldn't hear the creak of the spars; I couldn't think; I couldn't feel the sweat of my own death agony on my face—I could only look at the heavy charred top of the wick. It swelled, tottered, bent over to one side, dropped—red hot at the moment of its fall—black and harmless, even before the swing of the brig had canted it over into the bottom of the candlestick.

I caught myself laughing.

Yes! laughing at the safe fall of the bit of wick. But for the gag I should have screamed with laughing. As it was, I shook with it inside me—shook till the blood was in my head, and I was all but suffocated for want of breath. I had just sense enough left to feel that my own horrid laughter, at that awful moment, was a sign of my brain going at last. I had just sense enough left to make another struggle before my mind broke loose like a frightened horse, and ran away with me.

One comforting look at the blink of daylight through the hatch was what I tried for once more. The fight to force my eyes from the candle and to get that one look at the daylight, was the hardest I had had yet; and I lost the fight. The flame had hold of my eyes as fast as the lashings had hold of my hands. I couldn't look away from it. I couldn't even shut my eyes, when I tried that next, for the second time. There was the wick, growing tall once more. There was the space of unburnt candle between the light and the slow-match shortened to an inch or less.

How much life did that inch leave me? Three-quarters of an hour? Half an hour? Fifty minutes? Twenty minutes? Steady! an inch of tallow candle would burn longer than twenty minutes. An inch of tallow! the notion of a man's body and soul being kept together by an inch of tallow! Wonderful! Why, the greatest king that sits on a throne can't keep a man's body and soul together; and here's an inch of tallow that can do what the king can't! There's something to tell mother, when I get home, which will surprise her more than all the rest of my voyages put together. I laughed inwardly, again, at the thought of that; and shook and swelled and suffocated myself, till the light of the candle leaped in through my eyes, and licked up the laughter, and burnt it out of me, and made me all empty, and cold, and quiet once more.

Mother and Lizzie. I don't know when they came back; but they did come back—not, as it seemed to me, into my mind this time; but right down bodily before me, in the hold of the brig.

Yes: sure enough, there was Lizzie, just as light-hearted as usual, laughing at me. Laughing! Well, why not? Who is to blame Lizzie for thinking I'm lying on my back, drunk in the cellar, with the beer barrels all round me? Steady! she's crying now—spinning round and round in a fiery mist, wringing her hands, screeching out for help—fainter and fainter, like the splash of the schooner's sweeps. Gone!—burnt up in the fiery mist. Mist? fire? no: neither one nor the other. It's mother makes the light—mother knitting, with ten flaming points at the ends of her fingers and thumbs, and slow-matches hanging in bunches all round her face instead of her own grey hair. Mother in her old armchair, and the pilot's long skinny hands hanging over the back of the chair, dripping with gunpowder. No! no gunpowder, no chair, no mother—nothing but the pilot's face, shining red hot, like a sun, in the fiery mist; turning upside down in the fiery mist; running backwards and forwards along the slowmatch, in the fiery mist; spinning millions of miles in a minute, in the fiery mist—spinning itself smaller and smaller into one tiny point, and that point darting on a sudden straight into my head—and then, all fire and all mist—no hearing, no seeing, no thinking, no feeling—the brig, the sea, my own self, the whole world, all gone together!

After what I've just told you, I know nothing and remember nothing, till I woke up (as it seemed to me) in a comfortable bed, with two rough and ready men like myself sitting on each side of my pillow, and a gentleman standing watching me at the foot of the bed. It was about seven in the morning. My sleep (or what seemed like my sleep to me) had lasted better than eight months— I was among my own countrymen in the island of Trinidad—the men at each side of my pillow were my keepers, turn and turn about—and the gentleman standing at the foot of the bed was the doctor. What I said and did in those eight months, I never have known and never shall. I woke out of it as if it had been one long sleep—that's all I know.

It was another two months or more before the doctor thought it safe to answer the questions I asked him.

The brig had been anchored, just as I had supposed, off a part of the coast which was lonely enough to make the Spaniards pretty sure of no interruption, so long as they managed their murderous work quietly under cover of night.

My life had not been saved from the shore, but from the sea. An American vessel, becalmed in the offing, had made out the brig as the sun rose; and the captain having his time on his hands in consequence of the calm, and seeing a vessel anchored where no vessel had any reason to be, had manned one of his boats and sent his mate with it, to look a little closer into the matter, and bring back a report of what he saw.

What he saw, when he and his men found the brig deserted and boarded her, was a gleam of candlelight through the chink in the hatchway. The flame was within about a thread's breadth of the slow-match, when he lowered himself into the hold; and if he had not had the sense and coolness to cut the match in two with his knife, before he touched the candle, he and his men might have been blown up along with the brig, as well as me. The match caught and turned into sputtering red fire, in the very act of putting the candle out; and if the communication with the powder barrel had not been cut off, the Lord only knows what might have happened.

What became of the Spanish schooner and the pilot I have never heard from that day to this.

As for the brig, the Yankees took her, as they took me, to Trinidad, and claimed their salvage, and got it, I hope, for their own sakes. I was landed just in the same state as when they rescued me from the brig, that is to say, clean out of my senses. But, please to remember it was a long time ago; and, take my word for it, I was discharged cured, as I have told you. Bless your hearts, I'm all right now, as you may see. I'm a little shaken by telling the story, as is only natural—a little shaken, my good friends, that's all.

Mr. Lepel and the Housekeeper

First Epoch

The Italians are born actors.

At this conclusion I arrived, sitting in a Roman theatre—now many years since. My friend and travelling companion, Rothsay, cordially agreed with me. Experience had given us some claim to form an opinion. We had visited, at that time, nearly every city in Italy. Wherever a theatre was open, we had attended the performances of the companies which travel from place to place; and we had never seen bad acting from first to last. Men and women, whose names are absolutely unknown in England, played (in modern comedy and drama for the most part) with a general level of dramatic ability which I have never seen equalled in the theatres of other nations. Incapable Italian actors there must be, no doubt. For my own part I have only discovered them, by ones and twos, in England; appearing among the persons engaged to support Salvini and Ristori before the audiences of London.

On the occasion of which I am now writing, the night's performances consisted of two plays. An accident, to be presently related, prevented us from seeing more than the introductory part of the second piece. That one act—in respect of the influence which the remembrance of it afterwards exercised over Rothsay and myself—claims a place of its own in the opening pages of the present narrative.

The scene of the story was laid in one of the principalities of Italy, in the bygone days of the Carbonaro conspiracies. The chief persons were two young noblemen, friends affectionately attached to each other, and a beautiful girl born in the lower ranks of life.

On the rising of the curtain, the scene before us was the court-yard of a prison. We found the beautiful girl (called Celia as well as I can recollect) in great distress; confiding her sorrows to the gaoler's daughter. Her father was pining in the prison, charged with an offence of which he was innocent; and she herself was suffering the tortures of hopeless love. She was on the point of confiding her secret to her friend, when the appearance of the young nobleman closed her lips. The girls at once withdrew; and the two friends—whom I now only remember as the Marquis and the Count—began the dialogue which prepared us for the story of the play.

The Marquis had been tried for conspiracy against the reigning Prince and his government; had been found guilty, and is condemned to be shot that evening. He accepts his sentence with the resignation of a man who is weary of his life. Young as he is, he has tried the round of pleasures without enjoyment; he has no interests, no aspirations, no hopes; he looks on death as a welcome release. His friend the Count, admitted to a farewell interview, has invented a stratagem by which the prisoner may escape and take to flight. The Marquis expresses a grateful sense of obligation, and prefers being shot. "I don't value my life," he says; "I am not a happy man like you." Upon this the Count mentions circumstances which he has hitherto kept secret. He loves the charming Celia, and loves in vain. Her reputation is unsullied; she possesses every good quality that a man can desire in a wife—but the Count's social position forbids him to marry a woman of low birth. He is heartbroken; and he too finds life without hope a burden that is not to be borne. The Marquis at once sees a way of devoting himself to his friend's interests. He is rich; his money is at his own disposal; he will bequeath a marriage portion to Celia which will make her one of the richest women in Italy. The Count receives this proposal with a sigh. "No money," he says, "will remove the obstacle that still remains. My father's fatal objection to Celia is her rank in life." The Marquis walks apart—considers a little—consults his watch—and returns with a new idea. "I have nearly two hours of life still left," he says. "Send for Celia: she was here just now, and she is probably in her father's cell." The Count is at a loss to understand what this proposal means. The Marquis explains himself. "I ask your permission," he resumes, "to offer marriage to Celia—for your sake. The chaplain of the prison will perform the ceremony. Before dark, the girl you love will be my widow. My widow is a lady of title—a fit wife for the greatest

nobleman in the land." The Count protests and refuses in vain.
The gaoler is sent to find Celia. She appears. Unable to endure the
scene, the Count rushes out in horror. The Marquis takes the girl
into his confidence, and makes his excuses. If she becomes a
widow of rank, she may not only marry the Count, but will be in a
position to procure the liberty of the innocent old man, whose
strength is failing him under the rigours of imprisonment. Celia
hesitates. After a struggle with herself, filial love prevails, and she
consents. The gaoler announces that the chaplain is waiting; the
bride and bridegroom withdraw to the prison chapel. Left on the
stage, the gaoler hears a distant sound in the city, which he is at a
loss to understand. It sinks, increases again, travels nearer to the
prison, and now betrays itself as the sound of multitudinous voices
in a state of furious uproar. Has the conspiracy broken out again?
Yes! The whole population has risen; the soldiers have refused to
fire on the people; the terrified Prince has dismissed his ministers
and promises a constitution. The Marquis, returning from the
ceremony which has just made Celia his wife, is presented with a
free pardon, and with the offer of a high place in the reformed
ministry. A new life is opening before him—and he has innocently
ruined his friend's prospects! On this striking situation the drop-
curtain falls.

While we were still applauding the first act, Rothsay alarmed
me: he dropped from his seat at my side, like a man struck dead.
The stifling heat in the theatre had proved too much for him. We
carried him out at once into the fresh air. When he came to his
senses, my friend entreated me to leave him, and see the end of the
play. To my mind, he looked as if he might faint again. I insisted
on going back with him to our hotel.

On the next day I went to the theatre, to ascertain if the play
would be repeated. The box-office was closed. The dramatic company had left Rome.

My interest in discovering how the story ended led me next to
the booksellers' shops—in the hope of buying the play. Nobody
knew anything about it. Nobody could tell me whether it was the
original work of an Italian writer, or whether it had been stolen
(and probably disfigured) from the French. As a fragment I had
seen it. As a fragment it has remained from that time to this.

Second Epoch

One of my objects in writing these lines is to vindicate the character of an innocent woman (formerly in my service as housekeeper)
who has been cruelly slandered. Absorbed in the pursuit of my
purpose, it has only now occurred to me that strangers may desire
to know something more than they know now of myself and my
friend. "Give us some idea," they may say, "of what sort of persons you are, if you wish to interest us at the outset of your story."

A most reasonable suggestion, I admit. Unfortunately, I am not
the right man to comply with it.

In the first place, I cannot pretend to pronounce judgement on
my own character. In the second place, I am incapable of writing
impartially of my friend. At the imminent risk of his own life,
Rothsay rescued me from a dreadful death by accident, when we
were at college together. Who can expect me to speak of his faults?
I am not even capable of seeing them.

Under these embarrassing circumstances—and not forgetting, at
the same time, that a servant's opinion of his master and his
master's friends may generally be trusted not to err on the favourable side—I am tempted to call my valet as a witness to character.

I slept badly on our first night at Rome; and I happened to be
awake while the man was talking of us confidentially in the courtyard of the hotel—just under my bedroom window. Here, to the
best of my recollection, is a faithful report of what he said to some
friend among the servants who understood English:

"My master's well connected, you must know—though he's only
plain Mr. Lepel. His uncle's the great lawyer, Lord Lepel; and his
late father was a banker. Rich, did you say. I should think he *was*
rich—and be hanged to him! No! not married, and not likely to
be. Owns he was forty last birthday; a regular old bachelor. Not a
bad sort, taking him altogether. The worst of him is, he is one of
the most indiscreet persons I ever met with. Does the queerest
things, when the whim takes him, and doesn't care what other
people think of it. They say the Lepels have all got a slate loose in
the upper story. Oh, no; not a very old family—I mean, nothing
compared to the family of his friend, young Rothsay. *They* count
back, as I have heard, to the ancient Kings of Scotland. Between
ourselves, the ancient Kings haven't left the Rothsays much

money. They would be glad, I'll be bound, to get my rich master for one of their daughters. Poor as Job, I tell you. This young fellow, travelling with us, has never had a spare five-pound note since he was born. Plenty of brains in his head, I grant you; and a little too apt sometimes to be suspicious of other people. But liberal—oh, give him his due—liberal in a small way. Tips me with a sovereign now and then. I take it—Lord bless you, I take it. What do you say? Has he got any employment? Not he! Dabbles in chemistry (experiments, and that sort of thing) by way of amusing himself; and tells the most infernal lies about it. The other day he showed me a bottle about as big as a thimble, with what looked like water in it, and said it was enough to poison everybody in the hotel. What rot! Isn't that the clock striking again? Near about bedtime, I should say. Wish you good night."

There are our characters—drawn on the principle of justice without mercy, by an impudent rascal who is the best valet in England. Now you know what sort of persons we are; and now we may go on again.

Rothsay and I parted, soon after our night at the theatre. He went to Civita Vecchia to join a friend's yacht, waiting for him in the harbour. I turned homeward, travelling at a leisurely rate through the Tyrol and Germany.

After my arrival in England certain events in my life occurred, which did not appear to have any connexion at the time. They led nevertheless to consequences which seriously altered the relations of happy past years between Rothsay and myself.

The first event took place on my return to my house in London. I found among the letters waiting for me, an invitation from Lord Lepel to spend a few weeks with him at his country seat in Sussex.

I had made so many excuses, in past years, when I received invitations from my uncle, that I was really ashamed to plead engagements in London again. There was no unfriendly feeling between us. My only motive for keeping away from him took its rise in dislike of the ordinary modes of life in an English country-house. A man who feels no interest in politics, who cares nothing for field sports, who is impatient of amateur music and incapable of small talk, is a man out of his element in country society. This was my unlucky case. I went to Lord Lepel's house sorely against my will; longing already for the day when it would be time to say good-bye.

The routine of my uncle's establishment had remained unaltered since my last experience of it.

I found my lord expressing the same pride in his collection of old masters, and telling the same story of the wonderful escape of his picture-gallery from fire—I renewed my acquaintance with the same members of Parliament among the guests, all on the same side in politics—I joined in the same dreary amusements—I saluted the same resident priest (the Lepels are all born and bred Roman Catholics)—I submitted to the same rigidly early breakfast hour; and inwardly cursed the same peremptory bell, ringing as a means of reminding us of our meals. The one change that presented itself was a change out of the house. Death had removed the lodge-keeper at the park-gate. His widow and daughter (Mrs. Rymer and little Susan) remained in their pretty cottage. They had been allowed by my lord's kindness to take charge of the gate.

Out walking, on the morning after my arrival, I was caught in a shower on my way back to the park, and took shelter in the lodge.

In the bygone days, I had respected Mrs. Rymer's husband as a thoroughly worthy man—but Mrs. Rymer herself was no great favourite of mine. She had married beneath her, as the phrase is, and she was a little too conscious of it. A woman with a sharp eye to her own interests; selfishly discontented with her position in life, and not very scrupulous in her choice of means when she had an end in view: that is how I describe Mrs. Rymer. Her daughter, whom I only remembered as a weakly child, astonished me when I saw her again after the interval that had elapsed. The backward flower had bloomed into perfect health. Susan was now a lovely little modest girl of seventeen—with a natural delicacy and refinement of manner, which marked her to my mind as one of Nature's gentlewomen. When I entered the lodge she was writing at a table in a corner, having some books on it, and rose to withdraw. I begged that she would proceed with her employment, and asked if I might know what it was. She answered me with a blush, and a pretty brightening of her clear blue eyes. "I am trying, sir, to teach myself French," she said. The weather showed no signs of improving—I volunteered to help her, and found her such an attentive and intelligent pupil that I looked in at the lodge from time to time afterwards, and continued my instructions. The younger men among my uncle's guests set their own stupid construction on my attentions "to the girl at the gate," as they called her—rather too familiarly, according to my notions of propriety. I contrived to remind them that I was old enough to be Susan's father, in a manner which put an end to their jokes; and I was pleased to hear, when I next went to the lodge, that Mrs. Rymer had been wise enough to keep these facetious gentlemen at their proper distance.

The day of my departure arrived. Lord Lepel took leave of me kindly, and asked for news of Rothsay. "Let me know when your friend returns," my uncle said; "he belongs to a good old stock. Put me in mind of him when I next invite you to come to my house."

On my way to the train I stopped of course at the lodge to say good-bye. Mrs. Rymer came out alone. I asked for Susan.

"My daughter is not very well to-day."

"Is she confined to her room?"

"She is in the parlour."

I might have been mistaken, but I thought Mrs. Rymer answered me in no very friendly way. Resolved to judge for myself, I entered the lodge, and found my poor little pupil sitting in a corner, crying. When I asked her what was the matter, the excuse of a "bad headache" was the only reply that I received. The natures of young girls are a hopeless puzzle to me. Susan seemed, for some reason which it was impossible to understand, to be afraid to look at me.

"Have you and your mother been quarrelling?" I asked.

"Oh, no!"

She denied it with such evident sincerity that I could not for a moment suspect her of deceiving me. Whatever the cause of her distress might be, it was plain that she had her own reasons for keeping it a secret.

Her French books were on the table. I tried a little allusion to her lessons.

"I hope you will go on regularly with your studies," I said.

"I will do my best, sir—without you to help me."

She said it so sadly that I proposed—purely from the wish to encourage her—a continuation of our lessons through the post.

"Send your exercises to me once a week," I suggested; "and I will return them corrected."

She thanked me in low tones, with a shyness of manner which I had never noticed in her before. I had done my best to cheer her— and I was conscious, as we shook hands at parting, that I had failed. A feeling of disappointment overcomes me when I see young people out of spirits. I was sorry for Susan.

Third Epoch

One of my faults (which has not been included in the list set forth by my valet) is a disinclination to occupy myself with my own domestic affairs. The proceedings of my footman, while I had been away from home, left me no alternative but to dismiss him on my return. With this exertion of authority my interference as chief of the household came to an end. I left it to my excellent house-keeper, Mrs. Mozeen, to find a sober successor to the drunken vagabond who had been sent away. She discovered a respectable young man—tall, plump, and rosy—whose name was Joseph, and whose character was beyond reproach. I have but one excuse for noticing such a trifling event as this. It took its place, at a later period, in the chain which was slowly winding itself round me.

My uncle had asked me to prolong my visit; and I should probably have consented, but for anxiety on the subject of a near and dear relative—my sister. Her health had been failing since the death of her husband, to whom she was tenderly attached. I heard news of her while I was in Sussex, which hurried me back to town. In a month more, her death deprived me of my last living relation. She left no children; and my two brothers had both died unmarried while they were still young men.

This affliction placed me in a position of serious embarrassment, in regard to the disposal of my property after my death.

I had hitherto made no will; being well aware that my fortune (which was entirely in money) would go in due course of law to the person of all others who would employ it to the best purpose—that is to say, to my sister as my nearest of kin. As I was now situated, my property would revert to my uncle if I died intestate. He was a richer man than I was. Of his two children, both sons, the eldest would inherit his estates: the youngest had already succeeded to his mother's ample fortune. Having literally no family claims on me, I felt bound to recognize the wider demands of poverty and misfortune, and to devote my superfluous wealth to increasing the revenues of charitable institutions. As to minor legacies, I owed it to my good housekeeper, Mrs. Mozeen, not to forget the faithful services of past years. Need I add—if I had been free to act as I pleased—that I should have gladly made Rothsay the object of a handsome bequest? But this was not to be. My friend was a man morbidly sensitive on the subject of money. In the early days of our intercourse, we had been for the first and only time on the verge of a quarrel, when I had asked (as a favour to myself) to be allowed to provide for him in my will.

"It is because I am poor," he explained, "that I refuse to profit by your kindness—though I feel it gratefully."

I failed to understand him—and said so plainly.

"You will understand this," he resumed; "I should never recover my sense of degradation, if a mercenary motive on my side was associated with our friendship. Don't say it's impossible! You know as well as I do that appearances would be against me, in the eyes of the world. Besides, I don't want money; my own small income is enough for me. Make me your executor if you like, and leave me the customary present of five hundred pounds. If you exceed that sum I declare on my word of honour that I will not touch one farthing of it." He took my hand, and pressed it fervently. "Do me a favour," he said. "Never let us speak of this again!"

I understood that I must yield—or lose my friend.

In now making my will, I accordingly appointed Rothsay one of my executors, on the terms that he had prescribed. The minor legacies having been next duly reduced to writing, I left the bulk of my fortune to public charities.

My lawyer laid the fair copy of the will on my table.

"A dreary disposition of property for a man of your age," he said. "I hope to receive a new set of instructions before you are a year older."

"What instructions?" I asked.

"To provide for your wife and children," he answered.

My wife and children! The idea seemed to be so absurd that I burst out laughing. It never occurred to me that there could be any absurdity from my own point of view.

I was sitting alone, after my legal adviser had taken his leave,

looking absently at the newly-engrossed will, when I heard a sharp
knock at the house-door which I thought I recognized. In another
minute Rothsay's bright face enlivened my dull room. He had
returned from the Mediterranean that morning.

"Am I interrupting you?" he asked, pointing to the leaves of
manuscript before me. "Are you writing a book?"

"I am making my will."

His manner changed; he looked at me seriously.

"Do you remember what I said, when we once talked of your
will?" he asked. I set his doubts at rest immediately—but he was
not quite satisfied yet. "Can't you put your will away?" he suggested. "I hate the sight of anything that reminds me of death."

"Give me a minute to sign it," I said—and rang to summon the
witnesses.

Mrs. Mozeen answered the bell. Rothsay looked at her, as if he
wished to have my housekeeper put away as well as my will. From
the first moment when he had seen her, he conceived a great
dislike to that good creature. There was nothing, I am sure, personally repellent about her. She was a little slim quiet woman, with a
pale complexion and bright brown eyes. Her movements were
gentle; her voice was low; her decent grey dress was adapted to her
age. Why Rothsay should dislike her was more than he could
explain himself. He turned his unreasonable prejudice into a
joke—and said he hated a woman who wore slate-coloured cap-
ribbons!

I explained to Mrs. Mozeen that I wanted witnesses to the
signature of my will. Naturally enough—being in the room at the
time—she asked if she could be one of them.

I was obliged to say No; and not to mortify her, I gave the
reason.

"My will recognizes what I owe to your good services," I said.
"If you are one of the witnesses, you will lose your legacy. Send up
the menservants."

With her customary tact, Mrs. Mozeen expressed her gratitude
silently, by a look—and left the room.

"Why couldn't you tell that woman to send the servants, without
mentioning her legacy?" Rothsay asked. "My friend Lepel, you
have done a very foolish thing."

"In what way?"

"You have given Mrs. Mozeen an interest in your death."

It was impossible to make a serious reply to this ridiculous exhibition of Rothsay's prejudice against poor Mrs. Mozeen.

"When am I to be murdered?" I asked. "And how is it to be done? Poison?"

"I'm not joking," Rothsay answered. "You are infatuated about your housekeeper. When you spoke of her legacy, did you notice her eyes?"

"Yes."

"Did nothing strike you?"

"It struck me that they were unusually well-preserved eyes for a woman of her age."

The appearance of the valet and the footman put an end to this idle talk. The will was executed, and locked up. Our conversation turned on Rothsay's travels by sea. The cruise had been in every way successful. The matchless shores of the Mediterranean defied description; the sailing of the famous yacht had proved to be worthy of her reputation; and, to crown all, Rothsay had come back to England, in a fair way, for the first time in his life, of making money.

"I have discovered a treasure," he announced.

"What is it?"

"It *was* a dirty little modern picture, picked up in a by-street at Palermo. It *is* a Virgin and Child, by Guido."

On further explanation it appeared that the picture exposed for sale was painted on copper. Noticing the contrast between the rare material and the wretchedly bad painting that covered it, Rothsay had called to mind some of the well-known stories of valuable works of art that had been painted over for purposes of disguise. The price asked for the picture amounted to little more than the value of the metal. Rothsay bought it. His knowledge of chemistry enabled him to put his suspicion successfully to the test; and one of the guests on board the yacht—a famous French artist—had declared his conviction that the picture now revealed to veiw was a genuine work by Guido. Such an opinion as this convinced me that it would be worth while to submit my friend's discovery to the judgement of other experts. Consulted independently, these critics confirmed the view taken by the celebrated personage who had first seen the work. This result having been obtained, Rothsay asked my advice next on the question of selling his picture. I at once thought of my uncle. An undoubted work by Guido would surely be an acquisition to his gallery. I had only (in accordance with his own request) to let him know that my friend had returned to England. We might take the picture with us, when we received our invitation to Lord Lepel's house.

Fourth Epoch

My uncle's answer arrived by return of post. Other engagements obliged him to defer receiving us for a month. At the end of that time, we were cordially invited to visit him, and to stay as long as we liked.

In the interval that now passed, other events occurred—still of the trifling kind.

One afternoon, just as I was thinking of taking my customary ride in the park, the servant appeared charged with a basket of flowers, and with a message from Mrs. Rymer, requesting me to honour her by accepting a little offering from her daughter. Hearing that she was then waiting in the hall, I told the man to show her in. Susan (as I ought to have already mentioned) had sent her exercises to me regularly every week. In returning them corrected, I had once or twice added a word of well-deserved approval. The offering of flowers was evidently intended to express my pupil's grateful sense of the interest taken in her by her teacher.

I had no reason, this time, to suppose that Mrs. Rymer entertained an unfriendly feeling towards me. At the first words of greeting that passed between us I perceived a change in her manner, which ran into the opposite extreme. She overwhelmed me with the most elaborate demonstrations of politeness and respect; dwelling on her gratitude for my kindness in receiving her, and on her pride at seeing her daughter's flowers on my table, until I made a resolute effort to stop her by asking (as if it was actually a matter of importance to me!) whether she was in London on business or on pleasure.

"Oh, on business, sir! My poor husband invested his little savings in bank stock, and I have just been drawing my dividend. I do hope you don't think my girl over-bold in venturing to send you a few flowers. She wouldn't allow me to interfere. I do assure you she would gather and arrange them with her own hands. In themselves I know they are hardly worth accepting; but if you will allow the motive to plead—— "

I made another effort to stop Mrs. Rymer; I said her daughter could not have sent me a prettier present.

The inexhaustible woman only went on more fluently than ever.

"She is so grateful, sir, and so proud of your goodness in looking at her exercises. The difficulties of the French language seem as nothing to her, now her motive is to please you. She is so devoted to her studies that I find it difficult to induce her to take the exercise necessary to her health; and, as you may perhaps remember, Susan was always rather weakly as a child. She inherits her father's constitution, Mr. Lepel—not mine."

Here, to my infinite relief, the servant appeared, announcing that my horse was at the door.

Mrs. Rymer opened her mouth. I saw a coming flood of aplogies on the point of pouring out—and seized my hat on the spot. I declared I had an appointment; I sent kind remembrances to Susan (pitying her for having such a mother with my whole heart); I said I hoped to return to my uncle's house soon, and to continue the French lessons. The one thing more that I remember was finding myself safe in the saddle, and out of the reach of Mrs. Rymer's tongue.

Reflecting on what had passed, it was plain to me that this woman had some private end in view, and that my abrupt departure had prevented her from finding the way to it. What motive could she possibly have for that obstinate persistence in presenting poor Susan under a favourable aspect, to a man who had already shown that he was honestly interested in her pretty modest daughter? I tried hard to penetrate the mystery—and gave it up in despair.

Three days before the date at which Rothsay and I were to pay our visit to Lord Lepel, I found myself compelled to undergo one of the minor miseries of human life. In other words, I became one of the guests at a large dinner-party. It was a rainy day in October. My position at the table placed me between a window that was open, and a door that was hardly ever shut. I went to bed shivering; and woke the next morning with a headache and a difficulty in breathing. On consulting the doctor, I found that I was suffering from an attack of bronchitis. There was no reason to be alarmed.

If I remained indoors, and submitted to the necessary treatment, I might hope to keep my engagement with my uncle in ten days or a fortnight.

There was no alternative but to submit. I accordingly arranged with Rothsay that he should present himself at Lord Lepel's house (taking the picture with him), on the date appointed for our visit, and that I should follow as soon as I was well enough to travel.

On the day when he was to leave London, my friend kindly came to keep me company for awhile. He was followed into my room by Mrs. Mozeen, with a bottle of medicine in her hand. This worthy creature, finding that the doctor's directions occasionally escaped my memory, devoted herself to the duty of administering the remedies at the prescribed intervals of time. When she left the room, having performed her duties as usual, I saw Rothsay's eyes follow her to the door with an expression of sardonic curiosity. He put a strange question to me as soon as we were alone.

"Who engaged that new servant of yours?" he asked. "I mean the fat fellow, with the curly flaxen hair."

"Hiring servants," I replied, "is not much in my way. I left the engagement of the new man to Mrs. Mozeen."

Rothsay walked gravely up to my bedside.

"Lepel," he said, "your respectable housekeeper is in love with the fat young footman."

It is not easy to amuse a man suffering from bronchitis. But this new outbreak of absurdity was more than I could resist, even with a mustard-plaster on my chest.

"I thought I should raise your spirits," Rothsay proceeded. "When I came to your house this morning, the valet opened the door to me. I expressed my surprise at his condescending to take that trouble. He informed me that Joseph was otherwise engaged. 'With anybody in particular?' I asked, humouring the joke. 'Yes, sir, with the housekeeper. She's teaching him how to brush his hair, so as to show off his good looks to the best advantage.' Make up your mind, my friend, to lose Mrs. Mozeen—especially if she happens to have any money."

"Nonsense, Rothsay! The poor woman is old enough to be Joseph's mother."

"My good fellow, that won't make any differences to Joseph. In the days when we were rich enough to keep a manservant, our footman—as handsome a fellow as ever you saw, and no older than I am—married a witch with a lame leg. When I asked him why he had made such a fool of himself he looked quite indignant, and said, 'Sir! she has got six hundred pounds.' He and the witch keep a public-house. What will you bet me that we don't see your housekeeper drawing beer at the bar, and Joseph getting drunk in the parlour, before we are a year older?"

I was not well enough to prolong my enjoyment of Rothsay's boyish humour. Besides, exaggeration to be really amusing must have some relation, no matter how slender it may be, to the truth. My housekeeper belonged to a respectable family, and was essentially a person accustomed to respect herself. Her brother occupied a position of responsibility in the establishment of a firm of chemists whom I had employed for years past. Her late husband had farmed his own land and had owed his ruin to calamities for which he was in no way responsible. Kind-hearted Mrs. Mozeen was just the woman to take a motherly interest in a well-disposed lad like Joseph; and it was equally characteristic of my valet—especially when Rothsay was thoughtless enough to encourage him—to pervert an innocent action for the sake of indulging in a stupid jest. I took advantage of my privilege as an invalid, and changed the subject.

A week passed. I had expected to hear from Rothsay. To my surprise and disappointment no letter arrived.

Susan was more considerate. She wrote, very modestly and prettily, to say that she and her mother had heard of my illness from Mr. Rothsay, and to express the hope that I should soon be restored to health. A few days later, Mrs. Rymer's politeness carried her to the length of taking the journey to London, to make inquiries at my door. I did not see her, of course. She left word that she would have the honour of calling again.

The second week followed. I had by that time perfectly recovered from my attack of bronchitis—and yet I was too ill to leave the house.

The doctor himself seemed to be at a loss to understand the symptoms that now presented themselves. A vile sensation of nausea tried my endurance, and an incomprehensible prostration of strength depressed my spirits. I felt such a strange reluctance to exert myself, that I actually left it to Mrs. Mozeen to write to my uncle in my name, and say that I was not yet well enough to visit him. My medical adviser tried various methods of treatment; my housekeeper administered the prescribed medicine with unremitting care; but nothing came of it. A physician of great authority was called into consultation. Being completely puzzled, he retreated to the last refuge of bewildered doctors. I asked him what was the matter with me. And he answered:

"Suppressed gout."

Fifth Epoch

Midway in the third week, my uncle wrote to me as follows:

"I have been obliged to request your friend Rothsay to bring his visit to a conclusion. Although he refuses to confess it, I have reason to believe that he has committed the folly of falling seriously in love with the young girl at my lodge gate. I have tried remonstrance in vain; and I write to his father at the same time that I write to you. There is much more that I might say. I reserve it for the time when I hope to have the pleasure of seeing you, restored to health."

Two days after the receipt of this alarming letter, Rothsay returned to me.

Ill as I was, I forgot my sufferings the moment I looked at him. Wild, and haggard, he stared at me with bloodshot eyes like a man demented.

"Do you think I am mad? I dare say I am. I can't live without her." Those were the first words he said when we shook hands.

But I had more influence over him than any other person; and, weak as I was, I exerted it. Little by little, he became more reasonable; he began to speak like his old self again.

To have expressed any surprise, on my part, at what had happened, would have been not only imprudent, but unworthy of him and of me. My first inquiry was suggested by the fear that he might have been hurried into openly confessing his passion to Susan— although his position forbade him to offer marriage. I had done him an injustice. His honourable nature had shrunk from the cruelty of raising hopes, which, for all he knew to the contrary, might never be realized. At the same time, he had his reasons for believing that he was at least personally acceptable to her.

"She was always glad to see me," said poor Rothsay. "We constantly talked of you. She spoke of your kindness so prettily and so gratefully. Oh, Lepel, it is not her beauty only that has won my heart! Her nature is the nature of an angel."

His voice failed him. For the first time in my remembrance of our long companionship, he burst into tears.

I was so shocked and distressed that I had the greatest difficulty in preserving my own self-control. In the effort to comfort him, I asked if he had ventured to confide in his father.

"You are the favourite son," I reminded him. "Is there no gleam of hope in the future?"

He had written to his father. In silence he gave me the letter in reply.

It was expressed with a moderation which I had hardly dared to expect. Mr. Rothsay the elder admitted that he had himself married for love, and that his wife's rank in the social scale (although higher than Susan's) had not been equal to his own.

"In such a family as ours," he wrote—perhaps with pardonable pride—"we raise our wives to our own degree. But this young person labours under a double disadvantage. She is obscure, and she is poor. What have you to offer her? Nothing. And what have I to give you? Nothing."

This meant, as I interpreted it, that the main obstacle in the way was Susan's poverty. And I was rich! In the excitement that possessed me, I followed the impulse of the moment headlong, like a child.

"While you were away from me," I said to Rothsay, "did you never once think of your old friend? Must I remind you that I can make Susan your wife with one stroke of my pen?" He looked at me in silent surprise. I took my cheque-book from the drawer of the table, and placed the inkstand within reach. "Susan's marriage portion," I said, "is a matter of a line of writing, with my name at the end of it."

He burst out with an exclamation that stopped me, just as my pen touched the paper.

"Good heavens!" he cried, "you are thinking of that play we saw at Rome! Are we on the stage? Are you performing the part of the Marquis—and am I the Count?"

I was so startled by this wild allusion to the past—I recognized with such astonishment the reproduction of one of the dramatic situations in the play, at a crisis in his life and mine—that the use of the pen remained suspended in my hand. For the first time in my life, I was conscious of a sensation which resembled superstitious dread.

Rothsay recovered himself first. He misinterpreted what was passing in my mind.

"Don't think me ungrateful," he said. "You dear, kind, good fellow, consider for a moment, and you will see that it can't be. What would be said of her and of me, if you made Susan rich with your money, and if I married her? The poor innocent would be called your cast-off mistress. People would say, 'He has behaved liberally to her, and his needy friend has taken advantage of it.'"

The point of view which I had failed to see was put with terrible directness of expression: the conviction that I was wrong was literally forced on me. What reply could I make? Rothsay evidently felt for me.

"You are ill," he said gently; "let me leave you to rest."

He held out his hand to say good-bye. I insisted on his taking up his abode with me, for the present at least. Ordinary persuasion failed to induce him to yield. I put it on selfish grounds next.

"You have noticed that I am ill," I said; "I want you to keep me company."

He gave way directly.

Through the wakeful night, I tried to consider what moral remedies might be within our reach. The one useful conclusion at which I could arrive was to induce Rothsay to try what absence and change might do to compose his mind. To advise him to travel alone was out of the question. I wrote to his one other old friend besides myself—the friend who had taken him on a cruise in the Mediterranean.

The owner of the yacht had that very day given directions to have his vessel laid up for the winter season. He at once countermanded the order by telegraph. "I am an idle man," he said, "and I am as fond of Rothsay as you are. I will take him wherever he likes to go." It was not easy to persuade the object of these kind intentions to profit by them. Nothing that I could say roused him. I spoke to him of his picture. He had left it at my uncle's house, and neither knew nor cared to know whether it had been sold or not. The one consideration which ultimately influenced Rothsay was presented by the doctor; speaking as follows (to quote his own explanation) in the interests of my health:—

"I warned your friend," he said, "that his conduct was causing anxiety which you were not strong enough to bear. On hearing this he at once promised to follow the advice which you had given to him, and to join the yacht. As you know, he has kept his word. May I ask if he has ever followed the medical profession?"

Replying in the negative, I begged the doctor to tell me why he had put his question.

He answered, "Mr. Rothsay requested me to tell him all that I knew about your illness. I complied, of course; mentioning that I had lately adopted a new method of treatment, and that I had every reason to feel confident of the results. He was so interested in the symptoms of your illness, and in the remedies being tried, that he took notes in his pocket-book of what I had said. When he paid me that compliment, I thought it possible that I might be speaking to a colleague."

I was pleased to hear of my friend's anxiety for my recovery. If I had been in better health, I might have asked myself what reason he could have had for making those entries in his pocket-book.

Three days later, another proof reached me of Rothsay's anxiety for my welfare.

The owner of the yacht wrote to beg that I would send him a report of my health, addressed to a port on the south coast of England, to which they were then bound. "If we don't hear good news," he added, "I have reason to fear that Rothsay will overthrow our plans for the recovery of his peace of mind by leaving the vessel, and making his own inquiries at your bedside."

With no small difficulty I roused myself sufficiently to write a few words with my own hand. They were words that lied—for my poor friend's sake. In a postscript, I begged my correspondent to let me hear if the effect produced on Rothsay had answered to our hopes and expectations.

Sixth Epoch

The weary days followed each other—and time failed to justify the doctor's confidence in his new remedies. I grew weaker and weaker.

My uncle came to see me. He was so alarmed that he insisted on a consultation being held with his own physician. Another great authority was called in, at the same time, by the urgent request of my own medical man. These distinguished persons held more than one privy council, before they would consent to give a positive opinion. It was an evasive opinion (encumbered with hard words of Greek and Roman origin) when it was at last pronounced. I waited until they had taken their leave, and then appealed to my own doctor. "What do those men really think?" I asked. "Shall I live, or die?"

The doctor answered for himself as well as for his illustrious colleagues. "We have great faith in the new prescriptions," he said.

I understood what that meant. They were afraid to tell me the truth. I insisted on the truth.

"How long shall I live?" I said. "Till the end of the year?"

The reply followed in one terrible word:

"Perhaps."

It was then the first week in December. I understood that I might reckon—at the utmost—on three weeks of life. What I felt, on arriving at this conclusion, I shall not say. It is the one secret I keep from the readers of these lines.

The next day, Mrs. Rymer called once more to make inquiries. Not satisfied with the servant's report, she entreated that I would consent to see her. My housekeeper, with her customary kindness, undertook to convey the message. If she had been a wicked woman, would she have acted in this way? "Mrs. Rymer seems to be sadly distressed," she pleaded. "As I understand, sir, she is suffering under some domestic anxiety which can only be mentioned to yourself."

Did this anxiety relate to Susan? The bare doubt of it decided me. I consented to see Mrs. Rymer. Feeling it necessary to control her in the use of her tongue, I spoke the moment the door was opened.

"I am suffering from illness; and I must ask you to spare me as much as possible. What do you wish to say to me?"

The tone in which I addressed Mrs. Rymer would have offended a more sensitive woman. The truth is, she had chosen an unfortunate time for her visit. There were fluctuations in the progress of my malady: there were days when I felt better, and days when I felt worse—and this was a bad day. Moreover, my uncle had tried my temper that morning. He had called to see me, on his way to winter in the south of France by his physician's advice; and he recommended a trial of change of air in my case also. His country house (only thirty miles from London) was entirely at my disposal; and the railway supplied beds for invalids. It was useless to answer that I was not equal to the effort. He reminded me that I had exerted myself to leave my bed-chamber for my armchair in the next room, and that a little additonal resolution would enable me to follow his advice. We parted in a state of irritation on either side which, so far as I was concerned, had not subsided yet.

"I wish to speak to you, sir, about my daughter," Mrs. Rymer answered.

The mere allusion to Susan had its composing effect on me. I said kindly that I hoped she was well.

"Well in body," Mrs. Rymer announced. "Far from it, sir, in mind."

Before I could ask what this meant, we were interrupted by the appearance of the servant, bringing the letters which had arrived for me by the afternoon post. I told the man, impatiently, to put them on the table at my side.

"What is distressing Susan?" I inquired, without stopping to look at the letters.

"She is fretting, sir, about your illness. Oh, Mr. Lepel, if you would only try the sweet country air! If you only had my good little Susan to nurse you!"

She too taking my uncle's view! And talking of Susan as my nurse!

"What are you thinking of?" I asked her. "A young girl like your daughter nursing Me! You ought to have more regard for Susan's good name!"

"I know what *you* ought to do!" She made that strange reply with a furtive look at me; half in anger, half in alarm.

"Go on," I said.

"Will you turn me out of your house for my impudence?" she asked.

"I will hear what you have to say to me. What ought I to do?"

"Marry Susan."

I heard the woman plainly—and yet, I declare I doubted the evidence of my senses.

"She's breaking her heart for you," Mrs. Rymer burst out. "She's been in love with you, since you first darkened our doors—and it will end in the neighbours finding it out. I did my duty to her; I tried to stop it; I tried to prevent you from seeing her, when you went away. Too late; the mischief was done. When I see my girl fading day by day—crying about you in secret, talking about you in her dreams—I can't stand it; I must speak out. Oh, yes, I know how far beneath you she is—the daughter of your uncle's servant. But she's your equal, sir, in the sight of Heaven. My lord's priest converted her only last year—and my Susan is as good a Papist as yourself."

How could I let this go on? I felt that I ought to have stopped it before.

"It's possible," I said, "that you may not be deliberately deceiving me. If you are yourself deceived, I am bound to tell you the truth. Mr. Rothsay loves your daughter, and, what is more, Mr. Rothsay has reason to know that Susan——"

"That Susan loves him?" she interposed, with a mocking laugh. "Oh, Mr. Lepel, is it possible that a clever man like you can't see clearer than that? My girl in love with Mr. Rothsay! She wouldn't have looked at him a second time if he hadn't talked to her about *you*. When I complained privately to my lord of Mr. Rothsay hanging about the lodge, do you think she turned as pale as ashes, and cried when *he* passed through the gate, and said goodbye?"

She had complained of Rothsay to Lord Lepel—I understood her at last! She knew that my friend and all his family were poor. She had put her own construction on the innocent interest that I had taken in her daughter. Careless of the difference in rank, blind to the malady that was killing me, she was now bent on separating Rothsay and Susan, by throwing the girl into the arms of a rich husband like myself!

"You are wasting your breath," I told her; "I don't believe one word you say to me."

"Believe Susan, then!" cried the reckless woman. "Let me bring her here. If she's too shamefaced to own the truth, look at her— that's all I ask—look at her, and judge for yourself!"

This was intolerable. In justice to Susan, in justice to Rothsay, I insisted on silence. "No more of it!" I said. "Take care how you provoke me. Don't you see that I am ill? don't you see that you are irritating me to no purpose?"

She altered her tone. "I'll wait," she said quietly, "while you compose yourself."

With those words, she walked to the window, and stood there with her back towards me. Was the wretch taking advantage of my helpless condition? I stretched out my hand to ring the bell, and have her sent away—and hesitated to degrade Susan's mother, for Susan's sake. In my state of prostration, how could I arrive at a decision? My mind was dreadfully disturbed; I felt the imperative necessity of turning my thoughts to some other subject. Looking about me, the letters on the table attracted my attention. Mechanically, I took them up; mechanically I put them down again. Two of them slipped from my trembling fingers; my eyes fell on the uppermost of the two. The address was in the handwriting of the good friend with whom Rothsay was sailing.

Just as I had been speaking of Rothsay, here was the news of him for which I had been waiting.

I opened the letter and read these words:

"There is, I fear, but little hope for our friend—unless this girl on whom he has set his heart can (by some lucky change of circumstances) become his wife. He has tried to master his weakness; but his own infatuation is too much for him. He is really and truly in a state of despair. Two evenings since—to give you a melancholy example of what I mean—I was in my cabin, when I heard the alarm of a man overboard. The man was Rothsay. My sailing-master, seeing that he was unable to swim, jumped into the sea and rescued him, as I got on deck. Rothsay declares it to have been an accident; and everybody believes him but myself. I know the state of his mind. Don't be alarmed; I will have him well looked after; and I won't give him up just yet. We are still bound southward, with a fair wind. If the new scenes which I hope to show him prove to be of no avail, I must reluctantly take him back to England. In that case, which I don't like to contemplate, you may see him again—perhaps in a month's time."

He might return in a month's time—return to hear of the death of the one friend, on whose power and will to help him he might have relied. If I failed to employ in his interests the short interval of life still left to me, could I doubt (after what I had just read) what the end would be? How could I help him? Oh, God! how could I help him?

Mrs. Rymer left the window, and returned to the chair which she had occupied when I first received her.

"Are you quieter in your mind now?" she asked.

I neither answered her nor looked at her.

Still determined to reach her end, she tried again to force her unhappy daughter on me. "Will you consent," she persisted, "to see Susan?"

If she had been a little nearer to me, I am afraid I should have struck her. "You wretch!" I said, "do you know that I am a dying man?"

"While there's life there's hope," Mrs. Rymer remarked.

I ought to have controlled myself; but it was not to be done.

"Hope of your daughter being my rich widow?" I asked.

Her bitter answer followed instantly.

"Even then," she said, "Susan wouldn't marry Rothsay."

A lie! If circumstances favoured her, I knew, on Rothsay's authority, what Susan would do.

The thought burst on my mind, like light bursting on the eyes of a man restored to sight. If Susan agreed to go through the form of marriage with a dying bridegroom, my rich widow could (and would) become Rothsay's wife. Once more, the remembrance of the play at Rome returned, and set the last embers of resolution, which sickness and suffering had left to me, in a flame. The devoted friend of that imaginary story had counted on death to complete his generous purpose in vain: *he* had been condemned by the tribunal of man, and had been reprieved. I—in his place, and with his self-sacrifice in my mind—might found a firmer trust in the future; for I had been condemned by the tribunal of God.

Encouraged by my silence, the obstinate woman persisted. "Won't you even send a message to Susan?" she asked.

Rashly, madly, without an instant's hesitation, I answered: "Go back to Susan, and say I leave it to *her*."

Mrs. Rymer started to her feet. "You leave it to Susan to be your wife, if she likes?"

"I do."

"And if she consents?"

"*I* consent."

In two weeks and a day from that time, the deed was done. When Rothsay returned to England, he would ask for Susan—and he would find my virgin-widow rich and free.

Seventh Epoch

Whatever may be thought of my conduct, let me say this in justice to myself—I was resolved that Susan should not be deceived.

Half an hour after Mrs. Rymer had left my house, I wrote to her daughter, plainly revealing the motive which led me to offer marriage, solely in the future interest of Rothsay and herself.

"If you refuse," I said, in conclusion, "you may depend on my understanding you and feeling for you. But, if you consent—then I have a favour to ask. Never let us speak to one another of the profanation that we have agreed to commit, for your faithful lover's sake."

I had formed a high opinion of Susan—too high an opinion as it seemed. Her reply surprised and disappointed me. In other words, she gave her consent.

I stipulated that the marriage should be kept strictly secret, for a certain period. In my own mind I decided that the interval should be held to expire, either on the day of my death, or on the day when Rothsay returned.

My next proceeding was to write in confidence to the priest whom I have already mentioned, in an earlier part of these pages. He has reasons of his own for not permitting me to disclose the motive which induced him to celebrate my marriage privately in the chapel at Lord Lepel's house. My uncle's desire that I should try change of air, as offering a last chance of recovery, was known to my medical attendant, and served as a sufficient reason (although he protested against the risk) for my removal to the country. I was carried to the station, and placed on a bed—slung by ropes to the ceiling of a saloon carriage, so as to prevent me from feeling the vibration when the train was in motion. Faithful Mrs. Mozeen entreated to be allowed to accompany me. I was reluctantly compelled to refuse compliance with this request, in justice to the claims of my lord's housekeeper; who had been accustomed to exercise undivided authority in the household, and who had made every preparation for my comfort. With her own hands, Mrs. Mozeen packed everything that I required, including the medicines prescribed for the occasion. She was deeply affected, poor soul, when we parted.

I bore the journey—happily for me, it was a short one—better than had been anticipated. For the first few days that followed, the purer air of the country seemed, in some degree, to revive me. But the deadly sense of weakness, the slow sinking of the vital power in me, returned as the time drew near for the marriage. The ceremony was performed at night. Only Susan and her mother were present. No persons in the house but ourselves had the faintest suspicion of what had happened.

I signed my new will (the priest and Mrs. Rymer being the witnesses) in my bed that night. It left everything that I possessed excepting a legacy to Mrs. Mozeen, to my wife.

Obliged, it is needless to say, to preserve appearances, Susan remained at the lodge as usual. But it was impossible to resist her entreaty to be allowed to attend on me, for a few hours daily, an assistant to the regular nurse. When she was alone with me, and had no inquisitive eyes to dread, the poor girl showed a depth of feeling, which I was unable to reconcile with the motives that could alone have induced her (as I then supposed) to consent to the mockery of our marriage. On occasions when I was so far able to resist the languor that oppressed me as to observe what was passing at my bedside—I saw Susan look at me, as if there were thoughts in her pressing for utterance which she hesitated to express. Once, she herself acknowledged this. "I have so much to say to you," she owned, "when you are stronger and fitter to hear me." At other times, her nerves seemed to be shaken by the spectacle of my sufferings. Her kind hands trembled and made mistakes, when they had any nursing duties to perform near me. The servants, noticing her, used to say, "That pretty girl seems to be the most awkward person in the house." On the day that followed the ceremony in the chapel, this want of self-control brought about an accident which led to serious results.

In removing the small chest which held my medicines from the shelf on which it was placed, Susan let it drop on the floor. The two full bottles still left were so completely shattered that not even a tea-spoonful of the contents was saved.

Shocked at what she had done, the poor girl volunteered to go herself to my chemist in London by the first train. I refused to allow it. What did it matter to me now, if my death from exhaustion was hastened by a day or two? Why need my life be prolonged artificially by drugs, when I had nothing left to live for? An excuse for me which would satisfy others was easily found. I said that I had been long weary of physic, and that the accident had decided me on refusing to take more.

That night I did not wake quite so often as usual. When she came to me the next day, Susan noticed that I looked better. The day after, the other nurse made the same observation. At the end of the week I was able to leave my bed, and sit by the fireside, while Susan read to me. Some mysterious change in my health had completely falsified the prediction of the medical men. I sent to London for my doctor—and told him that the improvement in me had begun on the day when I left off taking his remedies. "Can you explain it?" I asked.

He answered that no such "resurrection from the dead" (as he called it) had ever happened in his long experience. On leaving me, he asked for the latest prescriptions that had been written. I inquired what he was going to do with them. "I mean to go to the chemist," he replied, "and to satisfy myself that your medicines have been properly made up."

I owed it to Mrs. Mozeen's true interest in me, to tell her what had happened. The same day I wrote to her. I also mentioned what the doctor had said, and asked her to call on him, and ascertain if the prescriptions had been shown to the chemist, and if any mistake had been made.

A more innocently intended letter than this never was written. And yet there are people who have declared that it was inspired by suspicion of Mrs. Mozeen!

Eighth Epoch

Whether I was so weakened by illness as to be incapable of giving my mind to more than one subject for reflection at a time (that subject being now the extraordinary recovery of my health)—or whether I was preoccupied by the effort, which I was in honour bound to make, to resist the growing attraction to me of Susan's society—I cannot presume to say. This only I know: when the discovery of the terrible position towards Rothsay in which I now stood suddenly overwhelmed me, an interval of some days had passed. I cannot account for it. I can only say—so it was.

Susan was in the room. I was wholly unable to hide from her the sudden change of colour which betrayed the horror that had over-powered me. She said anxiously: "What has frightened you?"

I don't think I heard her. The play was in my memory again—the fatal play, which had wound itself into the texture of Rothsay's life and mine. In vivid remembrance, I saw once more the dra-matic situation of the first act, and shrank from the reflection of it in the disaster which had fallen on my friend and myself.

"What has frightened you?" Susan repeated.

I answered in one word—I whispered his name: "Rothsay!"

She looked at me in innocent surprise. "Has he met with some misfortune?" she asked quietly.

"Misfortune"—did she call it? Had I not said enough to disturb her tranquillity in mentioning Rothsay's name? "I am living!" I said. "Living—and likely to live!"

Her answer expressed fervent gratitude. "Thank God for it!"

I looked at her, astonished as she had been astonished when she looked at me.

"Susan, Susan," I cried—"must I own it? I love you!"

She came nearer to me with timid pleasure in her eyes—with the first faint light of a smile playing round her lips.

"You say it very strangely," she murmured. "Surely, my dear one, you ought to love me? Since the first day when you gave me my French lesson—haven't I loved You?"

"*You* love *me?*" I repeated. "Have you read——?" My voice failed me; I could say no more.

She turned pale. "Read—what?" she asked.

"My letter."

"What letter?"

"The letter I wrote to you before we were married."

Am I a coward? The bare recollection of what followed that reply makes me tremble. Time has passed. I am a new man now; my health is restored; my happiness is assured: I ought to be able to write on. No: it is not to be done. How can I think coolly? how

force myself to record the suffering that I innocently, most innocently, inflicted on the sweetest and truest of women? Nothing
saved us from a parting as absolute as the parting that follows
death, but the confession that had been rung from me at a time
when my motive spoke for itself. The artless avowal of her affection had been justified, had been honoured, by the words which
laid my heart at her feet when I said "I love you."

She had risen to leave me. In a last look, we had silently resigned
ourselves to wait, apart from each other, for the day of reckoning
that must follow Rothsay's return, when we heard the sound of
carriage-wheels on the drive that led to the house. In a minute
more, the man himself entered the room.

He looked first at Susan—then at me. In both of us he saw the
traces that told of agitation endured, but not yet composed. Worn
and weary he waited, hesitating, near the door.

"Am I intruding?" he asked.

"We were thinking of you, and speaking of you," I replied, "just
before you came in."

"We?" he repeated, turning towards Susan once more. After a
pause, he offered me his hand—and drew it back.

"You don't shake hands with me," he said.

"I am waiting, Rothsay, until I know that we are the same firm
friends as ever."

For the third time he looked at Susan.

"Will you shake hands?" he asked.

She gave him her hand cordially. "May I stay here?" she said,
addressing herself to me.

In my situation at that moment, I understood the generous
purpose that animated her. But she had suffered enough already—
I led her gently to the door. "It will be better," I whispered, "if you
will wait downstairs in the library."

She hesitated. "What will they say in the house?" she objected,
thinking of the servants, and of the humble position which she was
still supposed to occupy.

"It matters nothing what they say, now," I told her. She left us.

"There seems to be some private understanding between you,"
Rothsay said, when we were alone.

"You shall hear what it is," I answered. "But I must beg you to
excuse me if I speak first of myself."

"Are you alluding to your health?"

"Yes."

"Quite needless, Lepel. I met your doctor this morning. I know that a council of physicians decided you would die before the year was out."

He paused there.

"And they proved to be wrong," I added.

"They might have proved to be right," Rothsay rejoined, "but for the accident which spilt your medicine, and the despair of yourself which decided you on taking no more."

I could hardly believe that I understood him. "Do you assert," I said, "that my medicine would have killed me, if I had taken the rest of it?"

"I have no doubt that it would."

"Will you explain what you mean?"

"Let me have your explanation first. I was not prepared to find Susan in your room. I was surprised to see traces of tears in her face. Something has happened in my absence. Am I concerned in it?"

"You are."

I said it quietly—in full possession of myself. The trial of forti-tude through which I had already passed seemed to have blunted my customary sense of feeling. I approached the disclosure which I was now bound to make with steady resolution, resigned to the worst that could happen when the truth was known.

"Do you remember the time," I resumed, "when I was so eager to serve you that I proposed to make Susan your wife by making her rich?"

"Yes."

"Do you remember asking me if I was thinking of the play we saw together at Rome? Is the story as present to your mind now, as it was then?"

"Quite as present."

"You asked if I was performing the part of the Marquis—and if you were the Count. Rothsay! the devotion of that ideal character to his friend has been *my* devotion; his conviction that his death would justify what he had done for his friend's sake, has been *my* conviction; and as it ended with him, so it has ended with me—his terrible position is *my* terrible position towards you, at this mo-ment."

"Are you mad?" Rothsay asked sternly.

I passed over that first outbreak of his anger in silence.

"Do you mean to tell me you have married Susan?" he went on.

"Bear this in mind," I said. "When I married her, I was doomed to death. Nay, more. In your interests—as God is my witness—I welcomed death."

He stepped up to me, in silence, and raised his hand with a threatening gesture.

That action at once deprived me of my self-possession. I spoke with the ungovernable rashness of a boy.

"Carry out your intention," I said. "Insult me."

His hand dropped.

"Insult me," I repeated; "it is one way out of the unendurable situation in which we are placed. You may trust me to challenge you. Duels are still fought on the Continent; I will follow you abroad; I will choose pistols; I will take care that we fight on the fatal foreign system; and I will purposely miss you. Make her what I intended her to be—My rich widow."

He looked at me attentively.

"Is *that* your refuge?" he asked scornfully. "No! I won't help you to commit suicide."

God forgive me! I was possessed by a spirit of reckless despair; I did my best to provoke him.

"Reconsider your decision," I said; "and remember—you tried to commit suicide yourself."

He turned quickly to the door, as if he distrusted his own powers of self-control.

"I wish to speak to Susan," he said, keeping his back turned on me.

"You will find her in the library."

He left me.

I went to the window. I opened it, and let the cold wintry air blow over my burning head. I don't know how long I sat at the window. There came a time when I saw Rothsay on the house steps. He walked rapidly towards the park gate. His head was down; he never once looked back at the room in which he had left me.

As he passed out of my sight, I felt a hand laid gently on my shoulder. Susan had returned to me.

"He will not come back," she said. "Try still to remember him as your old friend. He asks you to forgive and forget."

She had made the peace between us. I was deeply touched; my eyes filled with tears as I looked at her. She kissed me on the forehead and went out. I afterwards asked what had passed between them when Rothsay spoke with her in the library. She never has told me what they said to each other; and she never will. She is right.

Later in the day, I was told that Mrs. Rymer had called, and wished to "pay her respects."

I refused to see her. Whatever claim she might have otherwise had on my consideration had been forfeited by the infamy of her conduct, when she intercepted my letter to Susan. Her sense of injury, on receiving my message, was expressed in writing, and was sent to me the same evening. The last sentence in her letter was characteristic of the woman.

"However your pride may despise me," she wrote, "I am indebted to you for the rise in life that I have always desired. You may refuse to see me—but you can't prevent my being the mother-in-law of a gentleman."

Soon afterwards, I received a visit which I had hardly ventured to expect. Busy as he was in London, my doctor came to see me. He was not in his usual good spirits.

"I hope you don't bring me any bad news," I said.

"You shall judge for yourself," he replied. "I come from Mr. Rothsay, to say for him what he is not able to say for himself."

"Where is he?"

"He has left England."

"For any purpose that you know of?"

"Yes. He has sailed to join the expedition of rescue—I ought rather to call it the forlorn hope—which is to search for the lost explorers in Central Australia."

In other words, he had gone to seek death in the fatal footsteps of Burke and Wills. I could not trust myself to speak.

The doctor saw that there was a reason for my silence, and that he would do well not to notice it. He changed the subject.

"May I ask," he said, "if you have heard from the servants left in charge at your house in London?"

"Has anything happened?"

"Something has happened which they are evidently afraid to tell you; knowing the high opinion which you have of Mrs. Mozeen.

She has suddenly quitted your service, and has gone, nobody knows where. I have taken charge of a letter which she left for you."

He handed me the letter. As soon as I had recovered myself, I looked at it.

There was this inscription on the address: "For my good master, to wait until he returns home."

The few lines in the letter itself ran thus:

"Distressing circumstances oblige me to leave you, sir, and do not permit me to enter into particulars. In asking your pardon, I offer my sincere thanks for your kindness, and my fervent prayers for your welfare."

That was all. The date had a special interest for me. Mrs. Mozeen had written on the day when she must have received my letter—the letter which has already appeared in these pages.

"Is there really nothing known of the poor woman's motives?" I asked.

"There are two explanations suggested," the doctor informed me. "One of them, which is offered by your female servants, seems to me absurd. They declare that Mrs. Mozeen, at her mature age, was in love with the young man who is your footman! It is even asserted that she tried to recommend herself to him, by speaking of the money which she expected to bring to the man who would make her his wife. The footman's reply, informing her that he was already engaged to be married, is alleged to be the cause which has driven her from your house."

I begged that the doctor would not trouble himself to repeat more of what my women servants had said.

"If the other explanation," I added, "is equally unworthy of notice——"

"The other explanation," the doctor interposed, "comes from Mr. Rothsay, and is of a very serious kind."

Rothsay's opinion demanded my respect.

"What view does he take?" I inquired.

"A view that startles me," the doctor said. "You remember my telling you of the interest he took in your symptoms, and in the remedies I had employed? Well! Mr. Rothsay accounts for the incomprehensible recovery of your health by asserting that poison—probably administered in small quantities, and intermitted at intervals in fear of discovery—has been mixed with your medicine; and he asserts that the guilty person is Mrs. Mozeen."

It was impossible that I could openly express the indignation that I felt on hearing this. My position towards Rothsay forced me to restrain myself.

"May I ask," the doctor continued, "if Mrs. Mozeen was aware that she had a legacy to expect at your death?"

"Certainly."

"Has she a brother who is one of the dispensers employed by your chemists?"

"Yes."

"Did she know that I doubted if my prescriptions had been properly prepared, and that I intended to make inquiries?"

"I wrote to her myself on the subject."

"Do you think her brother told her that I was referred to *him,* when I went to the chemists?"

"I have no means of knowing what her brother did."

"Can you at least tell me when she received your letter?"

"She must have received it on the day when she left my house."

The doctor rose with a grave face.

"These are rather extraordinary coincidences," he remarked.

I merely replied, "Mrs. Mozeen is as incapable of poisoning as I am."

The doctor wished me good morning.

I repeat here my conviction of my housekeeper's innocence. I protest against the cruelty which accuses her. And, whatever may have been her motive in suddenly leaving my service, I declare that she still possesses my sympathy and esteem, and I invite her to return to me if she ever sees these lines.

I have only to add, by way of postscript, that we have heard of the safe return of the expedition of rescue. Time, as my wife and I both hope, may yet convince Rothsay that he will not be wrong in counting on Susan's love—the love of a sister.

In the meanwhile, we possess a memorial of our absent friend. We have bought his picture.

Miss Bertha and the Yankee

Preliminary Statements of Witnesses for the Defence

1. MISS BERTHA LAROCHE OF NETTLEGROVE HALL TESTIFIES AND SAYS:

Towards the middle of June, in the year 1817, I went to take the waters at Maplesworth, in Derbyshire, accompanied by my nearest living relative—my aunt.

I am an only child; and I was twenty-one years old at my last birthday. On coming of age I inherited a house and lands in Derbyshire, together with a fortune in money of one hundred thousand pounds. The only education which I have received has been obtained within the last two or three years of my life; and I have thus far seen nothing of Society, in England or in any other civilized part of the world. I can be a competent witness, it seems, in spite of these disadvantages. Anyhow, I mean to tell the truth.

My father was a French colonist in the island of Saint Domingo. He died while I was very young; leaving to my mother and to me just enough to live on, in the remote part of the island in which our little property was situated. My mother was an Englishwoman. Her delicate health made it necessary for her to leave me, for many hours of the day, under the care of our household slaves. I can never forget their kindness to me; but, unfortunately, their ignorance equalled their kindness. If we had been rich enough to send to France or England for a competent governess we might have done very well. But we were not rich enough. I am ashamed to say that I was nearly thirteen years old before I had learnt to read and write correctly.

Four more years passed—and then there came a wonderful event in our lives, which was nothing less than the change from Saint Domingo to England.

My mother was distantly related to an ancient and wealthy

English family. She seriously offended those proud people by marrying an obscure foreigner, who had nothing to live on but his morsel of land in the West Indies. Having no expectations from her relatives, my mother preferred happiness with the man she loved to every other consideration; and I, for one, think she was right. From that moment she was cast off by the head of the family. For eighteen years of her life, as wife, mother, and widow, no letters came to her from her English home. We had just celebrated my seventeenth birthday when the first letter came. It informed my mother that no less than three lives, which stood between her and the inheritance of certain portions of the family property, had been swept away by death. The estate and the fortune which I have already mentioned had fallen to her in due course of law, and her surviving relatives were magnanimously ready to forgive her at last!

We wound up our affairs at Saint Domingo, and we went to England to take possession of our new wealth.

At first, the return to her native air seemed to have a beneficial effect on my mother's health. But it was a temporary improvement only. Her constitution had been fatally injured by the West Indian climate, and just as we had engaged a competent person to look after my neglected education, my constant attendance was needed at my mother's bedside. We loved each other dearly, and we wanted no strange nurses to come between us. My aunt (my mother's sister) relieved me of my cares in the intervals when I wanted rest.

For seven sad months our dear sufferer lingered. I have only one remembrance to comfort me; my mother's last kiss was mine—she died peacefully with her head on my bosom.

I was nearly nineteen years old before I had sufficiently rallied my courage to be able to think seriously of myself and my prospects.

At that age one does not willingly submit one's self for the first time to the authority of a governess. Having my aunt for a companion and protectress, I proposed to engage my own masters and to superintend my own education.

My plans failed to meet with the approval of the head of the family. He declared (most unjustly, as the event proved) that my aunt was not a fit person to take care of me. She had passed all the later years of her life in retirement. A good creature, he admitted, in her own way, but she had no knowledge of the world, and no firmness of character. The right person to act as my chaperon, and to superintend my education, was the high-minded and accomplished woman who had taught his own daughters.

I declined, with all needful gratitude and respect, to take his advice. The bare idea of living with a stranger so soon after my mother's death revolted me. Besides, I liked my aunt, and my aunt liked me. Being made acquainted with my decision, the head of the family cast me off, exactly as he had cast off my mother before me.

So I lived in retirement with my good aunt, and studied industriously to improve my mind until my twenty-first birthday came. I was now an heiress, privileged to think and act for myself. My aunt kissed me tenderly. We talked of my poor mother, and we cried in each other's arms on the memorable day that made a wealthy woman of me. In a little time more, other troubles than vain regrets for the dead were to try me, and other tears were to fill my eyes than the tears which I had given to the memory of my mother.

I may now return to my visit, in June, 1817, to the healing springs at Maplesworth.

This famous inland watering-place was only between nine and ten miles from my new home called Nettlegrove Hall. I had been feeling weak and out of spirits for some months, and our medical adviser recommended change of scene and a trial of the waters at Maplesworth. My aunt and I established ourselves in comfortable apartments, with a letter of introduction to the chief doctor in the place. This otherwise harmless and worthy man proved, strangely enough, to be the innocent cause of the trials and troubles which beset me at the outset of my new life.

The day after we had presented our letter of introduction, we met the doctor on the public walk. He was accompanied by two strangers, both young men, and both (so far as my ignorant opinion went) persons of some distinction, judging by their dress and manners. The doctor said a few kind words to us, and rejoined his two companions. Both the gentlemen looked at me, and both took off their hats as my aunt and I proceeded on our walk.

I own I thought occasionally of the well-bred strangers during the rest of the day, especially of the shortest of the two, who was also the handsomest of the two to my thinking. If this confession seems rather a bold one, remember, if you please, that I had never been taught to conceal my feelings at Saint Domingo, and that the events which followed our arrival in England had kept me completely secluded from the society of other young ladies of my age.

The next day, while I was drinking my glass of healing water (extremely nasty water, by the way), the doctor joined us.

While he was asking me about my health, the two strangers made their appearance again, and took off their hats again. They both looked expectantly at the doctor, and the doctor (in performance of a promise which he had already made, as I privately suspected) formally introduced them to my aunt and to me. First (I put the handsomest man first) Captain Arthur Stanwick, of the army, home from India on leave, and staying at Maplesworth to take the waters; secondly, Mr. Lionel Varleigh, of Boston, in America, visiting England, after travelling all over Europe, and stopping at Maplesworth to keep company with his friend the Captain.

On their introduction, the two gentlemen, observing, no doubt, that I was a little shy, forbore delicately from pressing their society on us.

Captain Stanwick, with a beautiful smile, and with teeth worthy of the smile, stroked his whiskers, and asked me if I had found any benefit from taking the waters. He afterwards spoke in great praise of the charming scenery in the neighbourhood of Maplesworth, and then turning away, addressed his next words to my aunt. Mr. Varleigh took his place. Speaking with perfect gravity, and with no whiskers to stroke, he said:

"I have once tried the waters here out of curiosity. I can sympathize, miss, with the expression which I observed on your face when you emptied your glass just now. Permit me to offer you something nice to take the taste of the waters out of your mouth." He produced from his pocket a beautiful little box filled with sugar-plums. "I bought it in Paris," he explained. "Having lived a good deal in France, I have got into a habit of making little presents of this sort to ladies and children. I wouldn't let the doctor see it, miss, if I were you. He has the usual medical prejudice against sugar-plums." With that quaint warning he, too, made his bow and discreetly withdrew.

Thinking it over afterwards, I acknowledged to myself that the English Captain—although he was the handsomest man of the two, and possessed the smoothest manners—had failed, nevertheless, to overcome my shyness. The American traveller's unaffected sincerity and good-humour, on the other hand, set me quite at my ease. I could look at him and thank him, and feel amused at his sympathy with the grimace I had made, after swallowing the ill-flavoured waters. And yet, while I lay awake at night, wondering whether we should meet our new acquaintances on the next day, it was the English Captain that I most wanted to see again, and not the American traveller! At the time, I set this down to nothing more important than my own perversity. Ah, dear! dear! I know better than that now.

The next morning brought the doctor to our hotel on a special visit to my aunt. He invented a pretext for sending me into the next room, which was so plainly a clumsy excuse, that my curiosity was aroused. I gratified my curiosity. Must I make my confession plainer still? Must I acknowledge that I was mean enough to listen on the other side of the door?

I heard my dear innocent old aunt say, "Doctor! I hope you don't see anything alarming in the state of Bertha's health."

The doctor burst out laughing. "My dear madam! there is nothing in the state of the young lady's health which need cause the smallest anxiety to you or to me. The object of my visit is to justify myself for presenting those two gentlemen to you yesterday. They are both greatly struck by Miss Bertha's beauty, and they both urgently entreated me to introduce them. Such introductions, I need hardly say, are marked exceptions to my general rule. In ninety-nine cases out of a hundred I should have said No. In the cases of Captain Stanwick and Mr. Varleigh, however, I saw no reason to hesitate. Permit me to assure you that I am not intruding on your notice two fortune-hunting adventurers. They are both men of position and men of property. The family of the Stanwicks has been well known to me for years; and Mr. Varleigh brought me a letter from my oldest living friend, answering for him as a gentlemen in the highest sense of the word. He is the wealthiest man of the two; and it speaks volumes for him, in my opinion, that he has preserved his simplicity of character after a long residence in such places as Paris and Vienna. Captain Stanwick has more polish and ease of manner, but, looking under the surface, I rather fancy there may be something a little impetuous and domineering in his temper. However, we all have our faults. I can only say, for both these young friends of mine, that you need feel no scruple about admitting them to your intimacy, if they happen to please you—and your niece. Having now, I hope, removed any doubts which may have troubled you, pray recall Miss Bertha. I am afraid I have interrupted you in discussing your plans for the day."

The smoothly eloquent doctor paused for the moment; and I darted away from the door.

Our plans for the day included a drive through the famous scenery near the town. My two admirers met us on horseback. Here, again, the Captain had the advantage over his friend. His seat in the saddle and his riding-dress were both perfect things in their way. The Englishman rode on one side of the carriage and the American on the other. They both talked well, but Mr. Varleigh had seen more of the world in general than Captain Stanwick, and he made himself certainly the most interesting and most amusing companion of the two.

On our way back my admiration was excited by a thick wood, beautifully situated on rising ground at a little distance from the high-road. "Oh, dear," I said, "how I should like to take a walk in that wood!" Idle thoughtless words; but, oh, what remembrances crowd on me as I think of them now!

Captain Stanwick and Mr. Varleigh at once dismounted and offered themselves as my escort. The coachman warned them to be careful; people had often lost themselves, he said, in that wood. I asked the name of it. The name was Herne Wood. My aunt was not very willing to leave her comfortable seat in the carriage, but it ended in her going with us.

Before we entered the wood, Mr. Varleigh noted the position of the high-road by his pocket-compass. Captain Stanwick laughed at him, and offered me his arm. Ignorant as I was of the ways of the world and the rules of coquetry, my instinct (I suppose) warned me not to distinguish one of the gentlemen too readily at the expense of the other. I took my aunt's arm and settled it in that way.

A winding path led us into the wood.

On a nearer view, the place disappointed me; the farther we advanced, the more horribly gloomy it grew. The thickly-growing trees shut out the light; the damp stole over me little by little until I shivered; the undergrowth of bushes and thickets rustled at intervals mysteriously, as some invisible creeping creature passed through it. At a turn in the path we reached a sort of clearing, and saw the sky and the sunshine once more. But, even here, a dis-agreeable incident occurred. A snake wound his undulating way across the open space, passing close by me, and I was fool enough to scream. The Captain killed the creature with his riding-cane, taking a pleasure in doing it which I did not like to see.

We left the clearing and tried another path, and then another. And still the horrid wood preyed on my spirits. I agreed with my aunt that we should do well to return to the carriage. On our way back we missed the right path, and lost ourselves for the moment. Mr. Varleigh consulted his compass, and pointed in one direction. Captain Stanwick consulting nothing but his own jealous humour, pointed in the other. We followed Mr. Varleigh's guidance, and got back to the clearing. He turned to the Captain, and said good-humouredly, "You see the compass was right." Captain Stanwick answered sharply, "There are more ways than one out of an English wood; you talk as if we were in one of your American forests."

Mr. Varleigh seemed to be at a loss to understand his rudeness: there was a pause. The two men looked at each other, standing face to face on the brown earth of the clearing—the Englishman's ruddy countenance, light auburn hair and whiskers, and well-opened bold blue eyes, contrasting with the pale complexion, the keenly-observant look, the dark closely-cut hair, and the deli-cately-lined face of the American. It was only for a moment: I had barely time to feel uneasy before they controlled themselves and led us back to the carriage, talking as pleasantly as if nothing had happened. For days afterwards, nevertheless, that scene in the clearing—the faces and figures of the two men, the dark line of trees hemming them in on all sides, the brown circular patch of ground on which they stood—haunted my memory, and got in the way of my brighter and happier thoughts. When my aunt inquired if I had enjoyed the day, I surprised her by saying, No. And when she asked why, I could only answer, "It was all spoilt by Herne Wood."

Three weeks passed.

The terror of those dreadful days creeps over me again when I think of them. I mean to tell the truth without shrinking; but I may at least consult my own feelings by dwelling on certain particulars as briefly as I can. I shall describe my conduct towards the two

men who courted me, in the plainest terms, if I say that I distinguished neither of them. Innocently and stupidly I encouraged
them both.

In books, women are generally represented as knowing their
own minds in matters which relate to love and marriage. This is
not my experience of myself. Day followed day; and, ridiculous as
it may appear, I could not decide which of my two admirers I liked
best!

Captain Stanwick was, at first, the man of my choice. While he
kept his temper under control, he charmed me. But when he let it
escape him, he sometimes disappointed, sometimes irritated me. In
that frame of mind I turned for relief to Lionel Varleigh, feeling
that he was the more gentle and the more worthy man of the two,
and honestly believing, at such times, that I preferred him to his
rival. For the first few days after our visit to Herne Wood I had
excellent opportunties of comparing them. They paid their visits to
us together, and they divided their attentions carefully between me
and my aunt. At the end of the week, however, they began to
present themselves separately. If I had possessed any experience of
the natures of men, I might have known what this meant, and
might have seen the future possibility of some more serious estrangement between the two friends, of which I might be the
unfortunate cause. As it was, I never once troubled my head about
what might be passing out of my presence. Whether they came
together, or whether they came separately, their visits were always
agreeable to me, and I thought of nothing and cared for nothing
more.

But the time that was to enlighten me was not far off.

One day Captain Stanwick called much earlier than usual. My
aunt had not yet returned from her morning walk. The Captain
made some excuse for presenting himself under these circumstances which I have now forgotten.

Without actually committing himself to a proposal of marriage,
he spoke with such tender feeling, he managed his hold on my
inexperience so delicately, that he entrapped me into saying some
words, on my side, which I remembered with a certain dismay as
soon as I was left alone again. In half an hour more, Mr. Lionel
Varleigh was announced as my next visitor. I at once noticed a
certain disturbance in his look and manner which was quite new in

my experience of him. I offered him a chair. To my surprise he declined to take it.

"I must trust to your indulgence to permit me to put an embarrassing question to you," he began. "It rests with you, Miss Laroche, to decide whether I shall remain here, or whether I shall relieve you of my presence by leaving the room."

"What can you possibly mean?" I asked.

"Is it your wish," he went on, "that I should pay you no more visits except in Captain Stanwick's company, or by Captain Stanwick's express permission?"

My astonishment deprived me for the moment of the power of answering him. "Do you really mean that Captain Stanwick has forbidden you to call on me?" I asked as soon as I could speak.

"I have exactly repeated what Captain Stanwick said to me half an hour since," Lionel Varleigh answered.

In my indignation at hearing this, I entirely forgot the rash words of encouragement which the Captain had entrapped me into speaking to him. When I think of it now, I am ashamed to repeat the language in which I resented this man's presumptuous assertion of authority over me. Having committed one act of indiscretion already, my anxiety to assert my freedom of action hurried me into committing another. I bade Mr. Varleigh welcome whenever he chose to visit me, in terms which made his face flush under the emotions of pleasure and surprise which I had aroused in him. My wounded vanity acknowledged no restraints. I signed to him to take a seat on the sofa at my side; I engaged to go to his lodgings the next day, with my aunt, and see the collection of curiosities which he had amassed in the course of his travels. I almost believe, if he had tried to kiss me, that I was angry enough with the Captain to have let him do it!

Remember what my life had been—remember how ignorantly I had passed the precious days of my youth, how insidiously a sudden accession of wealth and importance had encouraged my folly and my pride—and try, like good Christians, to make some allowance for me!

My aunt came in from her walk before Mr. Varleigh's visit had ended. She received him rather coldly, and he perceived it. After reminding me of our appointment for the next day, he took his leave.

"What appointment does Mr. Varleigh mean?" my aunt asked, as soon as we were alone. "Is it wise, under the circumstances, to make appointments with Mr. Varleigh?" she said, when I had answered her question. I naturally inquired what she meant. My aunt replied, "I have met Captain Stanwick while I was out walking. He has told me something which I am quite at a loss to understand. Is it possible, Bertha, that you have received a proposal of marriage from him favourably, without saying one word about your intentions to me?"

I instantly denied it. However rashly I might have spoken, I had certainly said nothing to justify Captain Stanwick in claiming me as his promised wife. In his mean fear of a fair rivalry with Mr. Varleigh, he had deliberately misinterpreted me. "If I marry either of the two," I said, "it will be Mr. Varleigh!"

My aunt shook her head. "These two gentlemen seem to be both in love with you, Bertha. It is a trying position for you between them, and I am afraid you have acted with some indiscretion. Captain Stanwick tells me that he and his friend have come to a separation already. I fear you are the cause of it. Mr. Varleigh has left the hotel at which he was staying with the Captain, in consequence of a disagreement between them this morning. You were not aware of that when you accepted his invitation. Shall I write an excuse for you? We must, at least, put off the visit, my dear, until you have set yourself right with Captain Stanwick."

I began to feel a little alarmed, but I was too obstinate to yield without a struggle. "Give me time to think over it," I said. "To write an excuse seems like acknowledging the Captain's authority. Let us wait till to-morrow morning.

The morning brought with it another visit from Captain Stanwick. This time my aunt was present. He looked at her without speaking, and turned to me, with his fiery temper showing itself already in his eyes.

"I have a word to say to you in private," he began.

"I have no secrets from my aunt," I answered. "Whatever you have to say, Captain Stanwick, may be said here."

He opened his lips to reply, and suddenly checked himself. He was controlling his anger by so violent an effort that it turned his ruddy face pale. For the moment he conquered his temper—he addressed himself to me with the outward appearance of respect at least.

"Has that man Varleigh lied?" he asked; "or have you given *him* hopes too—after what you said to me yesterday?"

"I said nothing to you yesterday which gives you any right to put that question to me," I rejoined. "You have entirely misunderstood me if you think so."

My aunt attempted to say a few temperate words, in the hope of soothing him. He waved his hand, refusing to listen to her, and advanced closer to me.

"*You* have misunderstood *me*," he said, "if you think I am a man to be made a plaything of in the hands of a coquette!"

My aunt interposed once more, with a resolution which I had not expected from her.

"Captain Stanwick," she said, "you are forgetting yourself."

He paid to heed to her; he persisted in speaking to me. "It is my misfortune to love you," he burst out. "My whole heart is set on you. I mean to be your husband, and no other man living shall stand in my way. After what you said to me yesterday, I have a right to consider that you have favoured my addresses. This is not a mere flirtation. Don't think it! I say it's the passion of a life! Do you hear? It's the passion of a man's whole life! I am not to be trifled with. I have had a night of sleepless misery about you—I have suffered enough for you—and you're not worth it. Don't laugh! This is no laughing matter. Take care, Bertha! Take care!"

My aunt rose from her chair. She astonished me. On all ordinary occasions the most retiring, the most feminine of women, she now walked up to Captain Stanwick and looked him full in the face, without flinching for an instant.

"You appear to have forgotten that you are speaking in the presence of two ladies," she said. "Alter your tone, sir, or I shall be obliged to take my niece out of the room."

Half angry, half frightened, I tried to speak in my turn. My aunt signed to me to be silent. The Captain drew back a step as if he felt her reproof. But his eyes, still fixed on me, were as fiercely bright as ever. *There* the gentleman's superficial good-breeding failed to hide the natural man beneath.

"I will leave you in undisturbed possession of the room," he said to my aunt with bitter politeness. "Before I go, permit me to give your niece an opportunity of reconsidering her conduct before it is too late." My aunt drew back, leaving him free to speak to me. After considering for a moment, he laid his hand firmly, but not roughly, on my arm. "You have accepted Lionel Varleigh's invitation to visit him," he said, "under pretence of seeing his curiosities. Think again before you decide on keeping that engagement. If you go to Varleigh to-morrow, you will repent it to the last day of your life." Saying those words, in a tone which made me tremble in spite of myself, he walked to the door. As he laid his hand on the lock, he turned towards me for the last time. "I forbid you to go to Varleigh's lodgings," he said, very distinctly and quietly. "Understand what I tell you. I forbid it."

With those words he left us.

My aunt sat down by me and took my hand kindly. "There is only one thing to be done," she said; "we must return at once to Nettlegrove. If Captain Stanwick attempts to annoy you in your own house, we have neighbours who will protect us, and we have Mr. Loring, our Rector, to appeal to for advice. As for Mr. Varleigh, I will write our excuses myself before we go away."

She put out her hand to ring the bell and order the carriage. I stopped her. My childish pride urged me to assert myself in some way, after the passive position that I had been forced to occupy during the interview with Captain Stanwick.

"No," I said, "it is not acting fairly towards Mr. Varleigh to break our engagement with him. Let us return to Nettlegrove by all means, but let us first call on Mr. Varleigh and take our leave. Are we to behave rudely to a gentleman who has always treated us with the utmost consideration, because Captain Stanwick has tried to frighten us by cowardly threats? The commonest feeling of self-respect forbids it."

My aunt protested against this outbreak of folly with perfect temper and good sense. But my obstinacy (my firmness as I thought it!) was immovable. I left her to choose between going with me to Mr. Varleigh, or letting me go to him by myself. Finding it useless to resist, she decided, it is needless to say, on going with me.

We found Mr. Varleigh very courteous, but more than usually grave and quiet. Our visit only lasted for a few minutes; my aunt using the influence of her age and her position to shorten it. She mentioned family affairs as the motive which recalled us to Nettlegrove. I took it on myself to invite Mr. Varleigh to visit me at my own house. He bowed and thanked me, without engaging himself to accept the invitation. When I offered him my hand at parting, he raised it to his lips, and kissed it with a fervour that agitated me. His eyes looked into mine with a sorrowful admiration, with a lingering regret, as if they were taking their leave of me for a long while. "Don't forget me!" he whispered, as he stood at the door, while I followed my aunt out. "Come to Nettlegrove," I whispered back. His eyes dropped to the ground; he let me go without a word more.

This, I declare solemnly, was all that passed at our visit. By some unexpressed consent among us, no allusion whatever was made to Captain Stanwick; not even his name was mentioned. I never knew that the two men had met, just before we called on Mr. Varleigh. Nothing was said which could suggest to me the slightest suspicion of any arrangement for another meeting between them later in the day. Beyond the vague threats which had escaped Captain Stanwick's lips—threats which I own I was rash enough to despise—I had no warning whatever of the dreadful events which happened at Maplesworth on the day after our return to Nettlegrove Hall.

I can only add that I am ready to submit to any questions that may be put on me. Pray don't think me a heartless woman. My worst fault was ignorance. In those days, I knew nothing of the false pretences under which men hide what is selfish and savage in their natures from the women whom it is their interest to deceive.

2. JULIUS BENDER, FENCING-MASTER, TESTIFIES AND SAYS:

I am of German nationality; established in England as teacher of the use of the sword and the pistol since the beginning of the present year.

Finding business slack in London, it unfortunately occurred to me to try what I could do in the country. I had heard of Maplesworth as a place largely frequented by visitors on account of the scenery, as well as by invalids in need of taking the waters; and I opened a gallery there at the beginning of the season of 1817, for fencing and pistol practice. About the visitors I had not been deceived; there were plenty of idle young gentlemen among them who might have been expected to patronize my establishment. They showed the most barbarous indifference to the noble art of attack and defence—came by twos and threes, looked at my gallery, and never returned. My small means began to fail me. After paying my expenses, I was really at my wits' end to find a few pounds to go on with, in the hope of better days.

One gentleman, I remember, who came to see me, and who behaved most liberally.

He described himself as an American, and said he had travelled a great deal. As my ill luck would have it, he stood in no need of my instructions. On the two or three occasions when he amused himself with my foils and my pistols, he proved to be one of the most expert swordsmen and one of the finest shots that I ever met with. It was not wonderful: he had by nature cool nerves and a quick eye; and he had been taught by the masters of the art in Vienna and Paris.

Early in July—the 9th or 10th of the month, I think—I was sitting alone in my gallery, looking ruefully enough at the last two sovereigns in my purse, when a gentleman was announced who wanted a lesson. "A *private* lesson," he said with emphasis, looking at the man who cleaned and took care of my weapons.

I sent the man out of the room. The stranger (an Englishman, and, as I fancied, judging by outward appearances, a military man as well) took from his pocket-book a fifty-pound bank-note and held it up before me. "I have a heavy wager depending on a fencing match," he said, "and I have no time to improve myself. Teach me a trick which will make me a match for a man skilled in the use of the foil, and keep the secret—and there are fifty pounds for you."

I hesitated. I did indeed hesitate, poor as I was. But this devil of a man held his bank-note before me whichever way I looked, and I had only two pounds left in the world!

"Are you going to fight a duel?" I asked.

"I have already told you what I am going to do," he answered.

I waited a little. The infernal bank-note still tempted me. In spite of myself, I tried him again.

"If I teach you the trick, " I persisted, "will you undertake to make no bad use of your lesson?"

"Yes," he said, impatiently enough.

I was not quite satisfied yet.

"Will you promise it, on your word of honour?" I asked.

"Of course I will," he answered. "Take the money, and don't keep me waiting any longer!"

I took the money, and I taught him the trick—and I regretted it almost as soon as it was done. Not that I knew, mind, of any serious consequences that followed; for I returned to London the next morning. My sentiments were those of a man of honour, who felt that he had degraded his art, and who could not be quite sure that he might not have armed the hand of an assassin as well. I have no more to say.

3. THOMAS OUTWATER, SERVANT TO CAPTAIN STANWICK, TESTIFIES AND SAYS:

If I did not firmly believe my master to be out of his senses, no punishment that I could receive would prevail upon me to tell of him what I am going to tell now.

But I say he is mad, and therefore not accountable for what he has done—mad for love of a young woman. If I could have my way, I should like to twist her neck, though she *is* a lady, and a great heiress into the bargain. Before she came between them, my master and Mr. Varleigh were more like brothers than anything else. She set them at variance, and whether she meant to do it or not is all the same to me. I own I took a dislike to her when I first saw her. She was one of the light-haired, blue-eyed sort, with an innocent look and a snaky waist—not at all to be depended on, as I have found them.

I hear I am not expected to give an account of the disagreement between the two gentlemen, of which this lady was the cause. I am to state what I did in Maplesworth, and what I saw afterwards in Herne Wood. Poor as I am, I would give a five-pound note to anybody who could do it for me. Unfortunately, I must do it for myself.

On the 10th of July, in the evening, my master went, for the second time that day, to Mr. Varleigh's lodgings.

I am certain of the date, because it was the day of publication of the town newspaper, and there was a law report in it which set everybody talking. There had been a duel with pistols, a day or two before, between a resident in the town and a visitor, caused by some dispute about horses. Nothing very serious came of the meeting. One of the men only was hurt, and the wound proved to be of no great importance. The awkward part of the matter was that the constables appeared on the ground, before the wounded man had been removed. He and his two seconds were caught, and the prisoners were committed for trial. Dueling (the magistrates said) was an inhuman and unchristian practice, and they were determined to put the law in force and stop it. This sentence made a great stir in the town, and fixed the date, as I have just said, in my mind.

Having been accidentally within hearing of some of the disputes concerning Miss Laroche between my master and Mr. Varleigh, I had my misgivings about the Captain's second visit to the friend with whom he had quarrelled already. A gentleman called on him, soon after he had gone out, on important business. This gave me an excuse for following him to Mr. Varleigh's rooms with the visitor's card, and I took the opportunity.

I heard them at high words on my way upstairs, and waited a little on the landing. The Captain was in one of his furious rages; Mr. Varleigh was firm and cool as usual. After listening for a minute or so, I heard enough (in my opinion) to justify me in entering the room. I caught my master in the act of lifting his cane—threatening to strike Mr. Varleigh. He instantly dropped his hand, and turned on me in a fury at my intrusion. Taking no notice of this outbreak of temper, I gave him his friend's card, and went out. A talk followed in voices too low for me to hear outside the room, and then the Captain approached the door. I got out of his way, feeling very uneasy about what was to come next. I could not presume to question Mr. Varleigh. The only thing I could think of was to tell the young lady's aunt what I had seen and heard, and to plead with Miss Laroche herself to make peace between them. When I inquired for the ladies at their lodgings, I was told that they had left Maplesworth.

I saw no more of the Captain that night.

The next morning he seemed to be quite himself again. He said to me, "Thomas, I am going sketching in Herne Wood. Take the paint-box and the rest of it, and put this into the carriage."

He handed me a packet as thick as my arm, and about three feet long, done up in many folds of canvas. I made bold to ask what it was. He answered that it was an artist's sketching umbrella, packed for travelling.

In an hour's time, the carriage stopped on the road below Herne Wood. My master said he would carry his sketching things himself, and I was to wait with the carriage. In giving him the so-called umbrella, I took the occasion of his eye being off me for the moment to pass my hand over it carefully; and I felt, through the canvas, the hilt of a sword. As an old soldier, I could not be mistaken—the hilt of a sword.

What I thought, on making this discovery, does not much matter. What I did was to watch the Captain into the wood, and then to follow him.

I tracked him along the path to where there was a clearing in the midst of the trees. There he stopped, and I got behind a tree. He undid the canvas, and produced *two* swords concealed in the packet. If I had felt any doubts before, I was certain of what was coming now. A duel without seconds or witnesses, by way of keeping the town magistrates in the dark—a duel between my master and Mr. Varleigh! As his name came into my mind, the man himself appeared, making his way into the clearing from the other side of the wood.

What could I do to stop it? No human creature was in sight. The nearest village was a mile away, reckoning from the farther side of the wood. The coachman was a stupid old man, quite useless in a difficulty, even if I had had time enough to go back to the road and summon him to help me. While I was thinking about it, the Captain and Mr. Varleigh had stripped to their shirts and trousers. When they crossed their swords, I could stand it no longer—I burst in on them. "For God Almighty's sake, gentlemen," I cried out, "don't fight without seconds!" My master turned on me like the madman he was, and threatened me with the point of his sword. Mr. Varleigh pulled me back out of harm's way. "Don't be afraid," he whispered, as he led me back to the verge of the clearing; "I have chosen the sword instead of the pistol expressly to spare his life."

Those noble words (spoken by as brave and true a man as ever breathed) quieted me. I knew Mr. Varleigh had earned the repute of being one of the finest swordsmen in Europe.

The duel began. I was placed behind my master, and was consequently opposite to his antagonist. The Captain stood on his defence, waiting for the other to attack. Mr. Varleigh made a pass. I was opposite the point of his sword; I saw it touch the Captain's left shoulder. In the same instant of time my master struck up his opponent's sword with his own weapon, seized Mr. Varleigh's right wrist in his left hand, and passed his sword clean through Mr.

Varleigh's breast. He fell, the victim of a murderous trick—fell without a word or a cry.

The Captain turned slowly, and faced me with his bloody sword in his hand. I can't tell you how he looked; I can only say that the sight of him turned me faint with terror. I was at Waterloo—I am no coward. But I tell you the cold sweat poured down my face like water. I should have dropped if I had not held by the branch of a tree.

My master waited until I had in a measure recovered myself. "Feel if his heart beats," he said, pointing to the man on the ground.

I obeyed. He was dead—the heart was still; the beat of the pulse was gone. I said, "You have killed him!"

The Captain made no answer. He packed up the two swords again in the canvas, and put them under his arm. Then he told me to follow him with the sketching materials. I drew back from him without speaking; there was a horrid hollow sound in his voice that I did not like. "Do as I tell you," he said, "you have yourself to thank for it if I refuse to lose sight of you now." I managed to say that he might trust me to say nothing. He refused to trust me; he put his hand to take hold of me. I could not stand that. "I'll go with you," I said; "don't touch me!" We reached the carriage and returned to Maplesworth. The same day we travelled by post to London.

In London I contrived to give the Captain the slip. By the first coach the next morning I went back to Maplesworth, eager to hear what had happened, and if the body had been found. Not a word of news reached me; nothing seemed to be known of the duel in Herne Wood.

I went to the wood—on foot, fearing that I might be traced if I hired a carriage. The country round was as solitary as usual. Not a creature was near when I entered the wood; not a creature was near when I looked into the clearing.

There was nothing on the ground. The body was gone.

4. THE REVEREND ALFRED LORING, RECTOR OF NETTLEGROVE, TESTIFIES AND SAYS:

Early in the month of October, 1817, I was informed that Miss Bertha Laroche had called at my house, and wished to see me in private.

I had first been presented to Miss Laroche on her arrival, with her aunt, to take possession of her property at Nettlegrove Hall. My opportunities of improving my acquaintance with her had not been so numerous as I could have desired, and I sincerely regretted it. She had produced a very favourable impression on me. Singularly inexperienced and impulsive—with an odd mixture of shyness and vivacity in her manner, and subject now and then to outbursts of vanity and petulance which she was divertingly incapable of concealing—I could detect, nevertheless, under the surface the signs which told of a true and generous nature, of a simple and pure heart. Her personal appearance, I should add, was attractive in a remarkable degree. There was something in it so peculiar, and at the same time so fascinating, that I am conscious it may have prejudiced me in her favour. For fear of this acknowledgment being misunderstood, I think it right to add that I am old enough to be her grandfather, and that I am also a married man.

I told the servant to show Miss Laroche into my study.

The moment she entered the room, her appearance alarmed me: she looked literally panic-stricken. I offered to send for my wife; she refused the proposal. I entreated her to take time at least to compose herself. It was not in her impulsive nature to do this. She said, "Give me your hand to encourage me, and let me speak while I can." I gave her my hand, poor soul. I said, "Speak to me, my dear, as if I were your father."

So far as I could understand the incoherent statement which she addressed to me, she had been the object of admiration (while visiting Maplesworth) to two gentlemen, who both desired to marry her. Hesitating between them, and perfectly inexperienced in such matters, she had been the unfortunate cause of enmity between the rivals, and had returned to Nettlegrove, at her aunt's suggestion, as the best means of extricating herself from a very embarrassing position. The removal failing to alleviate her distressing recollections of what had happened, she and her aunt had tried a further change by making a tour of two months on the Continent. She had returned in a more quiet frame of mind. To her great surprise, she had heard nothing of either of her two suitors, from the day when she left Maplesworth to the day when she presented herself at my rectory.

Early that morning she was walking, after breakfast, in the park at Nettlegrove when she heard footsteps behind her. She turned and found herself face to face with one of her suitors at Maplesworth. I am informed that there is no necessity now for my suppressing the name. The gentleman was Captain Stanwick.

He was so fearfully changed for the worse that she hardly knew him again.

After his first glance at her, he held his hand over his bloodshot eyes as if the sunlight hurt them. Without a word to prepare her for the disclosure, he confessed that he had killed Mr. Varleigh in a duel. His remorse (he declared) had unsettled his reason: only a few days had passed since he had been released from confinement in an asylum.

"You are the cause of it," he said wildly. "It is for love of you. I have but one hope left to live for—my hope in you. If you cast me off, my mind is made up. I will give my life for the life that I have taken; I will die by my own hand. Look at me, and you will see that I am in earnest. My future as a living man depends on your decision. Think of it to-day, and meet me here to-morrow. Not at this time; the horrid daylight feels like fire in my eyes, and goes like fire to my brain. Wait till sunset—you will find me here."

He left her as suddenly as he had appeared. When she had sufficiently recovered herself to be able to think, she decided on saying nothing of what had happened to her aunt. She took her way to the rectory, to seek my advice.

It is needless to encumber my narrative by any statement of the questions which I felt it my duty to put to her, under these circumstances.

My inquiries informed me that Captain Stanwick had, in the first instance, produced a favourable impression on her. The less showy qualities of Mr. Varleigh had afterwards grown on her liking; aided greatly by the repelling effect on her mind of the Captain's violent language and conduct when he had reason to suspect that his rival was being preferred to him. When she knew the horrible news of Mr. Varleigh's death, she "knew her own heart" (to repeat her exact words to me) by the shock that she felt. Towards Captain Stanwick the only feeling of which she was now conscious was, naturally, a feeling of the strongest aversion.

My own course in this difficult and painful matter appeared to me to be clear.

"It is your duty as a Christian to see this miserable man again," I said. "And it is my duty, as your friend and pastor, to sustain you under the trial. I will go with you to-morrow to the place of meeting."

The next evening we found Captain Stanwick waiting for us in the park.

He drew back on seeing me. I explained to him, temperately and firmly, what my position was. With sullen looks he resigned himself to endure my presence. By degrees I won his confidence. My first impression of him remains unshaken—the man's reason was unsettled. I suspected that the assertion of his release was a falsehood, and that he had really escaped from the asylum. It was impossible to lure him into telling me where the place was. He was too cunning to do this—too cunning to say anything about his relations, when I tried to turn the talk that way next. On the other hand, he spoke with a revolting readiness of the crime that he had committed, and of his settled resolution to destroy himself if Miss Laroche refused to be his wife. "I have nothing else to live for; I am alone in the world," he said. "Even my servant has deserted me. He knows how I killed Lionel Varleigh." He paused, and spoke his next words in a whisper to me. "I killed him by a trick—he was the best swordsman of the two."

This confession was so horrible that I could only attribute it to an insane delusion. On pressing my inquiries, I found that the same idea must have occurred to the poor wretch's relations, and to the doctors who signed the certificates for placing him under medical care. This conclusion (as I afterwards heard) was greatly strengthened by the fact that Mr. Varleigh's body had not been found on the reported scene of the duel. As to the servant, he had deserted his master in London, and had never reappeared. So far as my poor judgment went, the question before me was not of delivering a self-accused murderer to justice (with no corpse to testify against him), but of restoring an insane man to the care of the persons who had been appointed to restrain him.

I tried to test the strength of his delusion in an interval when he was not urging his shocking entreaties on Miss Laroche.

"How do you know that you killed Mr. Varleigh?" I said.

He looked at me with a wild terror in his eyes. Suddenly he lifted his right hand, and shook it in the air, with a moaning cry, which was unmistakably a cry of pain. "Should I see his ghost," he asked, "if I had not killed him? I know it, by the pain that wrings me in the hand that stabbed him. Always in my right hand! always the same pain at the moment when I see him!" He stopped, and ground his teeth in the agony and reality of his delusion. "Look!" he cried. "Look between the two trees behind you. There he is— with his dark hair, and his shaven face, and his steady look! There he is, standing before me as he stood in the wood, with his eyes on my eyes, and his sword feeling mine!" He turned to Miss Laroche. "Do *you* see him too?" he asked eagerly. "Tell me the truth. My whole life depends on your telling me the truth."

She controlled herself with a wonderful courage. "I don't see him," she answered.

He took out his handkerchief, and passed it over his face with a gasp of relief. "There is my last chance!" he said. "If she will be true to me—if she will be always near me, morning, noon, and night, I shall be released from the sight of him. See! he is fading away already. Gone!" he cried, with a scream of exultation. He fell on his knees, and looked at Miss Laroche like a savage adoring his idol. "Will you cast me off now?" he asked humbly. "Lionel was fond of you in his lifetime. His spirit is a merciful spirit. He shrinks from frightening you; he has left me for your sake; he will release me for your sake. Pity me, take me to live with you—and I shall never see him again!"

It was dreadful to hear him. I saw that the poor girl could endure no more. "Leave us," I whispered to her; "I will join you at the house."

He heard me, and instantly placed himself between us. "Let her promise, or she shan't go."

She felt, as I felt, the imperative necessity of saying anything that might soothe him. At a sign from me she gave him her promise to return.

He was satisfied—he insisted on kissing her hand, and then he let her go. I had by this time succeeded in inducing him to trust me. He proposed, of his own accord, that I should accompany him to the inn in the village at which he had been staying. The landlord (naturally enough distrusting his wretched guest) had warned him that morning to find some other place of shelter. I engaged to use my influence with the man to make him change his purpose, and I succeeded in effecting the necessary arrangements for having the poor wretch properly looked after. On my return to my own house, I wrote to a brother magistrate living near me, and to the superintendent of our county asylum, requesting them to consult with me on the best means of lawfully restraining Captain Stanwick until we could communicate with his relations. Could I have done more than this? The event of the next morning answered that question—answered it at once and for ever.

Presenting myself at Nettlegrove Hall towards sunset, to take charge of Miss Laroche, I was met by an obstacle in the shape of a protest from her aunt.

This good lady had been informed of the appearance of Captain Stanwick in the park, and she strongly disapproved of encouraging any further communication with him on the part of her niece. She also considered that I had failed in my duty in still leaving the Captain at liberty. I told her that I was only waiting to act on the advice of competent persons, who would arrive the next day to consult with me; and I did my best to persuade her of the wisdom of the course that I had taken in the meantime. Miss Laroche, on her side, was resolved to be true to the promise that she had given. Between us, we induced her aunt to yield on certain conditions.

"I know the part of the park in which the meeting is to take place," the old lady said; "it is my niece's favourite walk. If she is not brought back to me in half an hour's time, I shall send the men-servants to protect her."

The twilight was falling when we reached the appointed place. We found Captain Stanwick angry and suspicious; it was not easy to pacify him on the subject of our delay. His insanity seemed to me to be now more marked than ever. He had seen, or dreamed of seeing, the ghost during the past night. For the first time (he said) the apparition of the dead man had spoken to him. In solemn words it had condemned him to expiate his crime by giving his life for the life that he had taken. It had warned him not to insist on marriage with Bertha Laroche: "She shall share your punishment if she shares your life. And you shall know it by this sign—*She shall see me as you see me.*"

I tried to compose him. He shook his head in immovable despair, "No," he answered; "if she sees him when I see him, there ends the one hope of release that holds me to life. It will be good-bye between us, and good-bye for ever!"

We had walked on, while we were speaking, to a part of the park through which there flowed a rivulet of clear water. On the farther bank the open ground led down into a wooded valley. On our side of the stream rose a thick plantation of fir-trees, intersected by a winding path. Captain Stanwick stopped as we reached the place. His eyes rested, in the darkening twilight, on the narrow space pierced by the path among the trees. On a sudden he lifted his right hand, with the same cry of pain which we had heard before: with his left hand he took Miss Laroche by the arm. "There!" he said. "Look where I look! Do you see him there?"

As the words passed his lips, a dimly-visible figure appeared, advancing towards us along the path.

Was it the figure of a living man? or was it the creation of my own excited fancy? Before I could ask myself the question, the man advanced a step nearer to us. A last gleam of the dying light fell on his face through an opening in the trees. At the same instant Miss Laroche started back from Captain Stanwick with a scream of terror. She would have fallen if I had not been near enough to support her. The Captain was instantly at her side again. "Speak!" he cried. "Do *you* see it too?"

She was just able to say "Yes," before she fainted in my arms.

He stooped over her, and touched her cold cheek with his lips. "Good-bye!" he said, in tones suddenly and strangely changed to the most exquisite tenderness. "Good-bye, for ever!"

He leapt the rivulet; he crossed the open ground; he was lost to sight in the valley beyond.

As he disappeared, the visionary man among the fir-trees advanced; passed in silence; crossed the rivulet at a bound; and vanished as the figure of the Captain had vanished before him.

I was left alone with the swooning woman. Not a sound, far or near, broke the stillness of the coming night.

5. MR. FREDERIC DARNEL, MEMBER OF THE COLLEGE OF SURGEONS, TESTIFIES AND SAYS:

In the intervals of my professional duty I am accustomed to occupy myself in studying Botany, assisted by a friend and neighbour, whose tastes in this respect resemble my own. When I can spare an hour or two from my patients, we go out together searching for specimens. Our favourite place is Herne Wood. It is rich in material for the botanist, and it is only a mile distant from the village in which I live.

Early in July, my friend and I made a discovery in the wood of a very alarming and unexpected kind. We found a man in the clearing, prostrated by a dangerous wound, and to all appearance dead.

We carried him to the gamekeeper's cottage, on the outskirts of the wood, and on the side of it nearest to our village. He and his boy were out, but the light cart in which he makes his rounds, in the remoter part of his master's property, was in the out-house. While my friend was putting the horse to, I examined the stranger's wound. It had been quite recently inflicted, and I doubted whether it had (as yet, at any rate) really killed him. I did what I could with the linen and cold water which the gamekeeper's wife offered to me, and then my friend and I removed him carefully to my house in the cart. I applied the necessary restoratives, and I had the pleasure of satisfying myself that the vital powers had revived. He was perfectly unconscious, of course, but the action of the heart became distinctly perceptible, and I had hopes.

In a few days more I felt fairly sure of him. Then the usual fever set in. I was obliged, in justice to his friends, to search his clothes in presence of a witness. We found his handkerchief, his purse, and his cigar-case, and nothing more. No letters or visiting cards; nothing marked on his clothes but initials. There was no help for it but to wait to identify him until he could speak.

When that time came, he acknowledged to me that he had divested himself purposely of any clue to his identity, in the fear (if some mischance happened to him) of the news of it reaching his father and mother abruptly, by means of the newspapers. He had sent a letter to his bankers in London, to be forwarded to his parents, if the bankers neither saw him nor heard from him in a month's time. His first act was to withdraw this letter. The other particulars which he communicated to me are, I am told, already known. I need only add that I willingly kept his secret, simply speaking of him in the neighbourhood as a traveller from foreign parts who had met with an accident.

His convalescence was a long one. It was the beginning of October before he was completely restored to health. When he left us he went to London. He behaved most liberally to me; and we parted with sincere good wishes on either side.

6 MR. LIONEL VARLEIGH, OF BOSTON, U.S.A., TESTIFIES AND SAYS:

My first proceeding, on my recovery, was to go to the relations of Captain Stanwick in London, for the purpose of making inquiries about him.

I do not wish to justify myself at the expense of that miserable man. It is true that I loved Miss Laroche too dearly to yield her to any rival except at her own wish. It is also true that Captain Stanwick more than once insulted me, and that I endured it. He had suffered from sunstroke in India, and in his angry moments he was hardly a responsible being. It was only when he threatened me with personal chastisement that my patience gave way. We met sword in hand. In my mind was the resolution to spare his life. In his mind was the resolution to kill me. I have forgiven him. I will say no more.

His relations informed me of the symptoms of insane delusion which he had shown after the duel; of his escape from the asylum in which he had been confined; and of the failure to find him again.

The moment I heard this news the dread crossed my mind that Stanwick had found his way to Miss Laroche. In an hour more I was travelling to Nettlegrove Hall.

I arrived late in the evening, and found Miss Laroche's aunt in great alarm about her niece's safety. The young lady was at that very moment speaking to Stanwick in the park, with only an old man (the Rector) to protect her. I volunteered to go at once, and assist in taking care of her. A servant accompanied me to show me the place of meeting. We heard voices indistinctly, but saw no one. The servant pointed to a path through the fir-trees. I went on quickly by myself, leaving the man within call. In a few minutes I came upon them suddenly, at a little distance from me, on the bank of a stream.

The fear of seriously alarming Miss Laroche, if I showed myself too suddenly, deprived me for a moment of my presence of mind. Pausing to consider what it might be best to do, I was less completely protected from discovery by the trees than I had supposed. She had seen me; I heard her cry of alarm. The instant afterwards I saw Stanwick leap over the rivulet and take to flight. That action roused me. Without stopping for a word of explanation, I pursued him.

Unhappily, I missed my footing in the obscure light, and fell on the open ground beyond the stream. When I had gained my feet once more, Stanwick had disappeared among the trees which marked the boundary of the park beyond me. I could see nothing of him, and I could hear nothing of him, when I came out on the high-road. There I met with a labouring man who showed me the way to the village. From the inn I sent a letter to Miss Laroche's aunt, explaining what had happened, and asking leave to call at the Hall on the next day.

Early in the morning the Rector came to me at the inn. He brought sad news. Miss Laroche was suffering from a nervous attack, and my visit to the Hall must be deferred. Speaking next of the missing man, I heard all that Mr. Loring could tell me. My intimate knowledge of Stanwick enabled me to draw my own conclusion from the facts. The thought instantly crossed my mind that the poor wretch might have committed his expiatory suicide at the very spot on which he had attempted to kill me. Leaving the Rector to institute the necessary inquiries, I took post-horses to Maplesworth on my way to Herne Wood.

Advancing from the high-road to the wood, I saw two persons at a little distance from me—a man in the dress of a gamekeeper, and a lad. I was too much agitated to take any special notice of them; I hurried along the path which led to the clearing. My presentiment had not misled me. There he lay, dead on the scene of the duel, with a blood-stained razor by his side! I fell on my knees by the corpse; I took his cold hand in mine; and I thanked God that I had forgiven him in the first days of my recovery.

I was still kneeling, when I felt myself seized from behind. I struggled to my feet, and confronted the gamekeeper. He had noticed my hurry in entering the wood; his suspicions had been aroused, and he and the lad had followed me. There was blood on my clothes, there was horror in my face. Appearances were plainly against me; I had no choice but to accompany the gamekeeper to the nearest magistrate.

My instructions to my solicitor forbade him to vindicate my innocence by taking any technical legal objections to the action of the magistrate or of the coroner. I insisted on my witnesses being summoned to the lawyer's office, and allowed to state, in their own way, what they could truly declare on my behalf; and I left my defence to be founded upon the materials thus obtained. In the meanwhile I was detained in custody, as a matter of course.

With this event the tragedy of the duel reached its culminating point. I was accused of murdering the man who had attempted to take my life!

This last incident having been related, all that is worth noticing in my contribution to the present narrative comes to an end. I was tried in due course of law. The evidence taken at my solicitor's office was necessarily altered in form, though not in substance, by the examination to which the witnesses were subjected in a court of justice. So thoroughly did our defence satisfy the jury, that they became restless towards the close of the proceedings, and returned their verdict of Not Guilty without quitting the box.

When I was a free man again, it is surely needless to dwell on the first use that I made of my honourable acquittal. Whether I deserved the enviable place that I occupied in Bertha's estimation, it is not for me to say. Let me leave the decision to the lady who has ceased to be Miss Laroche—I mean the lady who has been good enough to become my wife.

Mr. Policeman and the Cook

A First Word for Myself

Before the doctor left me one evening, I asked him how much longer I was likely to live. He answered: "It's not easy to say; you may die before I can get back to you in the morning, or you may live to the end of the month."

I was alive enough on the next morning to think of the needs of my soul, and (being a member of the Roman Catholic Church) to send for the priest.

The history of my sins, related in confession, included blameworthy neglect of a duty which I owed to the laws of my country. In the priest's opinion—and I agreed with him—I was bound to make public acknowledgment of my fault, as an act of penance becoming to a Catholic Englishman. We concluded, thereupon, to try a division of labour. I related the circumstances, while his reverence took the pen, and put the matter into shape.

Here follows what came of it:

1. When I was a young man of five-and-twenty, I became a member of the London police force. After nearly two year's ordinary experience of the responsible and ill-paid duties of that vocation, I found myself employed on my first serious and terrible case of official inquiry—relating to nothing less than the crime of Murder.

The circumstances were these:

I was then attached to a station in the northern district of London—which I beg permission not to mention more particularly. On a certain Monday in the week, I took my turn of night duty. Up to four in the morning, nothing occurred at the station-house out of the ordinary way. It was then spring time, and, between the gas and the fire, the room became rather hot. I went to the door to get a breath of fresh air—much to the surprise of our Inspector on duty, who was constitutionally a chilly man. There was a fine rain falling; and a nasty damp in the air sent me back to the fireside. I don't suppose I had sat down for more than a minute when the swinging-door was violently pushed open. A frantic woman ran in with a scream, and said: "Is this the station-house?"

Our Inspector (otherwise an excellent officer) had, by some perversity of nature, a hot temper in his chilly constitution. "Why, bless the woman, can't you *see* it is?" he says. "What's the matter now?"

"Murder's the matter!" she burst out. "For God's sake come back with me. It's at Mrs. Crosscapel's lodging-house, number 14, Lehigh Street. A young woman has murdered her husband in the night! With a knife, sir. She says she thinks she did it in her sleep."

I confess I was startled by this; and the third man on duty (a sergeant) seemed to feel it too. She was a nice-looking young woman, even in her terrified condition, just out of bed, with her clothes huddled on anyhow. I was partial in those days to a tall figure—and she was, as they say, my style. I put a chair for her; and the sergeant poked the fire. As for the Inspector, nothing ever upset *him*. He questioned her as coolly as if it had been a case of petty larceny.

"Have you seen the murdered man?" he asked.

"No, sir."

"Or the wife?"

"No sir. I didn't dare go into the room; I only heard about it!"

"Oh? And who are You? One of the lodgers?"

"No, sir. I'm the cook."

"Isn't there a master in the house?"

"Yes, sir. He's frightened out of his wits. And the housemaid's gone for the doctor. It all falls on the poor servants, of course. Oh, why did I ever set foot in that horrible house?"

The poor soul burst out crying, and shivered from head to foot. The Inspector made a note of her statement, and then asked her to read it, and sign it with her name. The object of this proceeding was to get her to come near enough to give him the opportunity of smelling her breath. "When people make extraordinary statements," he afterwards said to me, "it sometimes saves trouble to satisfy yourself that they are not drunk. I've known them to be mad—but not often. You will generally find *that* in their eyes."

She roused herself, and signed her name—"Priscilla Thurlby." The Inspector's own test proved her to be sober; and her eyes—a nice light blue colour, mild and pleasant, no doubt, when they were not staring with fear, and red with crying—satisfied him (as I supposed) that she was not mad. He turned the case over to me, in the first instance. I saw that he didn't believe in it, even yet.

"Go back with her to the house," he says. "This may be a stupid hoax, or a quarrel exaggerated. See to it yourself, and hear what the doctor says. If it *is* serious, send word back here directly, and let nobody enter the place or leave it till we come. Stop! You know the form if any statement is volunteered?"

"Yes, sir. I am to caution the persons that whatever they say will be taken down, and may be used against them."

"Quite right. You'll be an Inspector yourself one of these days. Now, miss!" With that he dismissed her, under my care.

Lehigh Street was not very far off—about twenty minutes' walk from the station. I confess I thought the Inspector had been rather hard on Priscilla. She was herself naturally angry with him. "What does he mean," she says, "by talking of a hoax? I wish he was as frightened as I am. This is the first time I have been out at service, sir—and I did think I had found a respectable place."

I said very little to her—feeling, if the truth must be told, rather anxious about the duty committed to me. On reaching the house the door was opened from within, before I could knock. A gentleman stepped out, who proved to be the doctor. He stopped the moment he saw me.

"You must be careful policeman," he says. "I found the man, lying on his back, in bed, dead—with the knife that had killed him left sticking in the wound."

Hearing this, I felt the necessity of sending at once to the station. Where could I find a trustworthy messenger? I took the liberty of asking the doctor if he would repeat to the police what he had already said to me. The station was not much out of his way home. He kindly granted my request.

The landlady (Mrs. Crosscapel) joined us while we were talking. She was still a young woman; not easily frightened, as far as I could see, even by a murder in the house. Her husband was in the passage behind her. He looked old enough to be her father; and he so trembled with terror that some people might have taken him for the guilty person. I removed the key from the street door, after locking it; and I said to the landlady: "Nobody must leave the house, or enter the house, till the Inspector comes. I must examine the premises to see if anyone has broken in."

"There is the key of the area gate," she said, in answer to me. "It's always kept locked. Come downstairs, and see for yourself." Priscilla went with us. Her mistress set her to work to light the kitchen fire. "Some of us," says Mrs. Crosscapel, "may be the better for a cup of tea." I remarked that she took things easy, under the circumstances. She answered that the landlady of a London lodging-house could not afford to lose her wits, no matter what might happen.

I found the gate locked, and the shutters of the kitchen window fastened. The back kitchen and back door were secured in the same way. No person was concealed anywhere. Returning upstairs, I examined the front parlour window. There again, the barred shutters answered for the security of that room. A cracked voice spoke through the door of the back parlour. "The policeman can come in," it said, "if he will promise not to look at me." I turned to the landlady for information. "It's my parlour lodger, Miss My-bus," she said, "a most respectable lady." Going into the room, I saw something rolled up perpendicularly in the bed curtains. Miss Mybus had made herself modestly invisible in that way. Having now satisfied my mind about the security of the lower part of the house, and having the keys safe in my pocket, I was ready to go upstairs.

On our way to the upper regions I asked if there had been any visitors on the previous day. There had been only two visitors, friends of the lodgers—and Mrs. Crosscapel herself had let them both out. My next inquiry related to the lodgers themselves. On the ground floor there was Miss Mybus. On the first floor (occupying both rooms) Mr. Barfield, an old bachelor, employed in a merchant's office. On the second floor, in the front room, Mr. John Zebedee, the murdered man, and his wife. In the back room, Mr. Deluc; described as a cigar agent, and supposed to be a Creole gentleman from Martinique. In the front garret, Mr. and Mrs. Crosscapel. In the back garret, the cook and the housemaid. These were the inhabitants, regularly accounted for. I asked about the servants. "Both excellent characters," says the landlady, "or they would not be in my service."

We reached the second floor, and found the housemaid on the watch outside the door of the front room. Not as nice a woman, personally, as the cook, and sadly frightened of course. Her mistress had posted her, to give the alarm in the case of an outbreak on the part of Mrs. Zebedee, kept locked up in the room. My arrival relieved the housemaid of further responsibility. She ran downstairs to her fellow-servant in the kitchen.

I asked Mrs. Crosscapel how and when the alarm of the murder had been given.

"Soon after three this morning," says she, "I was woke by the screams of Mrs. Zebedee. I found her out here on the landing, and Mr. Deluc, in great alarm, trying to quiet her. Sleeping in the next room, he had only to open his door, when her screams woke him. "My dear John's murdered! I am the miserable wretch—I did it in my sleep!" She repeated those frantic words over and over again, until she dropped in a swoon. Mr. Deluc and I carried her back into the bedroom. We both thought the poor creature had been driven distracted by some dreadful dream. But when we got to the bedside—don't ask me what we saw; the Doctor has told you about it already. I was once a nurse in a hospital, and accustomed, as such, to horrid sights. It turned me cold and giddy, notwithstanding. As for Mr. Deluc, I thought *he* would have had a fainting fit next."

Hearing this, I inquired if Mrs. Zebedee had said or done any strange things since she had been Mrs. Crosscapel's lodger.

"You think she's mad?" says the landlady. "And anybody would be of your mind, when a woman accuses herself of murdering her husband in her sleep. All I can say is that, up to this morning, a more quiet, sensible, well-behaved little person than Mrs. Zebedee I never met with. Only just married, mind, and as fond of her unfortunate husband as a woman could be. I should have called them a pattern couple, in their own line of life."

There was no more to be said on the landing. We unlocked the door and went into the room.

2. He lay in bed on his back as the doctor had described him. On the left side of his nightgown, just over his heart, the blood on the linen told its terrible tale. As well as one could judge, looking unwillingly at a dead face, he must have been a handsome young

man in his life-time. It was a sight to sadden anybody—but I think the most painful sensation was when my eyes fell next on his miserable wife.

She was down on the floor, crouched up in a corner—a dark little woman, smartly dressed in gay colours. Her black hair and her big brown eyes made the horrid paleness of her face look even more deadly white than perhaps it really was. She stared straight at us without appearing to see us. We spoke to her, and she never answered a word. She might have been dead—like her husband— except that she perpetually picked at her fingers, and shuddered every now and then as if she was cold. I went to her and tried to lift her up. She shrank back with a cry that wellnigh frightened me—not because it was loud, but because it was more like the cry of some animal than of a human being. However quietly she might have behaved in the landlady's previous experience of her, she was beside herself now. I might have been moved by a natural pity for her, or I might have been completely upset in my mind—I only know this, I could not persuade myself that she was guilty. I even said to Mrs. Crosscapel, "I don't believe she did it."

While I spoke, there was a knock at the door. I went downstairs at once, and admitted (to my great relief) the Inspector, accompanied by one of our men.

He waited downstairs to hear my report, and he approved of what I had done. "It looks as if the murder had been committed by somebody in the house." Saying this, he left the man below, and went up with me to the second floor.

Before he had been a minute in the room, he discovered an object which had escaped my observation.

It was the knife that had done the deed.

The doctor had found it left in the body—had withdrawn it to probe the wound—and had laid it on the bedside table. It was one of those useful knives which contain a saw, a corkscrew, and other like implements. The big blade fastened back, when open, with a spring. Except where the blood was on it, it was as bright as when it had been purchased. A small metal plate was fastened to the horn handle, containing an inscription, only partly engraved, which ran thus: "*To John Zebedee, from——*" There it stopped, strangely enough.

Who or what had interrupted the engraver's work? It was impossible even to guess. Nevertheless, the Inspector was encouraged.

"This ought to help us," he said—and then he gave an attentive ear (looking all the while at the poor creature in the corner) to what Mrs. Crosscapel had to tell him.

The landlady having done, he said he must now see the lodger who slept in the next bedchamber.

Mr. Deluc made his appearance, standing at the door of the room, and turning away his head with horror from the sight inside.

He was wrapped in a splendid blue dressing-gown, with a golden girdle and trimmings. His scanty brownish hair curled (whether artificially or not, I am unable to say) in little ringlets. His complexion was yellow; his greenish-brown eyes were of the sort called "goggle"—they looked as if they might drop out of his face, if you held a spoon under them. His moustache and goat's beard were beautifully oiled; and, to complete his equipment, he had a long black cigar in his mouth.

"It isn't insensibility to this terrible tragedy," he explained. "My nerves have been shattered, Mr. Policeman, and I can only repair the mischief in this way. Be pleased to excuse and feel for me."

The Inspector questioned this witness sharply and closely. He was not a man to be misled by appearances; but I could see that he was far from liking, or even trusting, Mr. Deluc. Nothing came of the examination, except what Mrs. Crosscapel had in substance already mentioned to me. Mr. Deluc returned to his room.

"How long has he been lodging with you?" the Inspector asked as soon as his back was turned.

"Nearly a year," the landlady answered.

"Did he give you a reference?"

"As good a reference as I could wish for." Thereupon, she mentioned the names of a well-known firm of cigar merchants in the City. The Inspector noted the information in his pocket-book.

I would rather not relate in detail what happened next: it is too distressing to be dwelt on. Let me only say that the poor demented woman was taken away in a cab to the station-house. The Inspector possessed himself of the knife, and of a book found on the floor, called *The World of Sleep*. The portmanteau containing the luggage was locked—and then the door of the room was secured, the keys in both cases being left in my charge. My instructions were to remain in the house, and allow nobody to leave it, until I heard again shortly from the Inspector.

3. The coroner's inquest was adjourned; and the examination before the magistrate ended in a remand—Mrs. Zebedee being in no condition to understand the proceedings in either case. The surgeon reported her to be completely prostrated by a terrible nervous shock. When he was asked if he considered her to have been a sane woman before the murder took place, he refused to answer positively at that time.

A week passed. The murdered man was buried; his old father attending the funeral. I occasionally saw Mrs. Crosscapel, and the two servants, for the purpose of getting such further information as was thought desirable. Both the cook and the housemaid had given their month's notice to quit; declining, in the interest of their characters, to remain in a house which had been the scene of a murder. Mr. Deluc's nerves led also to his removal; his rest was now disturbed by frightful dreams. He paid the necessary forfeit-money, and left without notice. The first-floor lodger, Mr. Barfield, kept his rooms, but obtained leave of absence from his employers, and took refuge with some friends in the country. Miss Mybus alone remained in the parlours. "When I am comfortable," the old lady said, "nothing moves me, at my age. A murder up two pairs of stairs is nearly the same thing as a murder in the next house. Distance, you see, makes all the difference."

It mattered little to the police what the lodgers did. We had men in plain clothes watching the house night and day. Everybody who went away was privately followed; and the police in the district to which they retired were warned to keep an eye on them, after that. As long as we failed to put Mrs. Zebedee's extraordinary statement to any sort of test—to say nothing of having proved unsuccessful, thus far, in tracing the knife to its purchaser—we were bound to let no person living under Mr. Crosscapel's roof, on the night of the murder, slip through our fingers.

4. In a fortnight more, Mrs. Zebedee had sufficiently recovered to make the necessary statement—after the preliminary caution addressed to persons in such cases. The surgeon had no hesitation, now, in reporting her to be a sane woman.

Her station in life had been domestic service. She had lived for four years in her last place as lady's-maid, with a family residing in Dorsetshire. The one objection to her had been the occasional infirmity of sleep-walking, which made it necessary that one of the other female servants should sleep in the same room, with the door locked and the key under her pillow. In all other respects the lady's-maid was described by her mistress as "a perfect treasure."

In the last six months of her service, a young man named John Zebedee entered the house (with a written character) as a footman. He soon fell in love with the nice little lady's-maid, and she heartily returned the feeling. They might have waited for years before they were in a pecuniary position to marry, but for the death of Zebedee's uncle, who left him a little fortune of two thousand pounds. They were now, for persons in their station, rich enough to please themselves; and they were married from the house in which they had served together, the little daughters of the family showing their affection for Mrs. Zebedee, by acting as her bridesmaids.

The young husband was a careful man. He decided to employ his small capital to the best advantage, by sheep-farming in Australia. His wife made no objection; she was ready to go wherever John went.

Accordingly they spent their short honeymoon in London, so as to see for themselves the vessel in which their passage was to be taken. They went to Mrs. Crosscapel's lodging-house because Zebedee's uncle had always stayed there when in London. Ten days were to pass before the day of embarkation arrived. This gave the young couple a welcome holiday, and a prospect of amusing themselves to their hearts' content among the sights and shows of the great city.

On their first evening in London they went to the theatre. They were both accustomed to the fresh air of the country, and they felt half stifled by the heat and the gas. However, they were so pleased with an amusement which was new to them that they went to another theatre on the next evening. On this second occasion, John Zebedee found the heat unendurable. They left the theatre, and got back to their lodgings towards ten o'clock.

Let the rest be told in the words used by Mrs. Zebedee herself. She said:

"We sat talking for a little while in our room, and John's headache got worse and worse. I persuaded him to go to bed, and I put out the candle (the fire giving sufficient light to undress by), so that he might the sooner fall asleep. But he was too restless to sleep. He asked me to read him something. Books always made him drowsy at the best of times.

"I had not myself begun to undress. So I lit the candle again, and I opened the only book I had. John had noticed it at the railway bookstall by the name of *The World of Sleep*. He used to joke with me about my being a sleep-walker; and he said, 'Here's something that's sure to interest you'—and he made me a present of the book.

"Before I had read to him for more than half an hour he was fast asleep. Not feeling that way inclined, I went on reading to myself.

"The book did indeed interest me. There was one terrible story which took a hold on my mind—the story of a man who stabbed his own wife in a sleep-walking dream. I thought of putting down my book after that, and then changed my mind again and went on. The next chapters were not so interesting; they were full of learned accounts of why we fall asleep, and what our brains do in that state, and such like. It ended in my falling asleep, too, in my armchair by the fireside.

"I don't know what o'clock it was when I went to sleep. I don't know how long I slept, or whether I dreamed or not. The candle and the fire had both burned out, and it was pitch dark when I woke. I can't even say why I woke—unless it was the coldness of the room.

"There was a spare candle on the chimney-piece. I found the match-box, and got a light. Then for the first time, I turned round towards the bed; and I saw——"

She had seen the dead body of her husband, murdered while she was unconsciously at his side—and she fainted, poor creature, at the bare remembrance of it.

The proceedings were adjourned. She received every possible care and attention; the chaplain looking after her welfare as well as the surgeon.

I have said nothing of the evidence of the landlady and servants. It was taken as a mere formality. What little they knew proved nothing against Mrs. Zebedee. The police made no discoveries that supported her first frantic accusation of herself. Her master and mistress, where she had been last in service, spoke of her in the highest terms. We were at a complete deadlock.

It had been thought best not to surprise Mr. Deluc, as yet, by citing him as a witness. The action of the law was, however, hurried in this case by a private communication received from the chaplain.

After twice seeing, and speaking with, Mrs. Zebedee, the reverend gentleman was persuaded that she had no more to do than himself with the murder of her husband. He did not consider that he was justified in repeating a confidential communication—he would only recommend that Mr. Deluc should be summoned to appear at the next examination. This advice was followed.

The police had no evidence against Mrs. Zebedee when the inquiry was resumed. To assist the ends of justice she was now put into the witness-box. The discovery of her murdered husband, when she woke in the small hours of the morning was passed over as rapidly as possible. Only three questions of importance were put to her.

First, the knife was produced. Had she ever seen it in her husband's possession? Never. Did she know anything about it? Nothing whatever.

Secondly: Did she, or did her husband, lock the bedroom door when they returned from the theatre? No. Did she afterwards lock the door herself? No.

Thirdly: Had she any sort of reason to give for supposing that she had murdered her husband in a sleep-walking dream? No reason, except that she was beside herself at the time, and the book put the thought into her head.

After this the other witnesses were sent out of court. The motive for the chaplain's communication now appeared. Mrs. Zebedee was asked if anything unpleasant had occurred between Mr. Deluc and herself.

Yes. He had caught her alone on the stairs at the lodginghouse; had presumed to make love to her; and had carried the insult still further by attempting to kiss her. She had slapped his face, and had declared that her husband should know of it, if his misconduct was repeated. He was in a furious rage at having his face slapped; and he said to her: "Madam, you may live to regret this."

After consultation, and at the request of our Inspector, it was decided to keep Mr. Deluc in ignorance of Mrs. Zebedee's statement for the present. When the witnesses were recalled, he gave the same evidence which he had already given to the Inspector—and he was then asked if he knew anything of the knife. He looked at it without any guilty signs in his face, and swore that he had never seen it until that moment. The resumed inquiry ended, and still nothing had been discovered.

But we kept an eye on Mr. Deluc. Our next effort was to try if we could associate him with the purchase of the knife.

Here again (there really did seem to be a sort of fatality in this case) we reached no useful result. It was easy enough to find out the wholesale cutlers, who had manufactured the knife at Sheffield, by the mark on the blade. But they made tens of thousands of such knives, and disposed of them to retail dealers all over Great Britain—to say nothing of foreign parts. As to finding out the person who had engraved the imperfect inscription (without knowing where, or by whom, the knife had been purchased) we might as well have looked for the proverbial needle in the bundle of hay. Our last resource was to have the knife photographed, with the inscribed side uppermost, and to send copies to every police-station in the kingdom.

At the same time we reckoned up Mr. Deluc—I mean that we made investigations into his past life—on the chance that he and the murdered man might have known each other, and might have had a quarrel, or a rivalry about a woman, on some former occasion. No such discovery rewarded us.

We found Deluc to have led a dissipated life, and to have mixed with very bad company. But he had kept out of reach of the law. A man may be a profligate vagabond; may insult a lady; may say threatening things to her, in the first stinging sensation of having his face slapped—but it doesn't follow from these blots on his character that he has murdered her husband in the dead of the night.

Once more, then, when we were called upon to report ourselves, we had no evidence to produce. The photographs failed to discover the owner of the knife, and to explain its interrupted inscription. Poor Mrs. Zebedee was allowed to go back to her friends, on entering into her own recognizance to appear again if called upon. Articles in the newspapers began to inquire how many more murderers would succeed in baffling the police. The authorities at the Treasury offered a reward of a hundred pounds for the necessary information. And the weeks passed, and nobody claimed the reward.

Our Inspector was not a man to be easily beaten. More inquiries and examinations followed. It is needless to say anything about them. We were defeated—and there, so far as the police and the public were concerned, was an end of it.

The assassination of the poor young husband soon passed out of notice, like other undiscovered murders. One obscure person only was foolish enough, in his leisure hours, to persist in trying to solve the problem of Who Killed Zebedee? He felt that he might rise to the highest position in the police-force if he succeeded where his elders and betters had failed—and he held to his own little ambition, though everybody laughed at him. In plain English, I was the man.

5. Without meaning it, I have told my story ungratefully. There were two persons who saw nothing ridiculous in my resolution to continue the investigation, single-handed. One of them was Miss Mybus; and the other was the cook, Priscilla Thurlby.

Mentioning the lady first, Miss Mybus was indignant at the resigned manner in which the police accepted their defeat. She was a little bright-eyed wiry woman; and she spoke her mind freely.

"This comes home to me," she said. "Just look back for a year or two. I can call to mind two cases of persons found murdered in London—and the assassins have never been traced. I am a person, too; and I ask myself if my turn is not coming next. You're a nice-looking fellow—and I like your pluck and perseverance. Come here as often as you think right; and say you are my visitor, if they make any difficulty about letting you in. One thing more! I have nothing particular to do, and I am no fool. Here, in the parlours, I see everybody who comes into the house or goes out of the house. Leave me your address—I may get some information for you yet."

With the best intentions, Miss Mybus found no opportunity of helping me. Of the two, Priscilla Thurlby seemed more likely to be of use.

In the first place, she was sharp and active, and (not having succeeded in getting another situation as yet) was mistress of her own movements.

In the second place, she was a woman I could trust. Before she had left home to try domestic service in London, the parson of her native parish gave her a written testimonial, of which I append a copy. Thus it ran:

I gladly recommend Priscilla Thurlby for any respectable employment which she may be competent to undertake. Her father and mother are infirm old people, who have lately suffered a diminution of their income; and they have a younger daughter to maintain. Rather than be a burden on her parents, Priscilla goes to London to find domestic employment, and to devote her earnings to the assistance of her father and mother. This circumstance speaks for itself. I have known the family many years; and I only regret that I have no vacant place in my own household which I can offer to this good girl.

(Signed) HENRY DERRINGTON, Rector of Roth

After reading those words, I could safely ask Priscilla to help me in reopening the mysterious murder case to some good purpose.

My notion was that the proceedings of the persons in Mrs. Crosscapel's house, had not been closely enough inquired into yet. By way of continuing the investigation, I asked Priscilla if she could tell me anything which associated the housemaid with Mr. Deluc. She was unwilling to answer. "I may be casting suspicion on an innocent person," she said. "Besides, I was for so short a time the housemaid's fellow servant——"

"You slept in the same room with her," I remarked; "and you had opportunities of observing her conduct towards the lodgers. If they had asked you, at the examination, what I now ask, you would have answered as an honest woman."

To this argument she yielded. I heard from her certain particulars which threw a new light on Mr. Deluc, and on the case generally. On that information I acted. It was slow work, owing to the claims on me of my regular duties; but with Priscilla's help, I steadily advanced towards the end I had in view.

Besides this, I owed another obligation to Mrs. Crosscapel's nice-looking cook. The confession must be made sooner or later—and I may as well make it now. I first knew what love was, thanks to Priscilla. I had delicious kisses, thanks to Priscilla. And, when I asked if she would marry me, she didn't say No. She looked, I must own, a little sadly, and she said: "How can two such poor people as we are ever hope to marry?" To this I answered: "It won't be long before I lay my hand on the clue which my Inspector has failed to find. I shall be in a position to marry you, my dear, when that time comes."

At our next meeting we spoke of her parents. I was now her promised husband. Judging by what I had heard of the proceedings of other people in my position, it seemed to be only right that I should be made known to her father and mother. She entirely agreed with me; and she wrote home that day to tell them to expect us at the end of the week.

I took my turn of night-duty, and so gained my liberty for the greater part of the next day. I dressed myself in plain clothes and we took our tickets on the railway for Yateland, being the nearest station to the village in which Priscilla's parents lived.

6 The train stopped, as usual, at the big town of Waterbank. Supporting herself by her needle, while she was still unprovided with a situation, Priscilla had been at work late in the night—she was tired and thirsty. I left the carriage to get her some soda-water. The stupid girl in the refreshment room failed to pull the cork out of the bottle, and refused to let me help her. She took a corkscrew, and used it crookedly. I lost all patience, and snatched the bottle out of her hand. Just as I drew the cork, the bell rang on the platform. I only waited to pour the soda-water into a glass—but the train was moving as I left the refreshment-room. The porters stopped me when I tried to jump on to the step of the carriage. I was left behind.

As soon as I had recovered my temper, I looked at the timetable. We had reached Waterbank at five minutes past one. By good luck, the next train was due at forty-four minutes past one, and arrived at Yateland (the next station) ten minutes afterwards. I could only hope that Priscilla would look at the timetable too, and wait for me. If I had attempted to walk the distance between the two places, I should have lost time instead of saving it. The interval before me was not very long; I occupied it in looking over the town.

Speaking with all due respect to the inhabitants, Waterbank (to other people) is a dull place. I went up one street and down another—and stopped to look at a shop which struck me; not from anything in itself, but because it was the only shop in the street with the shutters closed.

A bill was posted on the shutters, announcing that the place was to let. The out-going tradesman's name and business, announced in the customary painted letters, ran thus:—*James Wycomb, Cutler, etc.*

For the first time, it occurred to me that we had forgotten an obstacle in our way, when we distributed our photographs of the knife. We had none of us remembered that a certain proportion of cutlers might be placed, by circumstances, out of our reach—either by retiring from business or by becoming bankrupt. I always carried a copy of the photograph about me; and I thought to myself, "Here is the ghost of a chance of tracing the knife to Mr. Deluc!"

The shop door was opened, after I had twice rung the bell, by an old man, very dirty and very deaf. He said: "You had better go upstairs and speak to Mr. Scorrier—top of the house."

I put my lips to the old fellow's ear-trumpet, and asked who Mr. Scorrier was.

"Brother-in-law to Mr. Wycomb. Mr. Wycomb's dead. If you want to buy the business apply to Mr. Scorrier."

Receiving that reply, I went upstairs, and found Mr. Scorrier engaged in engraving a brass door-plate. He was a middle-aged man, with a cadaverous face and dim eyes. After the necessary apologies, I produced my photograph.

"May I ask, sir, if you know anything of the inscription on that knife?" I said.

He took his magnifying glass to look at it.

"This is curious," he remarked quietly. "I remember the queer name—Zebedee. Yes, sir; I did the engraving, as far as it goes. I wonder what prevented me from finishing it?"

The name of Zebedee, and the unfinished inscription on the knife had appeared in every English newspaper. He took the matter so coolly, that I was doubtful how to interpret his answer. Was it possible that he had not seen the account of the murder? Or was he an accomplice with prodigious powers of self-control?

"Excuse me," I said, "do you read the newspapers?"

"Never! My eyesight is failing me. I abstain from reading, in the interests of my occupation."

"Have you not heard the name of Zebedee mentioned—particularly by people who do read the newspapers?"

"Very likely; but I didn't attend to it. When the day's work is done, I take my walk. Then I have my supper, my drop of grog, and my pipe. Then I go to bed: A dull existence you think I dare say! I had a miserable life, sir, when I was young. A bare subsistence, and a little rest, before the last perfect rest in the grave—

that is all I want. The world has gone by me long ago. So much the better."

The poor man spoke honestly. I was ashamed of having doubted him. I returned to the subject of the knife.

"Do you know where it was purchased, and by whom?" I asked.

"My memory is not so good as it was," he said; "but I have got something by me that helps it."

He took from a cupboard a dirty old scrap-book. Strips of paper, with writing on them, were pasted on the pages, as well as I could see. He turned to an index or table of contents, and, opened a page. Something like a flash of life showed itself on his dismal face.

"Ha! now I remember," he said. "The knife was bought of my late brother-in-law, in the shop downstairs. It all comes back to me, sir. A person in a state of frenzy burst into this very room, and snatched the knife away from me, when I was only half-way through the inscription!"

I felt that I was now close on discovery. "May I see what it is that has assisted your memory?" I asked.

"Oh yes. You must know, sir, I live by engraving inscriptions and addresses, and I paste in this book the manuscript instructions which I receive, with marks of my own on the margin. For one thing, they serve as a reference to new customers. And for another thing, they do certainly help my memory."

He turned the book towards me, and pointed to a slip of paper which occupied the lower half of a page.

I read the complete inscription, intended for the knife that killed Zebedee, and written as follows:

"To John Zebedee. From Priscilla Thurlby."

7. I declare that it is impossible for me to describe what I felt when Priscilla's name confronted me like a written confession of guilt. How long it was before I recovered myself in some degree, I cannot say. The only thing I can clearly call to mind is, that I frightened the poor engraver.

My first desire was to get possession of the manuscript inscription. I told him I was a policeman, and summoned him to assist me in the discovery of a crime. I even offered him money. He drew back from my hand. "You shall have it for nothing," he said, "if you will only go away and never come back here again." He tried to cut it out of the page—but his trembling hands were helpless. I cut it out myself, and attempted to thank him. He wouldn't hear me. "Go away!" he said, "I don't like the look of you."

It may be here objected that I ought not to have felt so sure as I did of the woman's guilt, until I had got more evidence against her. The knife might have been stolen from her, supposing she was the person who had snatched it out of the engraver's hands, and might have been afterwards used by the thief to commit the murder. All very true. But I never had a moment's doubt in my own mind, from the time when I read the damnable line in the engraver's book.

I went back to the railway without any plan in my head. The train by which I had proposed to follow her had left Waterbank. The next train that arrived was for London. I took my place in it—still without any plan in my head.

At Charing Cross a friend met me. He said, "You're looking miserably ill. Come and have a drink."

I went with him. The liquor was what I really wanted; it strung me up, and cleared my head. He went his way, and I went mine. In a little while more, I determined what I would do.

In the first place, I decided to resign my situation in the police, from a motive which will presently appear. In the second place, I took a bed at a public-house. She would no doubt return to London, and she would go to my lodgings to find out why I had broken my appointment. To bring to justice the one woman whom I had dearly loved was too cruel a duty for a poor creature like me. I preferred leaving the police force. On the other hand, if she and I met before time had helped me to control myself, I had a horrid fear that I might turn murderer next, and kill her then and there. The wretch had not only all but misled me into marrying her, but also into charging the innocent housemaid with being concerned in the murder.

The same night I hit on a way of clearing up such doubts as still harassed my mind. I wrote to the rector of Roth, informing him that I was engaged to marry her, and asking if he would tell me (in consideration of my position) what her former relations might have been with the person named John Zebedee.

By return of post I got this reply:

SIR,—Under the circumstances, I think I am bound to tell you confidentially what the friends and well-wishers of Priscilla have kept secret, for her sake.

Zebedee was in service in this neighbourhood. I am sorry to say it, of a man who has come to such a miserable end—but his behaviour to Priscilla proves him to have been a vicious and heartless wretch. They were engaged—and, I add with indignation, he tried to seduce her under a promise of marriage. Her virtue resisted him, and he pretended to be ashamed of himself. The banns were published in my church. On the next day Zebedee disappeared, and cruelly deserted her. He was a capable servant; and I believe he got another place. I leave you to imagine what the poor girl suffered under the outrage inflicted on her. Going to London, with my recommendation, she answered the first advertisement that she saw, and was unfortunate enough to begin her career in domestic service in the very lodging-house, to which (as I gather from the newspaper report of the murder) the man Zebedee took the person whom he married, after deserting Priscilla. Be assured that you are about to unite yourself to an excellent girl, and accept my best wishes for your happiness.

It was plain from this that neither the rector nor the parents and friends knew anything of the purchase of the knife. The one miserable man who knew the truth was the man who had asked her to be his wife.

I owed it to myself—at least so it seemed to me—not to let it be supposed that I, too, had meanly deserted her. Dreadful as the prospect was, I felt that I must see her once more, and for the last time.

She was at work when I went into her room. As I opened the door she started to her feet. Her cheeks reddened, and her eyes flashed with anger. I stepped forward—and she saw my face. My face silenced her.

I spoke in the fewest words I could find.

"I have been to the cutler's shop at Waterbank," I said. "There is the unfinished inscription on the knife, completely in your handwriting. I could hang you by a word. God forgive me—I can't say the word."

Her bright complexion turned to a dreadful clay-colour. Her

eyes were fixed and staring, like the eyes of a person in a fit. She stood before me, still and silent. Without saying more, I dropped the inscription into the fire. Without saying more, I left her.

I never saw her again.

8. But I heard from her a few days later.

The letter has long since burnt. I wish I could have forgotten it as well. It sticks to my memory. If I die with my senses about me, Priscilla's letter will be my last recollection on earth.

In substance it repeated what the rector had already told me. Further, it informed me that she had bought the knife as a keepsake for Zebedee, in place of a similar knife which he had lost. On the Saturday, she made the purchase, and left it to be engraved. On the Sunday, the banns were put up. On the Monday, she was deserted; and she snatched the knife from the table while the engraver was at work.

She only knew that Zebedee had added a new sting to the insult inflicted on her, when he arrived at the lodgings with his wife. Her duties as cook kept her in the kitchen—and Zebedee never discovered that she was in the house. I still remember the last lines of her confession:

"The devil entered into me when I tried their door, on my way up to bed, and found it unlocked, and listened awhile, and peeped in. I saw them by the dying light of the candle—one asleep on the bed, the other asleep by the fireside. I had the knife in my hand, and the thought came to me to do it, so that they might hang *her* for the murder. I couldn't take the knife out again, when I had done it. Mind this! I did really like you—I didn't say Yes, because you could hardly hang your own wife, if you found out who killed Zebedee."

Since the past time I have never heard again of Priscilla Thurlby; I don't know whether she is living or dead. Many people may think I deserve to be hanged myself for not having given her up to the gallows. They may, perhaps, be disappointed when they see this confession, and hear that I have died decently in my bed. I don't blame them. I am a penitent sinner. I wish all merciful Christians good-bye for ever.

Fauntleroy

Chapter One

It was certainly a dull little dinner-party. Of the four guests two of us were men between fifty and sixty, and two of us were youths between eighteen and twenty, and we had no subjects in common. We were all intimate with our host, but were only slightly acquainted with each other. Perhaps we should have got on better if there had been some ladies among us; but the master of the house was a bachelor, and, except the parlourmaid, who assisted in waiting on us at dinner, no daughter of Eve was present to brighten the dreary scene.

We tried all sorts of subjects, but they dropped one after the other. The elder gentlemen seemed to be afraid of committing themselves by talking too freely within hearing of us juniors, and we, on our side, restrained our youthful flow of spirits and youthful freedom of conversation out of deference to our host, who seemed once or twice to be feeling a little nervous about the continued propriety of our behaviour in the presence of his respectable guests. To make matters worse, we had dined at a sensible hour. When the bottles made their first round at dessert, the clock on the mantelpiece only struck eight. I counted the strokes, and felt certain, from the expression of his face, that the other junior guest, who sat on one side of me at the round table, was counting them also. When we came to the final eight, we exchanged looks of despair. "Two hours more of this! What on earth is to become of us?" In the language of the eyes, that was exactly what we said to each other.

The wine was excellent, and I think we all came separately and secretly to the same conclusion—that our chance of getting through the evening was intimately connected with our resolution in getting through the bottles.

As a matter of course, we talked wine. No company of Englishmen can assemble together for an evening without doing that. Every man in this country who is rich enough to pay income-tax has at one time or other in his life effected a very remarkable transaction in wine. Sometimes he has made such a bargain as he never expects to make again. Sometimes he is the only man in England, not a peer of the realm, who has got a single drop of a certain famous vintage which has perished from the face of the earth. Sometimes he has purchased, with a friend, a few last left dozens from the cellar of a deceased potentate, at a price so exorbitant that he can only wag his head and decline mentioning it; and, if you ask his friend, that friend will wag his head, and decline mentioning it also. Sometimes he has been at an out-of-the-way country inn; has found the sherry not drinkable; has asked if there is no other wine in the house; has been informed that there is some "sourish foreign stuff that nobody ever drinks"; has called for a bottle of it; has found it Burgundy, such as all France cannot now produce; has cunningly kept his own counsel with the widowed landlady, and has bought the whole stock for "an old song." Sometimes he knows the proprietor of a famous tavern in London, and he recommends his one or two particular friends, the next time they are passing that way, to go in and dine and give his compliments to the landlord, and ask for a bottle of the brown sherry with the light blue—as distinguished from the dark blue—seal. Thousands of people dine there every year, and think they have got the famous sherry when they get the dark blue seal; but the real wine, the famous wine, is the light blue seal, and nobody in England knows it but the landlord and his friends. In all these wine-conversations, whatever variety there may be in the various experiences related, one of two great first principles is invariably assumed by each speaker in succession. Either he knows more about it than any one else, or he has got better wine of his own even than the excellent wine he is now drinking. Men can get together sometimes without talking of women, without talking of horses, without talking of politics, but they cannot assemble to eat a meal together without talking of wine, and they cannot talk of wine without assuming to each one of themselves an absolute infallibility in connexion with that single subject which they would shrink from asserting in relation to any other topic under the sun.

How long the inevitable wine-talk lasted on the particular social occasion of which I am now writing is more than I can undertake to say. I had heard so many other conversations of the same sort at so many other tables that my attention wandered away wearily, and I began to forget all about the dull little dinner-party, and the badly-assorted company of guests of whom I formed one. How long I remained in this not over-courteous condition of mental oblivion is more than I can tell; but when my attention was recalled, in due course of time, to the little world around me, I found that the good wine had begun to do its good office.

The stream of talk on either side of the host's chair was now beginning to flow cheerfully and continuously; the wine-conversation had worn itself out; and one of the elder guests—Mr. Wendell—was occupied in telling the other guest—Mr. Trowbridge—of a small fraud which had lately been committed on him by a clerk in his employment. The first part of the story I missed altogether. The last part, which alone caught my attention, followed the career of the clerk to the dock of the Old Bailey.

"So, as I was telling you," continued Mr. Wendell, "I made up my mind to prosecute, and I did prosecute. Thoughtless people blamed me for sending the young man to prison, and I said I might just as well have forgiven him, seeing that the trifling sum of money I had lost by his breach of trust was barely as much as ten pounds. Of course, personally speaking, I would much rather not have gone into court; but I considered that my duty to society in general, and to my brother merchants in particular, absolutely compelled me to prosecute for the sake of example. I acted on that principle, and I don't regret that I did so. The circumstances under which the man robbed me were particularly disgraceful. He was a hardened reprobate, sir, if ever there was one yet; and I believe, in my conscience, that he wanted nothing but the opportunity to be as great a villain as Fauntleroy himself."

At the moment when Mr. Wendell personified his idea of consummate villainy by quoting the example of Fauntleroy, I saw the other middle-aged gentleman—Mr. Trowbridge—colour up on a sudden, and begin to fidget in his chair.

"The next time you want to produce an instance of a villain, sir," said Mr. Trowbridge, "I wish you could contrive to quote some other example than Fauntleroy."

Mr. Wendell naturally enough looked excessively astonished when he heard these words, which were firmly and, at the same time, very politely addressed to him.

"May I inquire why you object to my example?" he asked.

"I object to it, sir," said Mr. Trowbridge, "because it makes me very uncomfortable to hear Fauntleroy called a villain."

"Good heavens above!" exclaimed Mr. Wendell, utterly bewildered. "Uncomfortable!—you, a mercantile man like myself—you, whose character stands so high everywhere—you uncomfortable when you hear a man who was hanged for forgery called a villain! In the name of wonder, why?"

"Because," answered Mr. Trowbridge, with perfect composure, "Fauntleroy was a friend of mine."

"Excuse me, my dear sir," retorted Mr. Wendell, in as polished a tone of sarcasm as he could command; "but of all the friends whom you have made in the course of your useful and honourable career, I should have thought the friend you have just mentioned would have been the very last to whom you were likely to refer in respectable society, at least by name."

"Fauntleroy committed an unpardonable crime, and died a disgraceful death," said Mr. Trowbridge. "But, for all that, Fauntleroy was a friend of mine, and in that character I shall always acknowledge him boldly to my dying day. I have a tenderness for his memory, though he violated a sacred trust, and died for it on the gallows. Don't look shocked, Mr. Wendell. I will tell you, and our other friends here, if they will let me, why I feel that tenderness, which looks so strange and so discreditable in your eyes. It is rather a curious anecdote, sir, and has an interest, I think, for all observers of human nature quite apart from its connexion with the unhappy man of whom we have been talking. You young gentlemen," continued Mr. Trowbridge, addressing himself to us juniors, "have heard of Fauntleroy, though he sinned and suffered, and shocked all England long before your time?"

We answered that we had certainly heard of him as one of the famous criminals of his day. We knew that he had been a partner in a great London banking-house; that he had not led a very virtuous life; that he had possessed himself, by forgery, of trust-moneys which he was doubly bound to respect; and that he had been hanged for his offence, in the year eighteen hundred and twenty-four, when the gallows was still set up for other crimes than murder, and when Jack Ketch was in fashion as one of the hardworking reformers of the age.

"Very good," said Mr. Trowbridge. "You both of you know quite enough of Fauntleroy to be interested in what I am going to tell you. When the bottles have been round the table, I will start with my story."

The bottles went round—claret for the degenerate youngsters; port for the sterling, steady-headed, middle-aged gentlemen. Mr. Trowbridge sipped his wine—meditated a little—sipped again— and started with the promised anecdote in these terms:

Chapter Two

What I am going to tell you, gentlemen, happened when I was a very young man, and when I was just setting up in business on my own account.

My father had been well acquainted for many years with Mr. Fauntleroy, of the famous London banking-firm of Marsh, Stracey, Fauntleroy, and Graham. Thinking it might be of some future service to me to make my position known to a great man in the commercial world, my father mentioned to his highly-respected friend that I was about to start in business for myself in a very small way, and with very little money. Mr. Fauntleroy received the intimation with a kind appearance of interest, and said that he would have his eye on me. I expected from this that he would wait to see if I could keep on my legs at starting, and that, if he found I succeeded pretty well, he would then help me forward if it lay in his power. As events turned out, he proved to be a far better friend than that, and he soon showed me that I had very much underrated the hearty and generous interest which he had felt in my welfare from the first.

While I was still fighting with the difficulties of setting up my office, and recommending myself to my connexion, and so forth, I got a message from Mr. Fauntleroy telling me to call on him, at the banking-house, the first time I was passing that way. As you may easily imagine, I contrived to be passing that way on a particularly early occasion, and, on presenting myself at the bank, I was shown at once into Mr. Fauntleroy's private room.

He was as pleasant a man to speak to as ever I met with—bright, and gay, and companionable in his manner—with a sort of easy, hearty, jovial bluntness about him that attracted everybody. The clerks all liked him—and that is something to say of a partner in a banking-house, I can tell you!

"Well, young Trowbridge," says he, giving his papers on the table a brisk push away from him, "so you are going to set up in business for yourself, are you? I have a great regard for your father, and a great wish to see you succeed. Have you started yet? No? Just on the point of beginning, eh? Very good. You will have your difficulties, my friend, and I mean to smooth one of them away for you at the outset. A word of advice for your private ear— Bank with us."

"You are very kind, sir," I answered, "and I should ask nothing better than to profit by your suggestion, if I could. But my expenses are heavy at starting, and when they are all paid I am afraid I shall have very little left to put by for the first year. I doubt if I shall be able to muster much more than three hundred pounds of surplus cash in the world after paying what I must pay before I set up my office, and I should be ashamed to trouble your house, sir, to open an account for such a trifle as that."

"Stuff and nonsense!" says Mr. Fauntleroy. "Are *you* a banker? What business have you to offer an opinion on the matter? Do as I tell you—leave it to me—bank with us—and draw for what you like. Stop! I haven't done yet. When you open the account, speak to the head cashier. Perhaps you may find he has got something to tell you. There! there! go away—don't interrupt me—good bye— God bless you!"

That was his way—ah! poor fellow, that was his way.

I went to the head cashier the next morning when I opened my little modicum of an account. He had received orders to pay my drafts without reference to my balance. My cheques, when I had overdrawn, were to be privately shown to Mr. Fauntleroy. Do many young men who start in business find their prosperous superiors ready to help them in that way?

Well, I got on—got on very fairly and steadily, being careful not to venture out of my depth, and not to forget that small beginnings may lead in time to great ends. A prospect of one of those great ends—great, I mean, to such a small trader as I was at that period—showed itself to me when I had been some little time in business. In plain terms, I had a chance of joining in a first-rate transaction, which would give me profit, and position, and everything I wanted, provided I could qualify myself for engaging in it by getting good security beforehand for a very large amount.

In this emergency, I thought of my kind friend, Mr. Fauntleroy, and went to the bank, and saw him once more in his private room.

There he was at the same table, with the same heaps of papers about him, and the same hearty, easy way of speaking his mind to you at once, in the fewest possible words. I explained the business I came upon with some little hesitation and nervousness, for I was afraid he might think I was taking an unfair advantage of his former kindness to me. When I had done, he just nodded his head, snatched up a blank sheet of paper, scribbled a few lines on it in his rapid way, handed the writing to me, and pushed me out of the room by the two shoulders before I could say a single word. I looked at the paper in the outer office. It was my security from that great banking-house for the whole amount, and for more, if more was wanted.

I could not express my gratitude then, and I don't know that I can describe it now. I can only say that it has outlived the crime, the disgrace, and the awful death on the scaffold. I am grieved to speak of that death at all; but I have no other alternative. The course of my story must now lead me straight on to the later time, and to the terrible discovery which exposed my benefactor and my friend to all England as the forger Fauntleroy.

I must ask you to suppose a lapse of some time after the occurrence of the events that I have just been relating. During this interval, thanks to the kind assistance I had received at the outset, my position as a man of business had greatly improved. Imagine me now, if you please, on the high road to prosperity, with good large offices and a respectable staff of clerks, and picture me to yourselves sitting alone in my private room between four and five o'clock on a certain Saturday afternoon.

All my letters had been written, all the people who had appointments with me had been received. I was looking carelessly over the newspaper, and thinking about going home, when one of my clerks came in, and said that a stranger wished to see me immediately on very important business.

"Did he mention his name?" I inquired.

"No, sir."

"Did you not ask him for it?"

"Yes, sir. And he said you would be none the wiser if he told me what it was."

"Does he look like a begging-letter writer?"

"He looks a little shabby, sir, but he doesn't talk at all like a begging-letter writer. He spoke sharp and decided, sir, and said it was in your interests that he came, and that you would deeply regret it afterwards if you refused to see him."

"He said that, did he? Show him in at once, then."

He was shown in immediately: a middling-sized man, with a sharp, unwholesome-looking face, and with a flippant, reckless manner, dressed in a style of shabby smartness, eyeing me with a bold look, and not so overburdened with politeness as to trouble himself about taking off his hat when he came in. I had never seen him before in my life, and I could not form the slightest conjecture from his appearance to guide me towards guessing his position in the world. He was not a gentleman, evidently; but as to fixing his whereabouts in the infinite downward gradations of vagabond existence in London, that was a mystery which I was totally incompetent to solve.

"Is your name Trowbridge?" he began.

"Yes," I answered, dryly enough.

"Do you bank with Marsh, Stracey, Fauntleroy, and Graham?"

"Why do you ask?"

"Answer my question, and you will know!"

"Very well, I *do* bank with Marsh, Stracey, Fauntleroy, and Graham—and what then?"

"Draw out every farthing of balance you have got before the bank closes at five to-day."

I stared at him in speechless amazement. The words, for an instant, absolutely petrified me.

"Stare as much as you like," he proceeded cooly, "I mean what I say. Look at your clock there. In twenty minutes it will strike five, and the bank will be shut. Draw out every farthing, I tell you again, and look sharp about it."

"Draw out my money!" I exclaimed, partially recovering myself. "Are you in your right senses? Do you know that the firm I bank with represents one of the first houses in the world? What do you mean—you, who are a total stranger to me—by taking this extraordinary interest in my affairs? If you want me to act on your advice, why don't you explain yourself?"

"I have explained myself. Act on my advice or not, just as you like. It don't matter to me. I have done what I promised, and there's an end of it."

He turned to the door. The minute-hand of the clock was getting on from the twenty minutes to the quarter.

"Done what you promised?" I repeated, getting up to stop him.

"Yes," he said, with his hand on the lock. "I have given my message. Whatever happens, remember that. Good afternoon."

He was gone before I could speak again.

I tried to call after him, but my speech suddenly failed me. It was very foolish, it was very unaccountable, but there was something in the man's last words which had more than half frightened me.

I looked at the clock. The minute-hand was on the quarter.

My office was just far enough from the bank to make it necessary for me to decide on the instant. If I had had time to think, I am perfectly certain that I should not have profited by the extraordinary warning that had just been addressed to me. The suspicious appearance and manners of the stranger; the outrageous improbability of the inference against the credit of the bank towards which his words pointed; the chance that some underhand attempt was being made, by some enemy of mine, to frighten me into embroiling myself with one of my best friends, through showing an ignorant distrust of the firm with which he was associated as partner— all these considerations would unquestionably have occurred to me if I could have found time for reflection; and, as a necessary consequence, not one farthing of my balance would have been taken from the keeping of the bank on that memorable day.

As it was, I had just time enough to act, and not a spare moment for thinking. Some heavy payments made at the beginning of the week had so far decreased my balance that the sum to my credit in the banking-book barely reached fifteen hundred pounds. I snatched up my cheque-book, wrote a draft for the whole amount, and ordered one of my clerks to run to the bank and get it cashed before the doors closed. What impulse urged me on, except the blind impulse of hurry and bewilderment, I can't say. I acted mechanically, under the influence of the vague inexplicable fear which the man's extraordinary parting words had aroused in me, without stopping to analyse my own sensations—almost without knowing what I was about. In three minutes from the time when the stranger had closed my door the clerk had started for the bank, and I was alone again in my room, with my hands as cold as ice and my head all in a whirl.

I did not recover my control over myself until the clerk came back with the notes in his hand. He had just got to the bank in the nick of time. As the cash for my draft was handed to him over the counter, the clock struck five, and he heard the order given to close the doors.

When I had counted the bank-notes and had locked them up in the safe, my better sense seemed to come back to me on a sudden. Never have I reproached myself before or since as I reproached myself at that moment. What sort of return had I made for Mr. Fauntleroy's fatherly kindness to me? I had insulted him by the meanest, the grossest distrust of the honour and the credit of his house, and that on the word of an absolute stranger, of a vagabond, if ever there was one yet. It was madness—downright madness in any man to have acted as I had done. I could not account for my own inconceivably thoughtless proceeding. I could hardly believe in it myself. I opened the safe and looked at the bank-notes again. I locked it once more, and flung the key down on the table in a fury of vexation against myself. There the money was, upbraiding me with my own inconceivable folly, telling me in the plainest terms that I had risked depriving myself of my best and kindest friend henceforth and for ever.

It was necessary to do something at once towards making all the atonement that lay in my power. I felt that, as soon as I began to cool down a little. There was but one plain, straight-forward way left now out of the scrape in which I had been mad enough to involve myself. I took my hat, and, without stopping an instant to hesitate, hurried off to the bank to make a clean breast of it to Mr. Fauntleroy.

When I knocked at the private door and asked for him, I was told that he had not been at the bank for the last two days. One of the other partners was there, however, and was working at that moment in his own room.

I sent in my name at once, and asked to see him. He and I were little better than strangers to each other, and the interview was likely to be, on that account, unspeakably embarrassing and humiliating on my side. Still, I could not go home. I could not endure the inaction of the next day, the Sunday, without having done my best on the spot to repair the error into which my own folly had led me. Uncomfortable as I felt at the prospect of the approaching interview, I should have been far more uneasy in my mind if the partner had declined to see me.

To my relief, the bank porter returned with a message requesting me to walk in.

What particular form my explanations and apologies took when I tried to offer them is more than I can tell now. I was so confused and distressed that I hardly knew what I was talking about at the time. The one circumstance which I remember clearly is that I was ashamed to refer to my interview with the strange man, and that I tried to account for my sudden withdrawal of my balance by referring it to some inexplicable panic, caused by mischievous reports which I was unable to trace to their source, and which, for anything I knew to the contrary, might, after all, have been only started in jest. Greatly to my surprise, the partner did not seem to notice the lamentable lameness of my excuses, and did not additionally confuse me by asking any questions. A weary, absent look, which I had observed on his face when I came in, remained on it while I was speaking. It seemed to be an effort to him even to keep up the appearance of listening to me; and when, at last, I fairly broke down in the middle of a sentence, and gave up the hope of getting any further, all the answer he gave me was comprised in these few civil commonplace words:

"Never mind, Mr. Trowbridge; pray don't think of apologizing. We are all liable to make mistakes. Say nothing more about it, and bring the money back on Monday if you still honour us with your confidence."

He looked down at his papers as if he was anxious to be alone again, and I had no alternative, of course, but to take my leave immediately. I went home, feeling a little easier in my mind now that I had paved the way for making the best practical atonement in my power by bringing my balance back the first thing on

Monday morning. Still I passed a weary day on Sunday, reflecting, sadly enough that I had not yet made my peace with Mr. Fauntleroy. My anxiety to set myself right with my generous friend was so intense that I risked intruding myself on his privacy by calling at his town residence on the Sunday. He was not there, and his servant could tell me nothing of his whereabouts. There was no help for it now but to wait till his week-day duties brought him back to the bank.

I went to business on Monday morning half an hour earlier than usual, so great was my impatience to restore the amount of that unlucky draft to my account as soon as possible after the bank opened.

On entering my office, I stopped with a startled feeling just inside the door. Something serious had happened. The clerks, instead of being at their desks as usual, were all huddled together in a group, talking to each other with blank faces. When they saw me, they fell back behind my managing man, who stepped forward with a circular in his hand.

"Have you heard the news, sir?" he said.

"No. What is it?"

He handed me the circular. My heart gave one violent throb the instant I looked at it. I felt myself turn pale; I felt my knees trembling under me.

Marsh, Stracey, Fauntleroy, and Graham had stopped payment.

"The circular has not been issued more than half an hour," continued my managing clerk. "I have just come from the bank, sir. The doors are shut; there is no doubt about it. Marsh and Company have stopped this morning."

I hardly heard him; I hardly knew who was talking to me. My strange visitor of the Saturday had taken instant possession of all my thoughts, and his words of warning seemed to be sounding once more in my ears. This man had known the true condition of the bank when not another soul outside the doors was aware of it! The last draft paid across the counter of that ruined house, when the doors closed on Saturday, was the draft that I had so bitterly reproached myself for drawing; the one balance saved from the wreck was my balance. Where had the stranger got the information that had saved me? and why had he brought it to *my* ears?

I was still groping, like a man in the dark, for an answer to those two questions—I was still bewildered by the unfathomable mystery of doubt into which they had plunged me—when the discovery of the stopping of the bank was followed almost immediately by a second shock, far more dreadful, far heavier to bear, so far as I was concerned, than the first.

While I and my clerks were still discussing the failure of the firm, two mercantile men, who were friends of mine, ran into the office, and overwhelmed us with the news that one of the partners had been arrested for forgery. Never shall I forget the terrible Monday morning when those tidings reached me, and when I knew that the partner was Mr. Fauntleroy.

I was true to him—and I can honestly say I was true to my belief in my generous friend—when that fearful news reached me. My fellow-merchants had got all the particulars of the arrest. They told me that two of Mr. Fauntleroy's fellow-trustees had come up to London to make arrangements about selling out some stock. On inquiring for Mr. Fauntleroy at the bankinghouse, they had been informed that he was not there; and, after leaving a message for him, they had gone into the city to make an appointment with their stockbroker for a future day, when their fellow-trustee might be able to attend. The stockbroker volunteered to make certain business inquiries on the spot, with a view to saving as much time as possible, and left them at his office to await his return. He came back, looking very much amazed, with the information that the stock had been sold out down to the last five hundred pounds. The affair was instantly investigated; the document authorizing the selling out was produced; and the two trustees saw on it, side by side with Mr. Fauntleroy's signature, the forged signatures of their own names. This happened on the Friday; and the trustees, without losing a moment, sent the officers of justice in pursuit of Mr. Fauntleroy. He was arrested, brought up before the magistrate, and remanded on the Saturday. On the Monday I heard from my friends the particulars which I have just narrated.

But the events of that one morning were not destined to end even yet. I had discovered the failure of the bank and the arrest of Mr. Fauntleroy. I was next to be enlightened, in the strangest and the saddest manner, on the difficult question of his innocence or his guilt.

Before my friends had left my office—before I had exhausted the arguments which my gratitude rather than my reason suggested to me in favour of the unhappy prisoner, a note, marked immediate, was placed in my hands, which silenced me the instant I looked at it. It was written from the prison by Mr. Fauntleroy, and it contained two lines only, entreating me to apply for the necessary order, and to go and see him immediately.

I shall not attempt to describe the flutter of expectation, the strange mixture of dread and hope that agitated me when I recognized his handwriting, and discovered what it was that he desired me to do. I obtained the order and went to the prison. The authorities, knowing the dreadful situation in which he stood, were afraid of his attempting to destroy himself, and had set two men to watch him. One came out as they opened his cell door. The other, who was bound not to leave him, very delicately and considerately affected to be looking out of window the moment I was shown in.

He was sitting on the side of his bed, with his head drooping and his hands hanging listlessly over his knees when I first caught sight of him. At the sound of my approach he started to his feet, and, without speaking a word, flung both his arms round my neck.

My heart swelled up.

"Tell me it's not true, sir! For God's sake, tell me it's not true!" was all I could say to him.

He never answered—oh me! he never answered, and he turned away his face.

There was one dreadful moment of silence. He still held his arms round my neck, and on a sudden he put his lips close to my ear.

"Did you get your money out?" he whispered. "Were you in time on Saturday afternoon?"

I broke free from him in the astonishment of hearing those words.

"What!" I cried out loud, forgetting the third person at the window. "That man who brought the message——"

"Hush!" he said, putting his hand on my lips. "There was no better man to be found, after the officers had taken me—I know no more about him than you do—I paid him well, as a chance messenger, and risked his cheating me of his errand."

"*You* sent him, then!"

"I sent him."

My story is over, gentlemen. There is no need for me to tell you that Mr. Fauntleroy was found guilty, and that he died by the hangman's hand. It was in my power to soothe his last moments in this world by taking on myself the arrangement of some of his private affairs, which, while they remained unsettled, weighed heavily on his mind. They had no connexion with the crimes he had committed, so I could do him the last little service he was ever to accept at my hands with a clear conscience.

I say nothing in defence of his character—nothing in palliation of the offence for which he suffered. But I cannot forget that in the time of his most fearful extremity, when the strong arm of the law had already seized him, he thought of the young man whose humble fortunes he had helped to build; whose heartfelt gratitude he had fairly won; whose simple faith he was resolved never to betray. I leave it to greater intellects than mine to reconcile the anomaly of his reckless falsehood towards others and his steadfast truth towards me. It is as certain as that we sit here that one of Fauntleroy's last efforts in this world was the effort he made to preserve me from being a loser by the trust that I had placed in him. There is the secret of my strange tenderness for the memory of a felon; that is why the word villain does somehow still grate on my heart when I hear it associated with the name—the disgraced name, I grant you—of the forger Fauntleroy. Pass the bottles, young gentlemen, and pardon a man of the old school for having so long interrupted your conversation with a story of the old time.

A Stolen Letter

I served my time—never mind in whose office—and I started in business for myself in one of our English country towns, I decline stating which. I hadn't a farthing of capital, and my friends in the neighbourhood were poor and useless enough, with one exception. That exception was Mr. Frank Gatliffe, son of Mr. Gatliffe, member for the county, the richest man and the proudest for many a mile round about our parts. You won't trace any particulars by the name of Gatliffe. I'm not bound to commit myself or anybody else by mentioning names. I have given you the first that came into my head.

Well, Mr. Frank was a staunch friend of mine, and ready to recommend me whenever he got the chance. I had contrived to get him a little timely help—for a consideration of course—in borrowing money at a fair rate of interest; in fact, I had saved him from the Jews. The money was borrowed while Mr. Frank was at college. He came back from college, and stopped at home a little while, and then there got spread about all our neighbourhood a report that he had fallen in love, as the saying is, with his young sister's governess, and that his mind was made up to marry her. What! you're at it again! You want to know her name, don't you? What do you think of Smith?

Speaking as a lawyer, I consider report, in a general way, to be a fool and a liar. But in this case report turned out to be something very different. Mr. Frank told me he was really in love, and said upon his honour (an absurd expression which young chaps of his age are always using) he was determined to marry Smith, the governess—the sweet, darling girl, as *he* called her; but I'm not sentimental, and *I* call her Smith, the governess. Well, Mr. Frank's father, being as proud as Lucifer, said "No," as to marrying the governess, when Mr. Frank wanted him to say "Yes." He was a man of business, was old Gatliffe, and he took the proper business course. He sent the governess away with a first-rate character and a spanking present, and then he looked about him to get something for Mr. Frank to do. While he was looking about, Mr. Frank bolted to London after the governess, who had nobody alive belonging to her to go to but an aunt—her father's sister. The aunt refuses to let Mr. Frank in without the squire's permission. Mr. Frank writes to his father, and says he will marry the girl as soon as he is of age, or shoot himself. Up to town comes the squire and his wife and his daughter, and a lot of sentimentality, not in the slightest degree material to the present statement, takes place among them; and the upshot of it is that old Gatliffe is forced into withdrawing the word No, and substituting the word Yes.

I don't believe he would ever have done it, though, but for one lucky peculiarity in the case. The governesses's father was a man of good family—pretty nigh as good as Gatliffe's own. He had been in the army; had sold out; set up as a wine-merchant—failed—died; ditto his wife, as to the dying part of it. No relation, in fact, left for the squire to make inquiries about but the father's sister—who had behaved, as old Gatliffe said, like a thorough-bred gentlewoman in shutting the door against Mr. Frank in the first instance. So, to cut the matter short, things were at last made up pleasant enough. The time was fixed for the wedding, and an announcement about it—Marriage in High Life and all that—put into the county paper. There was a regular biography, besides, of the governesses's father, so as to stop people from talking—a great flourish about his pedigree, and a long account of his services in the army; but not a word, mind ye, of his having turned wine-merchant afterwards. Oh, no—not a word about that!

I knew it, though, for Mr. Frank told me. He hadn't a bit of pride about him. He introduced me to his future wife one day when I met him out walking, and asked me if I did not think he was a lucky fellow. I don't mind admitting that I did, and that I told him so. Ah! but she was one of my sort, was that governess. Stood, to the best of my recollection, five foot four. Good lissom figure, that looked as if it had never been boxed up in a pair of stays. Eyes that made me feel as if I was under a pretty stiff cross-examination the moment she looked at me. Fine red, kiss-and-come-again sort of lips. Cheeks and complexion——No, you wouldn't identify her by her cheeks and complexion, if I drew you a picture of them this very moment. She has had a family of children since the time I'm talking of; and her cheeks are a trifle fatter, and her complexion is a shade or two redder now, than when I first met her out walking with Mr. Frank.

The marriage was to take place on a Wednesday. I decline mentioning the year or the month. I had started as an attorney on my own account—say six weeks, more or less, and was sitting alone in my office on the Monday morning before the wedding-day, trying to see my way clear before me and not succeeding particularly well, when Mr. Frank suddenly bursts in, as white as any ghost that ever was painted, and says he's got the most dreadful case for me to advise on, and not an hour to lose in acting on my advice.

"Is this in the way of business, Mr. Frank?" says I, stopping him just as he was beginning to get sentimental. "Yes or no, Mr. Frank?" rapping my new office paper-knife on the table, to pull him up short all the sooner.

"My dear fellow"—he was always familiar with me—"it's in the way of business, certainly; but friendship——"

I was obliged to pull him up short again, and regularly examine him as if he had been in the witness-box, or he would have kept me talking to no purpose half the day.

"Now, Mr. Frank," says I, "I can't have any sentimentality mixed up with business matters. You please to stop talking, and let me ask questions. Answer in the fewest words you can use. Nod when nodding will do instead of words."

I fixed him with my eye for about three seconds, as he sat groaning and wriggling in his chair. When I'd done fixing him, I gave another rap with my paper-knife on the table to startle him up a bit. Then I went on.

"From what you have been stating up to the present time," says I, "I gather that you are in a scrape which is likely to interfere seriously with your marriage on Wednesday?"

(He nodded, and I cut in again before he could say a word):

"The scrape affects your young lady, and goes back to the period of a transaction in which her late father was engaged, doesn't it?"

(He nods, and I cut in once more):

"There is a party who turned up after seeing the announcement of your marriage in the paper, who is cognizant of what he oughtn't to know, and who is prepared to use his knowledge of the same to the prejudice of the young lady and of your marriage, unless he receives a sum of money to quiet him? Very well. Now, first of all, Mr. Frank, state what you have been told by the young lady herself about the transaction of her late father. How did you first come to have any knowledge of it?"

"She was talking to me about her father one day so tenderly and prettily, that she quite excited my interest about him," begins Mr. Frank; "and I asked her, among other things, what had occasioned his death. She said she believed it was distress of mind in the first instance; and added that this distress was connected with a shocking secret, which she and her mother had kept from everybody, but which she could not keep from me, because she was determined to begin her married life by having no secrets from her husband." Here Mr. Frank began to get sentimental again, and I pulled him up short once more with the paper-knife.

"She told me," Mr. Frank went on, "that the great mistake of her father's life was his selling out of the army and taking to the wine trade. He had no talent for business; things went wrong with him from the first. His clerk, it was strongly suspected, cheated him——"

"Stop a bit," says I. "What was that suspected clerk's name?"

"Davager," says he.

"Davager," says I, making a note of it. "Go on, Mr. Frank."

"His affairs got more and more entangled," says Mr. Frank; "he was pressed for money in all directions; bankruptcy, and consequent dishonour (as he considered it) stared him in the face. His mind was so affected by his troubles that both his wife and daughter, towards the last, considered him to be hardly responsible for his own acts. In this state of desperation and misery, he——"Here Mr. Frank began to hesitate.

We have two ways in the law of drawing evidence off nice and clear from an unwilling client or witness. We give him a fright, or we treat him to a joke. I treated Mr. Frank to a joke.

"Ah!" says I, "I know what he did. He had a signature to write; and, by the most natural mistake in the world, he wrote another gentleman's name instead of his own—eh?"

"It was to a bill," says Mr. Frank, looking very crestfallen, instead of taking the joke. "His principal creditor wouldn't wait till he could raise the money, or the greater part of it. But he was resolved, if he sold off everything, to get the amount and repay——"

"Of course," says I, "drop that. The forgery was discovered. When?"

"Before even the first attempt was made to negotiate the bill. He had done the whole thing in the most absurdly and innocently wrong way. The person whose name he had used was a staunch friend of his, and a relation of his wife's—a good man as well as a rich one. He had influence with the chief creditor, and he used it nobly. He had a real affection for the unfortunate man's wife, and he proved it generously."

"Come to the point," says I. "What did he do? In a business way, what did he do?"

"He put the false bill into the fire, drew a bill of his own to replace it, and then—only then—told my dear girl and her mother all that had happened. Can you imagine anything nobler?" asks Mr. Frank.

"Speaking in my professional capacity, I can't imagine anything greener," says I. "Where was the father? Off, I suppose?"

"Ill in bed," says Mr. Frank, colouring. "But he mustered strength enough to write a contrite and grateful letter the same day, promising to prove himself worthy of the noble moderation and forgiveness extended to him, by selling off everything he possessed to repay his money debt. He did sell off everything, down to some old family pictures that were heirlooms; down to the little plate he had; down to the very tables and chairs that furnished his drawing-room. Every farthing of the debt was paid; and he was left to begin the world again, with the kindest promises of help from the generous man who had forgiven him. It was too late. His crime of one rash moment—atoned for though it had been— preyed upon his mind. He became possessed with the idea that he had lowered himself for ever in the estimation of his wife and daughter, and——"

"He died," I cut in. "Yes, yes, we know that. Let's go back for a minute to the contrite and grateful letter that he wrote. My experience in the law, Mr. Frank, has convinced me that if everybody burned everybody else's letters, half the courts of justice in this country might shut up shop. Do you happen to know whether the letter we are now speaking of contained anything like an avowal or confession of the forgery?"

"Of course it did," says he. "Could the writer express his contrition properly without making some such confession?"

"Quite easy, if he had been a lawyer," says I. "But never mind that; I'm going to make a guess—a desperate guess, mind. Should I be altogether in error if I thought that this letter had been stolen; and that the fingers of Mr. Davager, of suspicious commercial celebrity, might possibly be the fingers which took it?"

"That is exactly what I wanted to make you understand," cried Mr. Frank.

"How did he communicate the interesting fact of the theft to you?"

"He has not ventured into my presence. The scoundrel actually had the audacity——"

"Aha!" says I. "The young lady herself! Sharp practitioner, Mr. Davager."

"Early this morning, when she was walking alone in the shrubbery," Mr. Frank goes on, "he had the assurance to approach her, and to say that he had been watching his opportunity of getting a private interview for days past. He then showed her—actually showed her—her unfortunate father's letter; put into her hands another letter directed to me; bowed, and walked off; leaving her half dead with astonishment and terror. If I'd only happened to be there at the time!" says Mr. Frank, shaking his fist murderously in the air, by way of a finish.

"It's the greatest luck in the world that you were not," says I. "Have you got that other letter?"

He handed it to me. It was so remarkably humorous and short, that I remember every word of it at this distance of time. It began in this way:

To Francis Gatliffe, Esq., Jun.

Sir—I have an extremely curious autograph letter to sell. The price is a five-hundred-pound note. The young lady to whom you are to be married on Wednesday will inform you of the nature of the letter, and the genuineness of the autograph. If you refuse to deal, I shall send a copy to the local paper, and shall wait on your highly respected father with the original curiosity, on the afternoon of Tuesday next. Having come down here on family business, I have put up at the family hotel—being to be heard of at the Gatliffe Arms. Your very obedient servant,

ALFRED DAVAGER

"A clever fellow that," says I, putting the letter into my private drawer.

"Clever!" cries Mr. Frank, "he ought to be horsewhipped within an inch of his life. I would have done it myself; but she made me promise, before she told me a word of the matter, to come straight to you."

"That was one of the wisest promises you ever made," says I. "We can't afford to bully this fellow, whatever else we may do with him. Do you think I am saying anything libellous against your excellent father's character when I assert that if he saw the letter he would certainly insist on your marriage being put off, at the very least?"

"Feeling as my father does about my marriage, he would insist on its being dropped altogether, if he saw this letter," says Mr. Frank, with a groan. "But even that is not the worst of it. The generous, noble girl herself says that if the letter appears in the paper, with all the unanswerable comments this scoundrel would be sure to add to it, she would rather die than hold me to my engagement, even if my father would let me keep it."

As he said this his eyes began to water. He was a weak young fellow, and ridiculously fond of her. I brought him back to business with another rap of the paper-knife.

"Hold up, Mr. Frank," says I. "I have a question or two more. Did you think of asking the young lady whether, to the best of her knowledge, this infernal letter was the only written evidence of the forgery now in existence?"

"Yes, I did think directly of asking her that," says he; "and she told me she was quite certain that there was no written evidence of the forgery except that one letter."

"Will you give Mr. Davager his price for it?" says I.

"Yes," says Mr. Frank, quite peevish with me for asking him such a question. He was an easy young chap in money matters, and talked of hundreds as most men talk of sixpences.

"Mr. Frank," says I, "you came here to get my help and advice in this extremely ticklish business, and you are ready, as I know without asking, to remunerate me for all and any of my services at the usual professional rate. Now, I've made up my mind to act boldly—desperately, if you like—on the hit or miss, win all or lose all principle—in dealing with this matter. Here is my proposal. I'm going to try if I can't do Mr. Davager out of his letter. If I don't succeed before to-morrow afternoon, you hand him the money, and I charge you nothing for professional services. If I do succeed, I hand you the letter instead of Mr. Davager, and you give me the money instead of giving it to him. It's a precious risk for me, but I'm ready to run it. You must pay your five hundred anyway. What do you say to my plan? Is it Yes, Mr. Frank, or No?"

"Hang your questions!" cries Mr. Frank, jumping up; "you know it's Yes ten thousand times over. Only you earn the money and——"

"And you will be too glad to give it to me. Very good. Now go home. Comfort the young lady—don't let Mr. Davager so much as set eyes on you—keep quiet—leave everything to me—and feel as certain as you please that all the letters in the world can't stop your being married on Wednesday." With these words I hustled him off out of the office, for I wanted to be left alone to make my mind up about what I should do.

The first thing, of course, was to have a look at the enemy. I wrote to Mr. Davager, telling him that I was privately appointed to arrange the little business matter between himself and "another party" (no names!) on friendly terms; and begging him to call on me at his earliest convenience. At the very beginning of the case, Mr. Davager bothered me. His answer was, that it would not be convenient to him to call till between six and seven in the evening. In this way, you see, he contrived to make me lose several precious hours, at a time when minutes almost were of importance. I had nothing for it but to be patient, and to give certain instructions, before Mr. Davager came, to my boy Tom.

There never was such a sharp boy of fourteen before, and there never will be again, as my boy Tom. A spy to look after Mr. Davager was, of course, the first requisite in a case of this kind; and Tom was the smallest, quickest, quietest, sharpest, stealthiest little snake of a chap that ever dogged a gentleman's steps and kept cleverly out of range of a gentleman's eyes. I settled it with the boy that he was not to show at all when Mr. Davager came; and that he was to wait to hear me ring the bell when Mr. Davager left. If I rang twice, he was to show the gentleman out. If I rang once, he was to keep out of the way, and follow the gentleman

wherever he went till he got back to the inn. Those were the only
preparations I could make to begin with; being obliged to wait,
and let myself be guided by what turned up.

About a quarter to seven my gentleman came.

In the profession of the law we get somehow quite remarkably
mixed up with ugly people, blackguard people, and dirty people.
But far away the ugliest and dirtiest blackguard I ever saw in my
life was Mr. Alfred Davager. He had greasy white hair and a
mottled face. He was low in the forehead, fat in the stomach,
hoarse in the voice, and weak in the legs. Both his eyes were
bloodshot, and one was fixed in his head. He smelled of spirits,
and carried a toothpick in his mouth. "How are you? I've just done
dinner," says he; and he lights a cigar, sits down with his legs
crossed, and winks at me.

I tried at first to take the measure of him in a wheedling,
confidential way; but it was no good. I asked him in a facetious,
smiling manner, how he had got hold of the letter. He only told me
in answer that he had been in the confidential employment of the
writer of it, and that he had always been famous since infancy for
a sharp eye to his own interests. I paid him some compliments; but
he was not to be flattered. I tried to make him lose his temper; but
he kept it in spite of me. It ended in his driving me to my last
resource—I made an attempt to frighten him.

"Before we say a word about the money," I began, "let me put a
case, Mr. Davager. The pull you have on Mr. Francis Gatliffe is,
that you can hinder his marriage on Wednesday. Now, suppose I
have got a magistrate's warrant to apprehend you in my pocket?
Suppose I have a constable to execute it in the next room? Suppose
I bring you up to-morrow—the day before the marriage—charge
you only generally with an attempt to extort money, and apply for
a day's remand to complete the case? Suppose, as a suspicious
stranger, you can't get bail in this town? Suppose——"

"Stop a bit," says Mr. Davager. "Suppose I should not be the
greenest fool that ever stood in shoes? Suppose I should not carry
the letter about me? Suppose I should have given a certain envelope to a certain friend of mine in a certain place in this town?
Suppose the letter should be inside that envelope, directed to old
Gatliffe, side by side with a copy of the letter directed to the editor
of the local paper? Suppose my friend should be instructed to open
the envelope, and take the letters to their right address, if I don't

appear to claim them from him this evening? In short, my dear sir, suppose you were born yesterday, and suppose I wasn't?" says Mr. Davager, and winks at me again.

He didn't take me by surprise, for I never expected that he had the letter about him. I made a pretence of being very much taken aback, and of being quite ready to give in. We settled our business about delivering the letter, and handing over the money, in no time. I was to draw out a document, which he was to sign. He knew the document was stuff and nonsense, just as well as I did, and told me I was only proposing it to swell my client's bill. Sharp as he was, he was wrong there. The document was not to be drawn out to gain money from Mr. Frank, but to gain time from Mr. Davager. It served me as an excuse to put off the payment of the five hundred pounds till three o'clock on the Tuesday afternoon. The Tuesday morning Mr. Davager said he should devote to his amusement, and asked me what sights were to be seen in the neighbourhood of the town. When I had told him, he pitched his toothpick into my grate, yawned, and went out.

I rang the bell once—waited till he had passed the window—and then looked after Tom. There was my jewel of a boy on the opposite side of the street, just setting his top going in the most playful manner possible. Mr. Davager walked away up the street towards the market-place. Tom whipped his top up the street towards the market-place, too.

In a quarter of an hour he came back, with all his evidence collected in a beautifully clear and compact state. Mr. Davager had walked to a public-house just outside the town, in a lane leading to the highroad. On a bench outside the public-house there sat a man smoking. He said "All right?" and gave a letter to Mr. Davager, who answered "All right!" and walked back to the inn. In the hall he ordered hot rum-and-water, cigars, slippers, and a fire to be lit in his room. After that he went upstairs, and Tom came away.

I now saw my road clear before me—not very far on, but still clear. I had housed the letter, in all probability for that night, at the Gatliffe Arms. After tipping Tom, I gave him directions to play about the door of the inn, and refresh himself when he was tired at the tart-shop opposite, eating as much as he pleased, on the under-standing that he crammed all the time with his eye on the window. If Mr. Davager went out, or Mr. Davager's friend called on him,

Tom was to let me know. He was also to take a little note from me to the head chambermaid—an old friend of mine—asking her to step over to my office, on a private matter of business, as soon as her work was done for that night. After settling these little matters, having half an hour to spare, I turned to and did myself a bloater at the office fire, and had a drop of gin-and-water hot, and felt comparatively happy.

When the head chambermaid came, it turned out, as good luck would have it, that Mr. Davager had drawn her attention rather too closely to his ugliness, by offering her a testimony of his regard in the shape of a kiss. I no sooner mentioned him than she flew into a passion; and when I added, by way of clinching the matter, that I was retained to defend the interests of a very beautiful and deserving young lady (name not referred to, of course) against the most cruel underhand treachery on the part of Mr. Davager, the head chambermaid was ready to go to any lengths that she safely could to serve my cause. In a few words I discovered that Boots was to call Mr. Davager at eight the next morning, and was to take his clothes downstairs to brush as usual. If Mr. D——had not emptied his own pockets overnight, we arranged that Boots was to forget to empty them for him, and was to bring the clothes downstairs just as he found them. If Mr. D——'s pockets were emptied, then, of course, it would be necessary to transfer the searching process to Mr. D——'s room. Under any circumstances, I was certain of the head chambermaid; and under any circumstances, also, the head chambermaid was certain of Boots.

I waited till Tom came home, looking very puffy and bilious about the face; but as to his intellects, if anything, rather sharper than ever. His report was uncommonly short and pleasant. The inn was shutting up; Mr. Davager was going to bed in rather a drunken condition; Mr. Davager's friend had never appeared. I sent Tom (properly instructed about keeping our man in view all the next morning) to his shake-down behind the office-desk, where I heard him hiccoughing half the night, as even the best boys will, when over-excited and too full of tarts.

At half-past seven next morning, I slipped quietly into Boots's pantry.

Down came the clothes. No pockets in trousers. Waistcoat-pockets empty. Coat-pockets with something in them. First, handkerchief; secondly, bunch of keys; thirdly, cigar-case; fourthly, pocketbook. Of course I wasn't such a fool as to expect to find the letter there, but I opened the pocketbook with a certain curiosity, notwithstanding.

Nothing in the two pockets of the book but some old advertisements cut out of newspapers, a lock of hair tied round with a dirty bit of ribbon, a circular letter about a loan society, and some copies of verses not likely to suit any company that was not of an extremely free-and-easy description. On the leaves of the pocketbook, people's addresses scrawled in pencil, and bets jotted down in red ink. On one leaf, by itself, this queer inscription:

"MEM. 5 ALONG. 4 ACROSS."

I understood everything but those words and figures, so of course I copied them out into my own book.

Then I waited in the pantry till Boots had brushed the clothes, and had taken them upstairs. His report when he came down was, that Mr. D——had asked if it was a fine morning. Being told that it was, he had ordered breakfast at nine, and a saddle-horse to be at the door at ten, to take him to Grimwith Abbey—one of the sights in our neighbourhood which I had told him of the evening before.

"I'll be here, coming in by the back way, at half-past ten," says I to the head chambermaid.

"What for?" says she.

"To take the responsibility of making Mr. Davager's bed off your hands for this morning only," says I.

"Any more orders?" says she.

"One more," says I. "I want to hire Sam for the morning. Put it down in the order-book that he's to be brought round to my office at ten."

In case you should think Sam was a man, I'd better perhaps tell you he was a pony. I'd made up my mind that it would be beneficial to Tom's health, after the tarts, if he took a constitutional airing on a nice hard saddle in the direction of Grimwith Abbey.

"Anything else?" says the head chambermaid.

"Only one more favour," says I. "Would my boy Tom be very much in the way if he came, from now till ten, to help with the boots and shoes, and stood at his work close by this window which looks out on the staircase?"

"Not a bit," says the head chambermaid.

"Thank you," says I; and stepped back to my office directly.

When I had sent Tom off to help with the boots and shoes, I reviewed the whole case exactly as it stood at that time.

There were three things Mr. Davager might do with the letter. He might give it to his friend again before ten—in which case Tom would most likely see the said friend on the stairs. He might take it to his friend, or to some other friend, after ten—in which case Tom was ready to follow him on Sam the pony. And lastly, he might leave it hidden somewhere in his room at the inn—in which case I was all ready for him with a search-warrant of my own granting, under favour always of my friend the head chambermaid. So far I had my business arrangements all gathered up nice and compact in my own hands. Only two things bothered me; the terrible shortness of the time at my disposal, in case I failed in my first experiments, for getting hold of the letter, and that queer inscription which I had copied out of the pocketbook:

"MEM. 5 ALONG. 4 ACROSS."

It was the measurement most likely of something, and he was afraid of forgetting it; therefore it was something important. Query—something about himself? Say "5" (inches) "along"—he doesn't wear a wig. Say "5" (feet) "along"—it can't be coat, waistcoat, trousers, or underclothing. Say "5" (yards) "along"—it can't be anything about himself, unless he wears round his body the rope that he's sure to be hanged with one of these days. Then it is *not* something about himself. What do I know of that is important to him besides? I know of nothing but the Letter. Can the memorandum be connected with that? Say, yes. What do "5 along" and "4 across" mean, then? The measurement of something he carries about with him? or the measurement of something in his room? I could get pretty satisfactorily to myself as far as that; but I could get no further.

Tom came back to the office, and reported him mounted for his ride. His friend had never appeared. I sent the boy off, with his proper instructions, on Sam's back—wrote an encouraging letter to Mr. Frank to keep him quiet—then slipped into the inn by the back way a little before half-past ten. The head chambermaid gave me a signal when the landing was clear. I got into his room without a soul but her seeing me, and locked the door immediately.

The case was, to a certain extent, simplified now. Either Mr. Davager had ridden out with the letter about him, or he had left it in some safe hiding-place in his room. I suspected it to be in his room, for a reason that will a little astonish you—his trunk, his dressing-case, and all the drawers and cupboards, were left open. I knew my customer, and I thought this extraordinary carelessness on his part rather suspicious.

Mr. Davager had taken one of the best bedrooms at the Gatliffe Arms. Floor carpeted all over, walls beautifully papered, four-poster, and general furniture first-rate. I searched, to begin with, on the usual plan, examining everything in every possible way, and taking more than an hour about it. No discovery. Then I pulled out a carpenter's rule which I had brought with me. Was there anything in the room which—either in inches, feet, or yards—answered to "5 along" and "4 across"? Nothing. I put the rule back in my pocket—measurement was no good, evidently. Was there anything in the room that would count up to 5 one way and 4 another, seeing that nothing would measure up to it? I had got obstinately persuaded by this time that the letter must be in the room—principally because of the trouble I had had in looking after it. And persuading myself of that, I took it into my head next, just as obstinately, that "5 along" and "4 across" must be the right clue to find the letter by—principally because I hadn't left myself, after all my searching and thinking, even so much as the ghost of another guide to go by. "Five along"—where could I count five along the room, in any part of it?

Not on the paper. The pattern there was pillars of trellis-work and flowers, enclosing a plain green ground—only four pillars along the wall and only two across. The furniture? There were not five chairs or five separate pieces of any furniture in the room altogether. The fringes that hung from the cornice of the bed? plenty of them, at any rate! Up I jumped on the counterpane, with my pen-knife in my hand. Every way that "5 along" and "4 across" could be reckoned on those unlucky fringes I reckoned on them—probed with my pen-knife—scratched with my nails—crunched with my fingers. No use; not a sign of a letter; and the time was getting on—oh, Lord! how the time did get on in Mr. Davager's room that morning!

I jumped down from the bed, so desperate at my ill luck that I hardly cared whether anybody heard me or not. Quite a little cloud of dust arose at my feet as they thumped on the carpet.

"Hullo!" thought I, "my friend the head chambermaid takes it easy here. Nice state for a carpet to be in, in one of the best bedrooms at the Gatliffe Arms." Carpet! I had been jumping up on the bed, and staring up at the walls, but I had never so much as given a glance down at the carpet. Think of me pretending to be a lawyer, and not knowing how to look low enough!

The carpet! It had been a stout article in its time; had evidently began in a drawing room; then descended to a coffee-room; then gone upstairs altogether to a bedroom. The ground was brown, and the pattern was bunches of leaves and roses speckled over the ground at regular distances. I reckoned up the bunches. Ten along the room—eight across it. When I had stepped out five one way and four the other, and was down on my knees on the centre bunch, as true as I sit on this chair I could hear my own heart beating so loud that it quite frightened me.

I looked narrowly all over the bunch, and I felt all over it with the ends of my fingers, and nothing came of that. Then I scraped it over slowly and gently with my nails. My second finger-nail stuck a little at one place. I parted the pile of the carpet over that place, and saw a thin slit which had been hidden by the pile being smoothed over it—a slit about half an inch long with a little end of brown thread, exactly the colour of the carpet ground, sticking out about a quarter of an inch from the middle of it. Just as I laid hold of the thread gently, I heard a footstep outside the door.

It was only the head chambermaid. "Haven't you done yet?" she whispers.

"Give me two minutes," says I, "and don't let anybody come near the door—whatever you do, don't let anybody startle me again by coming near the door."

I took a little pull at the thread, and heard something rustle. I took a longer pull, and out came a piece of paper, rolled up tight like those candle-lighters that the ladies make. I unrolled it—and, by George! there was the letter!

The original letter! I knew it by the colour of the ink. The letter that was worth five hundred pounds to me! It was all that I could do to keep myself at first from throwing my hat into the air, and hurrahing like mad. I had to take a chair and sit quiet in it for a minute or two, before I could cool myself down to my proper business level. I knew that I was safely down again when I found myself pondering how to let Mr. Davager know that he had been done by the innocent country attorney, after all.

It was not long before a nice little irritating plan occurred to me. I tore a blank leaf out of my pocketbook, wrote on it with my pencil, "Change for a five-hundred-pound note," folded up the paper, tied the thread to it, poked it back into the hiding-place, smoothed over the pile of the carpet, and then bolted off to Mr. Frank. He in his turn bolted off to show the letter to the young lady, who first certified to its genuineness, then dropped it into the fire, and then took the initiative for the first time since her marriage engagement, by flinging her arms round his neck, kissing him with all her might, and going into hysterics in his arms. So at least Mr. Frank told me, but that's not evidence. It is evidence, however, that I saw them married with my own eyes on the Wednesday; and that while they went off in a carriage-and-four to spend the honeymoon, I went off on my own legs to open a credit at the Town and County Bank with a five-hundred-pound note in my pocket.

As to Mr. Davager, I can tell you nothing more about him, except what is derived from hearsay evidence, which is always unsatisfactory evidence, even in a lawyer's mouth.

My inestimable boy, Tom, although twice kicked off by Sam the pony, never lost hold of the bridle, and kept his man in sight from first to last. He had nothing particular to report except that on the way out to the Abbey Mr. Davager had stopped at the public-house, had spoken a word or two to his friend of the night before, and had handed him what looked like a bit of paper. This was no doubt a clue to the thread that held the letter, to be used in case of accidents. In every other respect Mr. D. had ridden out and ridden in like an ordinary sightseer. Tom reported him to me as having dismounted at the hotel about two. At half-past I locked my office door, nailed a card under the knocker with "not at home till tomorrow" written on it, and retired to a friend's house a mile or so out of the town for the rest of the day.

Mr. Davager, I have been since given to understand, left the Gatliffe Arms that same night with his best clothes on his back, and with all the valuable contents of his dressing-case in his pockets. I am not in a condition to state whether he ever went through the form of asking for his bill or not; but I can positively testify that he never paid it, and that the effects left in his bedroom did not pay it either.

The Lady of Glenwith Grange

I have known Miss Welwyn long enough to be able to bear personal testimony to the truth of many of the particulars which I am now about to relate. I knew her father, and her younger sister Rosamond; and I was acquainted with the Frenchman who became Rosamond's husband. These are the persons of whom it will be principally necessary for me to speak. They are the only prominent characters in my story.

Miss Welwyn's father died some years since. I remember him very well—though he never excited in me, or in anyone else that I ever heard of, the slightest feeling of interest. When I have said that he inherited a very large fortune, amassed during his father's time, by speculations of a very daring, very fortunate, but not always very honourable kind, and that he bought this old house with the notion of raising his social position, by making himself a member of our landed aristocracy in these parts, I have told you as much about him, I suspect, as you would care to hear. He was a thoroughly commonplace man, with no great virtues and no great vices in him. He had a little heart, a feeble mind, an amiable temper, a tall figure, and a handsome face. More than this need not, and cannot, be said on the subject of Mr. Welwyn's character.

I must have seen the late Mrs. Welwyn very often as a child; but I cannot say that I remember anything more of her than that she was tall and handsome, and very generous and sweet-tempered towards me when I was in her company. She was her husband's superior in birth, as in everything else; was a great reader of books in all languages; and possessed such admirable talents as a musician, that her wonderful playing on the organ is remembered and talked of to this day among the old people in our country houses about here. All her friends, as I have heard, were disappointed when she married Mr. Welwyn, rich as he was; and were afterwards astonished to find her preserving the appearance, at least, of being perfectly happy with a husband who, neither in mind nor heart, was worthy of her.

It was generally supposed (and I have no doubt correctly) that she found her great happiness and her great consolation in her little girl Ida. The child took after her mother from the first— inheriting her mother's fondness for books, her mother's love of music, her mother's quick sensibilities, and, more than all, her mother's quiet firmness, patience, and loving kindness of disposition. From Ida's earliest years, Mrs. Welwyn undertook the whole superintendence of her education. The two were hardly ever apart, within doors or without. Neighbours and friends said that the little girl was being brought up too fancifully, and was not enough among other children, was sadly neglected as to all reasonable and practical teaching, and was perilously encouraged in those dreamy and imaginative tendencies of which she had naturally more than her due share. There was, perhaps, some truth in this; and there might have been still more, if Ida had possessed an ordinary character, or had been reserved for an ordinary destiny. But she was a strange child from the first, and a strange future was in store for her.

Little Ida reached her eleventh year without either brother or sister to be her playfellow and companion at home. Immediately after that period, however, her sister Rosamond was born. Though Mr. Welwyn's own desire was to have had a son, there were, nevertheless, great rejoicings yonder in the old house on the birth of this second daughter. But they were all turned, only a few months afterwards, to the bitterest grief and despair: the Grange lost its mistress. While Rosamond was still an infant in arms, her mother died.

Mrs. Welwyn had been afflicted with some disorder after the birth of her second child, the name of which I am not learned enough in medical science to be able to remember. I only know that she recovered from it, to all appearance, in an unexpectedly short time; that she suffered a fatal relapse, and that she died a lingering and a painful death. Mr. Welwyn (who, in after years, had a habit of vaingloriously describing his marriage as "a love-match on both sides") was really fond of his wife in his own frivolous, feeble way, and suffered as acutely as such a man could suffer, during the latter days of her illness, and at the terrible time when the doctors, one and all, confessed that her life was a thing to be despaired of. He burst into irrepressible passions of tears, and was always obliged to leave the sick-room whenever Mrs. Welwyn spoke of her approaching end. The last solemn words of the dying woman, the tenderest messages that she could give, the dearest parting wishes that she could express, the most earnest commands that she could leave behind her, the gentlest reasons for consolation that she could suggest to the survivors among those who loved her, were not poured into her husband's ear, but into her child's. From the first period of her illness, Ida had persisted in remaining in the sick-room, rarely speaking, never showing outwardly any signs of terror or grief, except when she was removed from it; and then bursting into hysterical passions of weeping, which no expostulations, no arguments, no commands—nothing, in short, but bringing her back to the bedside—ever availed to calm. Her mother had been her playfellow, her companion, her dearest and most familiar friend; and there seemed something in the remembrance of this which, instead of overwhelming the child with despair, strengthened her to watch faithfully and bravely by her dying parent to the very last.

When the parting moment was over, and when Mr. Welwyn, unable to bear the shock of being present in the house of death at the time of his wife's funeral, left home and went to stay with one of his relations in a distant part of England, Ida, whom it had been his wish to take away with him, petitioned earnestly to be left behind. "I promised mamma before she died that I would be as good to my little sister Rosamond as she had been to me," said the child, simply; "and she told me in return that I might wait here and see her laid in her grave." There happened to be an aunt of Mrs. Welwyn, and an old servant of the family, in the house at this time, who understood Ida much better than her father did, and they persuaded him not to take her away. I have heard my mother say that the effect of the child's appearance at the funeral on her, and on all who went to see it, was something that she could never think of without the tears coming into her eyes, and could never forget to the last day of her life.

It must have been very shortly after this period that I saw Ida for the first time.

I remember accompanying my mother on a visit to the old house we have just left, in the summer, when I was at home for the holidays. It was a lovely, sunshiny morning. There was nobody indoors, and we walked out into the garden. As we approached that lawn yonder, on the other side of the shrubbery, I saw, first, a young woman in mourning (apparently a servant) sitting reading; then a little girl, dressed all in black, moving towards us slowly over the bright turf, and holding up before her a baby, whom she was trying to teach to walk. She looked, to my ideas, so very young to be engaged in such an occupation as this, and her gloomy black frock appeared to be such an unnaturally grave garment for a mere child of her age, and looked so doubly dismal by contrast with the brilliant sunny lawn on which she stood, that I quite started when I first saw her, and eagerly asked my mother who she was. The answer informed me of the sad family story, which I have been just relating to you. Mrs. Welwyn had then been buried about three months; and Ida, in her childish way, was trying, as she had promised, to supply her mother's place to her infant sister Rosamond.

I only mention this simple incident, because it is necessary, before I proceed to the eventful part of my narrative, that you should know exactly in what relation the sisters stood towards one another from the first. Of all the last parting words that Mrs. Welwyn had spoken to her child, none had been oftener repeated, none more solemnly urged, than those which had commended the little Rosamond to Ida's love and care. To other persons, the full, the all-trusting dependence which the dying mother was known to have placed in a child hardly eleven years old, seemed merely a proof of that helpless desire to cling even to the feeblest consolations, which the approach of death so often brings with it. But the event showed that the trust so strangely placed had not been ventured vainly when it was committed to young and tender hands. The whole future existence of the child was one noble proof that she had been worthy of her mother's dying confidence, when it was first reposed in her. In that simple incident which I have just mentioned the new life of the two motherless sisters was all foreshadowed.

Time passed. I left school—went to college—travelled in Germany, and stayed there some time to learn the language. At every interval when I came home, and asked about the Welwyns, the answer was, in substance, almost always the same. Mr. Welwyn was giving his regular dinners, performing his regular duties as a county magistrate, enjoying his regular recreations as an amateur farmer and an eager sportsman. His two daughters were never separate. Ida was the same strange, quiet, retiring girl, that she had always been; and was still (as the phrase went) "spoiling" Rosamond in every way in which it was possible for an elder sister to spoil a younger by too much kindness.

I myself went to the Grange occasionally, when I was in this neighbourhood, in holiday and vacation time; and was able to test the correctness of the picture of life there which had been drawn for me. I remember the two sisters, when Rosamond was four or five years old; and when Ida seemed to me, even then, to be more like the child's mother than her sister. She bore with her little caprices as sisters do not bear with one another. She was so patient at lesson-time, so anxious to conceal any weariness that might overcome her in play hours, so proud when Rosamond's beauty was noticed, so grateful for Rosamond's kisses when the child thought of bestowing them, so quick to notice all that Rosamond did, and to attend to all that Rosamond said, even when visitors were in the room, that she seemed, to my boyish observation, altogether different from other elder sisters in other family circles into which I was then received.

I remember then, again, when Rosamond was just growing to womanhood, and was in high spirits at the prospect of spending a season in London, and being presented at Court. She was very beautiful at that time—much handsomer than Ida. Her "accomplishments" were talked of far and near in our country circles. Few, if any, of the people, however, who applauded her playing and singing, who admired her water-colour drawings, who were delighted at her fluency when she spoke French, and amazed at her ready comprehension when she read German, knew how little of all this elegant mental cultivation and nimble manual dexterity she owed to her governess and masters, and how much to her elder sister. It was Ida who really found out the means of stimulating her when she was idle; Ida who helped her through all her worst difficulties; Ida who gently conquered her defects of memory over her books, her inaccuracies of ear at the piano, her errors of taste when she took the brush and pencil in hand. It was Ida alone who worked these marvels, and whose all-sufficient reward for her hardest exertions was a chance word of kindness from her sister's lips. Rosamond was not unaffectionate, and not ungrateful; but she inherited much of her father's commonness and frivolity of character. She became so accustomed to owe everything to her sister—to resign all her most trifling difficulties to Ida's ever-ready care—to have all her tastes consulted by Ida's ever-watchful kindness—that she never appreciated, as it deserved, the deep, devoted love of which she was the object. When Ida refused two good offers of marriage, Rosamond was as much astonished as the veriest strangers, who wondered why the elder Miss Welwyn seemed bent on remaining single all her life.

When the journey to London, to which I have already alluded, took place, Ida accompanied her father and sister. If she had consulted her own tastes, she would have remained in the country; but Rosamond declared that she should feel quite lost and helpless twenty times a day, in town, without her sister. It was in the nature of Ida to sacrifice herself to anyone whom she loved, on the smallest occasions as well as the greatest. Her affection was as intuitively ready to sanctify Rosamond's slightest caprices as to excuse Rosamond's most thoughtless faults. So she went to London cheerfully, to witness with pride all the little triumphs won by her sister's beauty; to hear, and never tire of hearing, all that admiring friends could say in her sister's praise.

At the end of the season Mr. Welwyn and his daughters returned for a short time to the country; then left home again to spend the latter part of the autumn and the beginning of the winter in Paris.

They took with them excellent letters of introduction, and saw a great deal of the best society in Paris, foreign as well as English. At one of the first of the evening parties which they attended, the general topic of conversation was the conduct of a certain French nobleman, the Baron Franval, who had returned to his native country after a long absence, and who was spoken of in terms of high eulogy by the majority of the guests present. The history of who Franval was, and of what he had done, was readily communicated to Mr. Welwyn and his daughters, and was briefly this:

The baron inherited little from his ancestors besides his high rank and his ancient pedigree. On the death of his parents, he and his two unmarried sisters (their only surviving children) found the small territorial property of the Franvals, in Normandy, barely productive enough to afford a comfortable subsistence for the three. The baron, then a young man of three-and-twenty, endeavoured to obtain such military or civil employment as might become his rank; but, although the Bourbons were at that time restored to the throne of France, his efforts were ineffectual. Either his interest at court was bad, or secret enemies were at work to oppose his advancement. He failed to obtain even the slightest favour; and, irritated by undeserved neglect, resolved to leave France, and seek occupation for his energies in foreign countries, where his rank would be no bar to his bettering his fortunes, if he pleased, by engaging in commercial pursuits.

An opportunity of the kind that he wanted unexpectedly offered itself. He left his sisters in the care of an old male relative of the family at the château in Normandy, and sailed, in the first instance, to the West Indies; afterwards extending his wanderings to the continent of South America, and there engaging in mining transactions on a very large scale. After fifteen years of absence (during the latter part of which time false reports of his death had reached Normandy) he had just returned to France, having realized a handsome independence, with which he proposed to widen the limits of his ancestral property, and to give his sisters (who were still, like himself, unmarried) all the luxuries and advantages that affluence could bestow. The baron's independent spirit and generous devotion to the honour of his family and the happiness of his surviving relatives were themes of general admiration in most of the social circles of Paris. He was expected to arrive in the capital every day; and it was naturally enough predicted that his reception in society there could not fail to be of the most flattering and most brilliant kind.

The Welwyns listened to this story with some little interest; Rosamond, who was very romantic, being especially attracted by it, and openly avowing to her father and sister, when they got back to their hotel, that she felt as ardent a curiosity as anybody to see the adventurous and generous baron. The desire was soon gratified. Franval came to Paris, as had been anticipated—was introduced to the Welwyns—met them constantly in society—made no favourable impression on Ida, but won the good opinion of Rosamond from the first; and was regarded with such high approval by their father, that when he mentioned his intentions of visiting England in the spring of the new year, he was cordially invited to spend the hunting season at Glenwith Grange.

I came back from Germany about the same time that the Welwyns returned from Paris, and at once set myself to improve my neighbourly intimacy with the family. I was very fond of Ida; more fond, perhaps, than my vanity will now allow me to——; but that is of no consequence. It is much more to the purpose to tell you that I heard the whole of the baron's story enthusiastically related by Mr. Welwyn and Rosamond; that he came to the Grange at the appointed time; that I was introduced to him; and that he produced as unfavourable an impression upon me as he had already produced upon Ida.

It was whimsical enough; but I really could not tell why I disliked him, though I could account very easily, according to my own notions, for his winning the favour and approval of Rosamond and her father. He was certainly a handsome man, as far as features went; he had a winning gentleness and graceful respect in his manner when he spoke to women; and he sang remarkably well, with one of the sweetest tenor voices I ever heard. These qualities alone were quite sufficient to attract any girl of Rosamond's disposition; and I certainly never wondered why he was a favourite of hers.

Then, as to her father, the baron was not only fitted to win his sympathy and regard in the field, by proving himself an ardent sportsman and an excellent rider; but was also, in virtue of some of his minor personal peculiarities, just the man to gain the friendship of his host. Mr. Welwyn was as ridiculously prejudiced as most weak-headed Englishmen are, on the subject of foreigners in general. In spite of his visit to Paris, the vulgar notion of a Frenchman continued to be *his* notion, both while he was in France and when he returned from it. Now, the baron was as unlike the traditional "Mounseer" of English songs, plays, and satires, as a man could well be; and it was on account of this very dissimilarity that Mr. Welwyn first took a violent fancy to him, and then invited him to his house. Franval spoke English remarkably well; wore neither beard, moustache, nor whiskers; kept his hair cut almost unbecomingly short; dressed in the extreme of plainness and modest good taste; talked little in general society; uttered his words, when he did speak, with singular calmness and deliberation; and, to crown all, had the greater part of his acquired property invested in English securities. In Mr. Welwyn's estimation, such a man as this was a perfect miracle of a Frenchman, and he admired and encouraged him accordingly.

I have said that I disliked him, yet could not assign a reason for my dislike; and I can only repeat it now. He was remarkably polite to me; we often rode together in hunting, and sat near each other at the Grange table; but I could never become familiar with him. He always gave me the idea of a man who had some mental reservation in saying the most trifling thing. There was a constant restraint, hardly perceptible to most people, but plainly visible, nevertheless, to me, which seemed to accompany his lightest words, and to hang about his most familiar manner. This, however, was no just reason for my secretly disliking and distrusting him as I did. Ida said as much to me, I remember, when I confessed to her what my feelings towards him were, and tried (but vainly) to induce her to be equally candid with me in return. She seemed to shrink from the tacit condemnation of Rosamond's opinion which such a confidence on her part would have implied. And yet she watched the growth of that opinion—or, in other words, the growth of her sister's liking for the baron—with an apprehension and sorrow which she tried fruitlessly to conceal. Even her father began to notice that her spirits were not so good as usual, and to suspect the cause of her melancholy. I remember he jested, with all the dense insensibility of a stupid man, about Ida having invariably been jealous from a child, if Rosamond looked kindly upon anybody except her elder sister.

The spring began to get far advanced towards summer. Franval paid a visit to London; came back in the middle of the season to Glenwith Grange; wrote to put off his departure for France; and at last (not at all to the surprise of anybody who was intimate with the Welwyns) proposed to Rosamond, and was accepted. He was candour and generosity itself when the preliminaries of the marriage-settlement were under discussion. He quite overpowered Mr. Welwyn and the lawyers with references, papers, and statements of the distribution and extent of his property, which were found to be perfectly correct. His sisters were written to, and returned the most cordial answers; saying that the state of their health would not allow them to come to England for the marriage; but adding a warm invitation to Normandy for the bride and her family. Nothing, in short, could be more straightforward and satisfactory than the baron's behaviour, and the testimonies to his worth and integrity which the news of the approaching marriage produced from his relatives and his friends.

The only joyless face at the Grange now was Ida's. At any time it would have been a hard trial to her to resign that first and foremost place which she had held since childhood in her sister's heart, as she knew she must resign it when Rosamond married. But, secretly disliking and distrusting Franval as she did, the thought that he was soon to become the husband of her beloved sister filled her with a vague sense of terror which she could not explain to herself; which it was imperatively necessary that she should conceal; and which, on those very accounts, became a daily and hourly torment to her that was almost more than she could bear.

One consolation alone supported her: Rosamond and she were not to be separated. She knew that the baron secretly disliked her as much as she disliked him; she knew that she must bid farewell to the brighter and happier part of her life on the day when she went to live under the same roof with her sister's husband; but, true to the promise made years and years ago by her dying mother's bed—true to the affection which was the ruling and beautiful feeling of her whole existence—she never hesitated about indulging Rosamond's wish, when the girl, in her bright, light-hearted way, said that she could never get on comfortably in the marriage state unless she had Ida to live with her and help her just the same as ever. The baron was too polite a man even to *look* dissatisfied when he heard of the proposed arrangement; and it was therefore settled from the beginning that Ida was always to live with her sister.

The marriage took place in the summer, and the bride and bridegroom went to spend their honeymoon in Cumberland. On their return to Glenwith Grange, a visit to the baron's sisters in Normandy, was talked of; but the execution of this project was suddenly and disastrously suspended by the death of Mr. Welwyn, from an attack of pleurisy.

In consequence of this calamity, the projected journey was of course deferred; and when autumn and the shooting season came, the baron was unwilling to leave the well-stocked preserves of the Grange. He seemed, indeed, to grow less and less inclined, as time advanced, for the trip to Normandy; and wrote excuse after excuse to his sisters, when letters arrived from them urging him to pay the promised visit. In the winter-time, he said he would not allow his wife to risk a long journey. In the spring, his health was pronounced to be delicate. In the genial summertime, the accomplishment of the proposed visit would be impossible, for at that period the baroness expected to become a mother. Such were the apologies which Franval seemed almost glad to be able to send to his sisters in France.

The marriage was, in the strictest sense of the term, a happy one. The baron, though he never altogether lost the strange restraint and reserve of his manner, was, in his quiet, peculiar way, the fondest and kindest of husbands. He went to town occasionally on business, but always seemed glad to return to the baroness; he never varied in the politeness of his bearing towards his wife's sister; he behaved with the most courteous hospitality towards all the friends of the Welwyns; in short, he thoroughly justified the good opinion which Rosamond and her father had formed of him when they first met at Paris. And yet no experience of his character thoroughly reassured Ida. Months passed on quietly and pleasantly; and still that secret sadness, that indefinable, unreasonable apprehension on Rosamond's account hung heavily on her sister's heart.

At the beginning of the first summer months, a little domestic inconvenience happened, which showed the baroness, for the first time, that her husband's temper could be seriously ruffled—and that by the veriest trifle. He was in the habit of taking in two French provincial newspapers—one published at Bordeaux and the other at Havre. He always opened these journals the moment they came, looked at one particular column of each with the deepest attention, for a few minutes, then carelessly threw them aside into his waste-paper basket. His wife and her sister were at first rather surprised at the manner in which he read his two papers; but they thought no more of it when he explained that he only took them in to consult them about French commercial intelligence, which might be, occasionally, of importance to him.

These papers were published weekly. On the occasion to which I have just referred, the Bordeaux paper came on the proper day, as usual; but the Havre paper never made its appearance. This trifling circumstance seemed to make the baron seriously uneasy. He wrote off directly to the country post-office and to the newspaper agent in London. His wife, astonished to see his tranquility so completely overthrown by so slight a cause, tried to restore his good humour by jesting with him about the missing newspaper. He replied by the first angry and unfeeling words that she had heard issue from his lips. She was then within about six weeks of her confinement, and very unfit to bear harsh answers from anybody—least of all from her husband.

On the second day no answer came. On the afternoon of the third, the baron rode off to the post town to make inquiries. About an hour after he had gone, a strange gentleman came to the Grange and asked to see the baroness. On being informed that she was not well enough to receive visitors, he sent up a message that his business was of great importance, and that he would wait downstairs for a second answer.

On receiving this message, Rosamond turned, as usual, to her elder sister for advice. Ida went downstairs immediately to see the stranger. What I am now about to tell you of the extraordinary interview which took place between them, and of the shocking events that followed it, I have heard from Miss Welwyn's own lips.

She felt unaccountably nervous when she entered the room. The stranger bowed very politely, and asked, in a foreign accent, if she were the Baroness Franval. She set him right on this point, and told him she attended to all matters of business for the baroness; adding that, if his errand at all concerned her sister's husband, the baron was not then at home.

The stranger answered that he was aware of it when he called, and that the unpleasant business on which he came could not be confided to the baron—at least, in the first instance.

She asked why. He said he was there to explain; and expressed himself as feeling greatly relieved at having to open his business to her, because she would, doubtless, be best able to prepare her sister for the bad news that he was, unfortunately, obliged to bring. The sudden faintness which overcame her, as he spoke those words, prevented her from addressing him in return. He poured out some water for her from a bottle which happened to be standing on the table, and asked if he might depend on her fortitude. She tried to say "Yes"; but the violent throbbing of her heart seemed to choke her. He took a foreign newspaper from his pocket, saying that he was a secret agent of the French police—that the paper was the Havre *Journal*, for the past week, and that it had been expressly kept from reaching the baron, as usual, through his (the agent's) interference. He then opened the newspaper, and begged that she would nerve herself sufficiently (for her sister's sake) to read certain lines, which would give her some hint of the business that brought him there. He pointed to the passage as he spoke. It was among the "Shipping Entries," and was thus expressed:

Arrived, the *Berenice*, from San Francisco, with a valuable cargo of hides. She brings one passenger, the Baron Franval, of Chateau Franval, in Normandy.

As Miss Welwyn read the entry, her heart, which had been throbbing violently but the moment before, seemed suddenly to cease from all action, and she began to shiver, though it was a warm June evening. The agent held the tumbler to her lips, and made her drink a little of the water, entreating her very earnestly to take courage and listen to him. He then sat down, and referred again to the entry, every word he uttered seeming to burn itself in for ever (as she expressed it) on her memory and her heart.

He said: "It has been ascertained beyond the possibility of a doubt that there is no mistake about the name in the lines you have just read. And it is as certain as that we are here, that there is only *one* Baron Franval now alive. The question, therefore, is, whether the passenger by the *Berenice* is the true baron, or—I beg you most earnestly to bear with me and to compose yourself—or the husband of your sister. The person who arrived last week at Havre was scouted as an impostor by the ladies at the château, the moment he presented himself there as their brother, returning to them after sixteen years of absence. The authorities were communicated with, and I and my assistants were instantly sent for from Paris.

"We wasted no time in questioning the supposed impostor. He either was, or affected to be, in a perfect frenzy of grief and indignation. We just ascertained, from competent witnesses, that he bore an extraordinary resemblance to the real baron, and that he was perfectly familiar with places and persons in and about the château; we just ascertained that, and then proceeded to confer with the local authorities, and to examine their private entries of suspected persons in their jurisdiction, ranging back over a past period of twenty years or more. One of the entries thus consulted contained these particulars:

"Hector Auguste Monbrun, son of a respectable proprietor in Normandy. Well educated; gentleman-like manners. On bad terms with his family. Character: bold, cunning, unscrupulous, self-possessed. Is a clever mimic. May be easily recognized by his striking likeness to the Baron Franval. Imprisoned at twenty for theft and assault."

Miss Welwyn saw the agent look up at her after he had read this extract from the police-book to ascertain if she was still able to listen to him. He asked, with some appearance of alarm, as their eyes met, if she would like some more water. She was just able to make a sign in the negative. He took a second extract from his pocket-book, and went on.

He said: "The next entry under the same name was dated four years later, and ran thus,

"H. A. Monbrun, condemned to the galleys for life, for assassination, and other crimes not officially necessary to be here specified. Escaped from custody at Toulon. Is known, since the expiration of his first term of imprisonment, to have allowed his beard to grow, and to have worn his hair long, with the intention of rendering it impossible for those acquainted with him in his native province to recognize him, as heretofore, by his likeness to the Baron Franval.

"There were more particulars added, not important enough for extract. We immediately examined the supposed impostor; for, if he was Monbrun, we knew that we should find on his shoulder the two letters of the convict brand, "T.F.," standing for *Travaux Forcés*. After the minutest examination with the mechanical and chemical tests used on such occasions, not the slightest trace of the brand was to be found. The moment this astounding discovery was made, I started to lay an embargo on the forthcoming numbers of the Havre *Journal* for that week, which were about to be sent to the English agent in London. I arrived at Havre on Saturday (the morning of publication), in time to execute my design. I waited there long enough to communicate by telegraph with my superiors in Paris, then hastened to this place. What my errand here is, you may——"

He might have gone on speaking for some moments longer; but Miss Welwyn heard no more.

Her first sensation of returning consciousness was the feeling that water was being sprinkled on her face. Then she saw that all the windows in the room had been set wide open, to give her air; and that she and the agent were still alone. At first she felt bewildered, and hardly knew who he was; but he soon recalled to her mind the horrible realities that had brought him there, by apologizing for not having summoned assistance when she fainted. He said it was of the last importance, in Franval's absence, that no one in the house should imagine that anything unusual was taking place in it. Then, after giving her an interval of a minute or two to collect what little strength she had left, he added that he would not increase her sufferings by saying anything more, just then, on the shocking subject of the investigation which it was his duty to make—that he would leave her to recover herself, and to consider what was the best course to be taken with the baroness in the present terrible emergency—and that he would privately return to the house between eight and nine o'clock that evening, ready to act as Miss Welwyn wished, and to afford her and her sister any aid and protection of which they might stand in need. With these words he bowed, and noiselessly quitted the room.

For the first few awful minutes after she was left alone, Miss Welwyn sat helpless and speechless; utterly numbed in heart, and mind, and body—then a sort of instinct (she was incapable of thinking) seemed to urge her to conceal the fearful news from her sister as long as possible. She ran upstairs to Rosamond's sitting-room, and called through the door (for she dared not trust herself in her sister's presence) that the visitor had come on some troublesome business from their late father's lawyers, and that she was going to shut herself up, and write some long letters in connexion with that business. After she had got into her own room, she was never sensible of how time was passing—never conscious of any feeling within her, except a baseless, helpless hope that the French police might yet be proved to have made some terrible mistake—until she heard a violent shower of rain come on a little after sunset. The noise of the rain, and the freshness it brought with it in the air, seemed to awaken her as if from a painful and a fearful sleep. The power of reflection returned to her; her heart heaved and bounded with an overwhelming terror, as the thought of Rosamond came back vividly to it; her memory recurred despairingly to the long-past day of her mother's death, and to the farewell promise she had made by her mother's bedside. She burst into an hysterical passion of weeping that seemed to be tearing her to pieces. In the midst of it she heard the clatter of a horse's hoofs in the courtyard, and knew that Rosamond's husband had come back.

Dipping her handkerchief in cold water, and passing it over her eyes as she left the room, she instantly hastened to her sister.

Fortunately the daylight was fading in the old-fashioned chamber that Rosamond occupied. Before they could say two words to each other, Franval was in the room. He seemed violently irritated; he said that he had waited for the arrival of the mail—that the missing newspaper had not come by it—that he had got wet through—that he felt a shivering fit coming on—and that he believed he had caught a violent cold. His wife anxiously suggested some simple remedies. He roughly interrupted her, saying there was but one remedy, the remedy of going to bed; and so left them without another word. She just put her handkerchief to her eyes, and said softly to her sister, "How he is changed!" then spoke no more. They sat silent for half an hour or longer. After that, Rosamond went affectionately and forgivingly to see how her husband was. She returned, saying that he was in bed, and in a deep, heavy sleep; and predicting hopefully that he would wake up quite well the next morning. In a few minutes more the clock struck nine; and Ida heard the servant's step ascending the stairs. She suspected what his errand was, and went out to meet him. Her presentiment had not deceived her; the police agent had arrived, and was waiting for her downstairs.

He asked her if she had said anything to her sister, or had thought of any plan of action, the moment she entered the room; and, on receiving a reply in the negative, inquired, further, if "the baron" had come home yet. She answered that he had; that he was ill and tired, and vexed, and that he had gone to bed. The agent asked in an eager whisper if she knew that he was asleep, and alone in bed? and, when he received her reply, said that he must go up into the bedroom directly.

She began to feel the faintness coming over her again, and with it sensations of loathing and terror that she could neither express to others nor define to herself. He said that if she hesitated to let him avail himself of this unexpected opportunity, her scruples might lead to fatal results. He reminded her that if "the baron" were really the convict Monbrun, the claims of society and of justice demanded that he should be discovered by the first available means; and that if he were not—if some inconceivable mistake had really been committed—then such a plan for getting immediately at the truth as was now proposed would ensure the delivery of an innocent man from suspicion, and at the same time spare him the knowledge that he had ever been suspected. This last argument had its effect on Miss Welwyn. The baseless, helpless hope that the French authorities might yet be proved to be in error, which she had already felt in her own room, returned to her now. She suffered the agent to lead her upstairs.

He took the candle from her hand when she pointed to the door; opened it softly; and, leaving it ajar, went into the room.

She looked through the gap with a feverish, horrorstruck curiosity. Franval was lying on his side in a profound sleep, with his back turned towards the door. The agent softly placed the candle upon a small reading table between the door and the bedside, softly drew down the bedclothes a little away from the sleeper's back, then took a pair of scissors from the toilet-table, and very gently and slowly began to cut away, first the loose folds, then the intervening strips of linen, from the part of Franval's nightgown that was over his shoulders. When the upper part of his back had been bared in this way, the agent took the candle and held it near the flesh. Miss Welwyn heard him ejaculate some word under his breath, then saw him looking round to where she was standing, and beckoning her to come in.

Mechanically she obeyed; mechanically she looked down where his finger was pointing. It was the convict Monbrun—there, just visible under the bright light of the candle, were the fatal letters "T.F." branded on the villain's shoulder!

Though she could neither move nor speak, the horror of this discovery did not deprive her of her consciousness. She saw the agent softly draw up the bedclothes again into their proper position, replace the scissors on the toilet-table, and take from it a bottle of smelling-salts. She felt him removing her from the bedroom, and helping her quickly downstairs, giving her the salts to smell by the way. When they were alone again, he said, with the first appearance of agitation that he had yet exhibited, "Now, madam, for God's sake, collect all your courage, and be guided by me. You and your sister had better leave the house immediately. Have you any relatives in the neighbourhood with whom you could take refuge?" They had none. "What is the name of the nearest town where you could get good accommodation for the night?" Harleybrook (he wrote the name down on his tablets). "How far off is it?" Twelve miles. "You had better have the carriage out at once, to go there with as little delay as possible, leaving me to pass the night here. I will communicate with you to-morrow at the principal hotel. Can you compose yourself sufficiently to be able to tell the head servant, if I ring for him, that he is to obey my orders till further notice?"

The servant was summoned, and received his instructions, the agent going out with him to see that the carriage was got ready quietly and quickly. Miss Welwyn went upstairs to her sister.

How the fearful news was first broken to Rosamond, I cannot relate to you. Miss Welwyn has never confided to me, has never confided to anybody, what happened at the interview between her sister and herself that night. I can tell you nothing of the shock they both suffered, except that the younger and the weaker died under it; that the elder and the stronger has never recovered from it, and never will.

They went away the same night, with one attendant, to Harley-brook, as the agent had advised. Before daybreak Rosamond was seized with the pains of premature labour. She died three days after, unconscious of the horror of her situation, wandering in her mind about past times, and singing old tunes that Ida had taught her as she lay in her sister's arms.

The child was born alive, and lives still. You saw her at the window as we came in at the back way to the Grange. I surprised you, I daresay, by asking you not to speak of her to Miss Welwyn. Perhaps you noticed something vacant in the little girl's expression. I am sorry to say that her mind is more vacant still. If "idiot" did not sound like a mocking word, however tenderly and pityingly one may wish to utter it, I should tell you that the poor thing had been an idiot from her birth.

You will, doubtless, want to hear now what happened at Glen-with Grange after Miss Welwyn and her sister left it. I have seen the letter which the police agent sent the next morning to Harley-brook; and, speaking from my recollection of that, I shall be able to relate all you can desire to know.

First, as to the past history of the scoundrel Monbrun, I need only tell you that he was identical with an escaped convict, who, for a long term of years, had successfully eluded the vigilance of the authorities all over Europe, and in America as well. In conjunction with two accomplices, he had succeeded in possessing himself of large sums of money by the most criminal means. He also acted secretly as the "banker" of his convict brethren, whose dishonest gains were all confided to his hands for safe-keeping. He would have been certainly captured, on venturing back to France, along with his two associates, but for the daring imposture in which he took refuge; and which, if the true Baron Franval had really died abroad, as was reported, would, in all probability, never have been found out.

Besides his extraordinary likeness to the baron, he had every other requisite for carrying on his deception successfully. Though his parents were not wealthy, he had received a good education. He was so notorious for his gentleman-like manners among the villainous associates of his crimes and excesses, that they nicknamed him "the Prince." All his early life had been passed in the neighbourhood of the Château Franval. He knew what were the circumstances which had induced the baron to leave it. He had been in the country to which the baron had emigrated. He was able to refer familiarly to persons and localities, at home and abroad, with which the baron was sure to be acquainted. And, lastly, he had an expatriation of fifteen years to plead for him as his all-sufficient excuse, if he made any slight mistakes before the baron's sisters, in his assumed character of their long-absent brother. It will be, of course, hardly necessary for me to tell you, in relation to this part of the subject, that the true Franval was immediately and honourably reinstated in the family rights of which the impostor had succeeded for a time in depriving him.

According to Monbrun's own account, he had married poor Rosamond purely for love; and the probabilities certainly are, that the pretty, innocent English girl had really struck the villain's fancy for the time; and that the easy, quiet life he was leading at the Grange pleased him, by contrast with his perilous and vagabond existence of former days. What might have happened if he had had time enough to grow wearied of his ill-fated wife and his English home, it is now useless to inquire. What really did happen on the morning when he awoke after the flight of Ida and her sister can be briefly told.

As soon as his eyes opened they rested on the police agent sitting quietly by the bedside, with a loaded pistol in his hand.

Monbrun knew immediately that he was discovered; but he never for an instant lost the self-possession for which he was famous. He said he wished to have five minutes allowed him to deliberate quietly in bed, whether he should resist the French authorities on English ground, and so gain time by obliging the one Government to apply specially to have him delivered up by the other—or whether he should accept the terms officially offered to him by the agent, if he quietly allowed himself to be captured. He chose the latter course—it was suspected, because he wished to communicate personally with some of his convict associates in France, whose fraudulent gains were in his keeping, and because he felt boastfully confident of being able to escape again, whenever he pleased. Be his secret motives, however, what they might, he allowed the agent to conduct him peaceably from the Grange; first writing a farewell letter to poor Rosamond, full of heartless French sentiment and glib sophistries about Fate and Society. His own fate was not long in overtaking him. He attempted to escape again, as it had been expected he would, and was shot by the sentinel on duty at the time. I remember hearing that the bullet entered his head and killed him on the spot.

My story is done. It is ten years now since Rosamond was buried in the churchyard yonder; and it is ten years also since Miss Welwyn returned to be the lonely inhabitant of Glenwith Grange. She now lives but in the remembrances that it calls up before her of her happier existence of former days. There is hardly an object in the old house which does not tenderly and solemnly remind her of the mother, whose last wishes she lived to obey; of the sister, whose happiness was once her dearest earthly care. Those prints that you noticed on the library walls Rosamond used to copy in the past time, when her pencil was often guided by Ida's hand. Those music-books that you were looking over, she and her mother have played from together through many a long and quiet summer's evening. She has no ties now to bind her to the present but the poor child whose affliction it is her constant effort to lighten, and the little peasant population around her, whose humble cares and wants and sorrows she is always ready to relieve. Far and near her modest charities have penetrated among us; and far and near she is heartily beloved and blessed in many a labourer's household. There is no poor man's hearth, not in this village only, but for miles away from it as well, at which you would not be received with the welcome given to an old friend, if you only told the cottagers that you knew the Lady of Glenwith Grange!

Mad Monkton

Chapter One

The Monktons of Wincot Abbey bore a sad character for want of sociability in our county. They held no friendly intercourse with their neighbours; and, excepting my father, and a lady and her daughter living near them, they never received anyone under their own roof.

Proud as they all certainly were, it was not pride but dread which kept them thus apart from their neighbours. The family had suffered for generations past from the horrible affliction of heredi-tary insanity, and the members of it shrank from exposing their calamity to others, as they must have exposed it if they had mingled with the busy little world around them. There is a frightful story of a crime committed in past times by two of the Monktons, near relatives, from which the first appearance of the insanity was always supposed to date, but it is needless for me to shock anyone by repeating it. It is enough to say that at intervals almost every form of madness appeared in the family; monomania being the most frequent manifestation of the affliction among them. I have these particulars, and one or two yet to be related, from my father.

At the period of my youth but three of the Monktons were left at the Abbey: Mr. and Mrs. Monkton, and their only child, Alfred, heir to the property. The one other member of this, the elder, branch of the family who was then alive, was Mr. Monkton's younger brother, Stephen. He was an unmarried man, possessing a fine estate in Scotland; but he lived almost entirely on the Conti-nent, and bore the reputation of being a shameless profligate. The family at Wincot held almost as little communication with him as with their neighbours.

I have already mentioned my father, and a lady and her daughter, as the only privileged people who were admitted into Wincot Abbey.

My father had been an old school and college friend of Mr. Monkton, and accident had brought them so much together in later life, that their continued intimacy at Wincot was quite intelligible. I am not so well able to account for the friendly terms on which Mrs. Elmslie (the lady to whom I have alluded) lived with the Monktons. Her late husband had been distantly related to Mrs. Monkton, and my father was her daughter's guardian. But even these claims to friendship and regard never seemed to me strong enough to explain the intimacy between Mrs. Elmslie and the inhabitants of the Abbey. Intimate, however, they certainly were, and one result of the constant interchange of visits between the two families in due time declared itself—Mr. Monkton's son and Mrs. Elmslie's daughter became attached to each other.

I had no opportunities of seeing much of the young lady; I only remember her at that time as a delicate, gentle, lovable girl, the very opposite in appearance, and apparently in character also, to Alfred Monkton. But perhaps that was one reason why they fell in love with each other. The attachment was soon discovered, and was far from being disapproved by the parents on either side. In all essential points, except that of wealth, the Elmslies were nearly the equals of the Monktons, and want of money in a bride was of no consequence to the heir of Wincot. Alfred, it was well known, would succeed to thirty thousand a year on his father's death.

Thus, though the parents on both sides thought the young people not old enough to be married at once, they saw no reason why Ada and Alfred should not be engaged to each other, with the understanding that they should be united when young Monkton came of age, in two years' time. The person to be consulted in the matter, after the parents, was my father in his capacity of Ada's guardian. He knew that the family misery had shown itself many years ago in Mrs. Monkton, who was her husband's cousin. The *illness,* as it was significantly called, had been palliated by careful treatment, and was reported to have passed away. But my father was not to be deceived. He knew where the hereditary taint still lurked; he viewed with horror the bare possibility of its reappearing one day in the children of his friend's only daughter; and he positively refused his consent to the marriage engagement.

The result was that the doors of the Abbey and the doors of Mrs. Elmslie's house were closed to him. This suspension of friendly intercourse had lasted but a very short time, when Mrs. Monkton died. Her husband, who was fondly attached to her, caught a violent cold while attending her funeral. The cold was neglected, and settled on his lungs. In a few months' time, he followed his wife to the grave, and Alfred was left master of the grand old Abbey, and the fair lands that spread all around it.

At this period Mrs. Elmslie had the indelicacy to endeavour a second time to procure my father's consent to the marriage engagement. He refused it again more positively than before. More than a year passed away. The time was approaching fast when Alfred would be of age. I returned from college to spend the long vacation at home, and made some advances towards bettering my acquaintance with young Monkton. They were evaded—certainly with perfect politeness, but still in such a way as to prevent me from offering my friendship to him again. Any mortification I might have felt at this petty repulse, under ordinary circumstances, was dismissed from my mind by the occurrence of a real misfortune in our household. For some months past my father's health had been failing, and, just at the time of which I am now writing, his sons had to mourn the irreparable calamity of his death.

This event (through some informality or error in the late Mr. Elmslie's will) left the future of Ada's life entirely at her mother's disposal. The consequence was the immediate ratification of the marriage engagement to which my father had so steadily refused his consent. As soon as the fact was publicly announced, some of Mrs. Elmslie's more intimate friends, who were acquainted with the reports affecting the Monkton family, ventured to mingle with their former congratulations one or two significant references to the late Mrs. Monkton, and some searching inquiries as to the disposition of her son.

Mrs. Elmslie always met these polite hints with one bold form of answer. She first admitted the existence of those reports about the Monktons which her friends were unwilling to specify distinctly; and then declared that they were infamous calumnies. The hereditary taint had died out of the family generations back. Alfred was the best, the kindest, the sanest of human beings. He loved study and retirement; Ada sympathised with his tastes, and had made her choice unbiassed; if any more hints were dropped about sacrificing her by her marriage, those hints would be viewed as so many insults to her mother, whose affection for her it was monstrous to call in question. This way of talking silenced people, but did not convince them. They began to suspect, what was indeed the actual truth, that Mrs. Elmslie was a selfish, worldly, grasping woman, who wanted to get her daughter well married, and cared nothing for consequences as long as she saw Ada mistress of the greatest establishment in the whole county.

It seemed, however, as if there was some fatality at work to prevent the attainment of Mrs. Elmslie's great object in life. Hardly was one obstacle to the ill-omened marriage removed by my father's death, before another succeeded it, in the shape of anxieties and difficulties caused by the delicate state of Ada's health. Doctors were consulted in all directions, and the result of their advice was that the marriage must be deferred, and that Miss Elmslie must leave England for a certain time, to reside in a warmer climate; the South of France, if I remember rightly. Thus it happened that just before Alfred came of age, Ada and her mother departed for the Continent, and the union of the two young people was understood to be indefinitely postponed.

Some curiosity was felt in the neighbourhood as to what Alfred Monkton would do under these circumstances. Would he follow his lady-love? Would he go yachting? Would he throw open the doors of the old Abbey at last, and endeavour to forget the absence of Ada, and the postponement of his marriage, in a round of gaieties? He did none of these things. He simply remained at Wincot, living as suspiciously strange and solitary a life as his father had lived before him. Literally, there was now no companion for him at the Abbey but the old priest (the Monktons, I should have mentioned before, were Roman Catholics) who had held the office of tutor to Alfred from his earliest years. He came of age, and there was not even so much as a private dinner-party at Wincot to celebrate the event. Families in the neighbourhood determined to forget the offence which his father's reserve had given them, and invited him to their houses. The invitations were politely declined. Civil visitors called resolutely at the Abbey, and were resolutely bowed away from the doors as soon as they had left their cards. Under this combination of sinister and aggravating circumstances, people in all directions took to shaking their heads mysteriously when the name of Mr. Alfred Monkton was mentioned, hinting at the family calamity, and wondering peevishly or sadly, as their tempers inclined them, what he could possibly do to occupy himself month after month in the lonely old house.

The right answer to this question was not easy to find. It was quite useless, for example, to apply to the priest for it. He was a very quiet, polite old gentleman; his replies were always excessively ready and civil, and appeared at the time to convey a reasonable amount of information; but when they were tested by after-reflection, it was universally observed that nothing tangible could be extracted from them. The housekeeper, a weird old woman, with a very abrupt and repelling manner, was too fierce and taciturn to be safely approached. The few indoor servants had all been long enough in the family to have learnt to hold their tongues in public as a regular habit. It was only from the farm-servants who supplied the table at the Abbey, that any information could be obtained; and vague enough it was when they came to communicate it.

Some of them had observed the "young master" walking about the library with heaps of dusty papers in his hands. Others had heard odd noises in the uninhabited parts of the Abbey, had looked up, and had seen him forcing open the old windows, as if to let light and air into rooms supposed to have been shut close for years and years; or had discovered him standing on the perilous summit of one of the crumbling turrets, never ascended before within their memories, and popularly considered to be inhabited by the ghosts of the monks who had once possessed the building. The result of these observations and discoveries, when they were communicated to others, was of course to impress every one with a firm belief that "poor young Monkton was going the way that the rest of the family had gone before him": which opinion always appeared to be immensely strengthened in the popular mind by a conviction—founded on no particle of evidence—that the priest was at the bottom of all the mischief.

Thus far I have spoken from hearsay evidence mostly. What I have next to tell will be the result of my own personal experience.

Chapter Two

About five months after Alfred Monkton came of age I left college, and resolved to amuse and instruct myself a little by travelling abroad.

At the time when I quitted England, young Monkton was still leading his secluded life at the Abbey, and was, in the opinion of everybody, sinking rapidly, if he had not already succumbed, under the hereditary curse of his family. As to the Elmslies, report said that Ada had benefited by her sojourn abroad, and that mother and daugher were on their way back to England to resume their old relations with the heir of Wincot. Before they returned, I was away on my travels, and wandered half over Europe, hardly ever planning whither I should shape my course beforehand. Chance, which thus led me everywhere, led me at last to Naples. There I met with an old school friend, who was one of the *attachés* at the English embassy; and there began the extraordinary events in connection with Alfred Monkton which form the main interest of the story I am now relating.

I was idling away the time one morning with my friend the *attaché*, in the garden of the Villa Reale, when we were passed by a young man, walking alone, who exchanged bows with my friend.

I thought I recognised the dark eager eyes, the colourless cheeks, the strangely-vigilant, anxious expression which I remembered in past times as characteristic of Alfred Monkton's face, and was about to question my friend on the subject, when he gave me unasked the information of which I was in search.

"That is Alfred Monkton," said he; "he comes from your part of England. You ought to know him."

"I do know a little of him," I answered; "he was engaged to Miss Elmslie when I was last in the neighbourhood of Wincot. Is he married to her yet?"

"No; and he never ought to be. He has gone the way of the rest of the family; or, in plainer words, he has gone mad."

"Mad! But I ought not to be surprised at hearing that, after the reports about him in England."

"I speak from no reports; I speak from what he has said and done here before me, and before hundreds of other people. Surely you must have heard of it?"

"Never. I have been out of the way of news from Naples or England for months past."

"Then I have a very extraordinary story to tell you. You know, of course, that Alfred had an uncle, Stephen Monkton. Well, some time ago, this uncle fought a duel in the Roman states, with a Frenchman, who shot him dead. The seconds and the Frenchman (who was unhurt) took to flight in different directions, as it is supposed. We heard nothing here of the details of the duel till a month after it happened, when one of the French journals published an account of it, taken from papers left by Monkton's second, who died at Paris of consumption. These papers stated the manner in which the duel was fought, and how it terminated, but nothing more. The surviving second and the Frenchman have never been traced from that time to this. All that anybody knows, therefore, of the duel is that Stephen Monkton was shot; an event which nobody can regret, for a greater scoundrel never existed. The exact place where he died, and what was done with his body, are still mysteries not to be penetrated."

"But what has all this to do with Alfred?"

"Wait a moment, and you will hear. Soon after the news of his uncle's death reached England, what do you think Alfred did? He actually put off his marriage with Miss Elmslie, which was then about to be celebrated, to come out here in search of the burial-place of his wretched scamp of an uncle. And no power on earth will now induce him to return to England and to Miss Elmslie, until he has found the body and can take it back with him to be buried with all the other dead Monktons, in the vault under Wincot Abbey Chapel. He has squandered his money, pestered the police, exposed himself to the ridicule of the men and the indignation of the women for the last three months, in trying to achieve his insane purpose, and is now as far from it as ever. He will not assign to anybody the smallest motive for his conduct. You can't laugh him out of it, or reason him out of it. When we met him just now, I happen to know that he was on his way to the office of the police minister, to send out fresh agents to search and inquire through the Roman states for the place where his uncle was shot. And mind, all this time he professes to be passionately in love with Miss Elmslie, and to be miserable at his separation from her. Just think of that! And then think of his self-imposed absence from her here, to hunt after the remains of a wretch who was a disgrace to the family, and whom he never saw but once or twice in his life. Of all the 'Mad Monktons,' as they used to call them in England, Alfred is the maddest. He is actually our principal excitement in this dull opera season, though, for my own part, when I think of the poor girl in England, I am a great deal more ready to despise him than to laugh at him."

"You know the Elmslies, then?"

"Intimately. The other day, my mother wrote to me from England, after having seen Ada. This escapade of Monkton's has outraged all her friends. They have been entreating her to break off the match, which it seems she could do if she liked. Even her mother, sordid and selfish as she is, has been obliged at last, in common decency, to side with the rest of the family; but the good faithful girl won't give Monkton up. She humours his insanity, declares he gave her a good reason, in secret, for going away; says she could always make him happy when they were together in the old Abbey, and can make him still happier when they are married; in short, she loves him dearly, and will therefore believe in him to the last. Nothing shakes her; she has made up her mind to throw away her life on him, and she will do it."

"I hope not. Mad as his conduct looks to us, he may have some sensible reason for it that we cannot imagine. Does his mind seem at all disordered when he talks on ordinary topics?"

"Not in the least. When you can get him to say anything, which is not often, he talks like a sensible, well-educated man. Keep silence about his precious errand here, and you would fancy him the gentlest and most temperate of human beings. But touch the subject of his vagabond of an uncle, and the Monkton madness comes out directly. The other night a lady asked him, jestingly of course, whether he had even seen his uncle's ghost. He scowled at her like a perfect fiend, and said that he and his uncle would answer her question together some day, if they came from hell to do it. We laughed at his words, but the lady fainted at his looks, and we had a scene of hysterics and hartshorn in consequence. Any other man would have been kicked out of the room for nearly frightening a pretty woman to death in that way; but "Mad Monkton," as we have christened him, is a privileged lunatic in Neapolitan society, because he is English, good-looking, and worth thirty thousand a year. He goes out everywhere, under the impression that he may meet with somebody who has been let into the secret of the place where the mysterious duel was fought. If you are introduced to him, he is sure to ask you whether you know anything about it; but beware of following up the subject after you have answered him, unless you want to make sure that he is out of his senses. In that case, only talk of his uncle, and the result will rather more than satisfy you."

A day or two after this conversation with my friend the *attaché*, I met Monkton at an evening party.

The moment he heard my name mentioned, his face flushed up; he drew me away into a corner, and referring to his cool reception of my advance, years ago, towards making his acquaintance, asked my pardon for what he termed his inexcusable ingratitude, with an earnestness and an agitation which utterly astonished me. His next proceeding was to question me, as my friend had said he would, about the place of the mysterious duel.

An extraordinary change came over him while he interrogated me on this point. Instead of looking into my face as they had looked hitherto, his eyes wandered away, and fixed themselves intensely, almost fiercely, either on the perfectly empty wall at our side, or on the vacant space between the wall and ourselves—it was impossible to say which. I had come to Naples from Spain by sea, and briefly told him so, as the best way of satisfying him that I could not assist his inquiries. He pursued them no further; and mindful of my friend's warning, I took care to lead the conversation to general topics. He looked back at me directly, and as long as we stood in our corner, his eyes never wandered away again to the empty wall or the vacant space at our side.

Though more ready to listen than to speak, his conversation, when he did talk, had no trace of anything the least like insanity about it. He had evidently read, not generally only, but deeply as well, and could apply his reading with singular felicity to the illustration of almost any subject under discussion, neither obtruding his knowledge absurdly, nor concealing it affectedly. His manner was in itself a standing protest against such a nickname as "Mad Monkton." He was so shy, so quiet, so composed and gentle in all his actions, that at times I should have been almost inclined to call him effeminate. We had a long talk together on the first evening of our meeting; we often saw each other afterwards, and never lost a single opportunity of bettering our acquaintance. I felt that he had taken a liking to me; and in spite of what I had heard about his behaviour to Miss Elmslie, in spite of the suspicions which the history of his family and his own conduct had arrayed against him, I began to like "Mad Monkton" as much as he liked me. We took many a quiet ride together in the country, and sailed often along the shores of the Bay on either side. But for two eccentricities in his conduct, which I could not at all understand, I should soon have felt as much at my ease in his society as if he had been my own brother.

The first of these eccentricities consisted in the reappearance on several occasions of the odd expression in his eyes, which I had first seen when he asked me whether I knew anything about the duel. No matter what we were talking about, or where we happened to be, there were times when he would suddenly look away from my face, now on one side of me, now on the other, but always where there was nothing to see, and always with the same intensity and fierceness in his eyes. This looked so like madness—or hypochondria, at the least—that I felt afraid to ask him about it, and always pretended not to observe him.

The second peculiarity in his conduct was that he never referred while in my company, to the reports about his errand at Naples, and never once spoke of Miss Elmslie, or of his life at Wincot Abbey. This not only astonished me, but amazed those who had noticed our intimacy, and who had made sure that I must be the depositary of all his secrets. But the time was near at hand when this mystery, and some other mysteries of which I had no suspicion at that period, were all to be revealed.

I met him one night at a large ball, given by a Russian nobleman, whose name I could not pronounce then, and cannot remember now. I had wandered away from reception-room, ballroom, and card-room to a small apartment at one extremity of the palace, which was half conservatory, half boudoir, and which had been prettily illuminated for the occasion with Chinese lanthorns. Nobody was in the room when I got there. The view over the Mediterranean, bathed in the bright softness of Italian moonlight, was so lovely, that I remained for a long time at the window, looking out, and listening to the dance music which faintly reached me from the ballroom. My thoughts were far away with the relations I had left in England, when I was startled out of them by hearing my name softly pronounced.

I looked round directly, and saw Monkton standing in the room. A livid paleness overspread his face, and his eyes were turned away from me with the same extraordinary expression in them to which I have already alluded.

"Do you mind leaving the ball early no-night?" he asked, still not looking at me.

"Not at all," said I. "Can I do anything for you? Are you ill?"

"No, at least nothing to speak of. Will you come to my rooms?"

"At once, if you like."

"No, not at once. *I* must go home directly; but don't you come to me for half an hour yet. You have not been at my rooms before, I know; but you will easily find them out, they are close by. There is a card with my address. I *must* speak to you to-night; my life depends on it. Pray come! for God's sake come when the half hour is up!"

I promised to be punctual, and he left me directly.

Most people will be easily able to imagine the state of nervous impatience and vague expectation in which I passed the allotted period of delay, after hearing such words as those Monkton had spoken to me. Before the half hour had quite expired, I began to make my way out through the ballroom.

At the head of the staircase, my friend the *attaché* met me.

"What! going away already?" said he.

"Yes; and on a very curious expedition. I am going to Monkton's rooms, by his own invitation."

"You don't mean it! Upon my honour, you're a bold fellow to trust yourself alone with 'Mad Monkton' when the moon is at the full."

"He is ill, poor fellow. Besides, I don't think him half as mad as you do."

"We won't dispute about that; but mark my words, he has not asked you to go where no visitor has ever been admitted before, without a special purpose. I predict that you will see or hear something to-night which you will remember for the rest of your life."

We parted. When I knocked at the courtyard gate of the house where Monkton lived, my friend's last words on the palace staircase occurred to me; and though I had laughed at him when he had spoken them, I began to suspect even then that his prediction would be fulfilled.

Chapter Three

The porter who let me into the house where Monkton lived, directed me to the floor on which his rooms were situated. On getting upstairs, I found his door on the landing ajar. He heard my footsteps, I suppose, for he called to me to come in before I could knock.

I entered, and found him sitting by the table, with some loose letters in his hand, which he was just tying together in a packet. I noticed, as he asked me to sit down, that his expression looked more composed, though the paleness had not yet left his face. He thanked me for coming; repeated that he had something very important to say to me; and then stopped short, apparently too much embarrassed to proceed. I tried to set him at ease by assuring him that if my assistance or advice could be of any use, I was ready to place myself and my time heartily and unreservedly at his service.

As I said this, I saw his eyes beginning to wander away from my face—to wander slowly, inch by inch as it were, until they stopped at a certain point, with the same fixed stare into vacancy which had so often startled me on former occasions. The whole expression of his face altered as I had never yet seen it alter; he sat before me, looking like a man in a death-trance.

"You are very kind," he said, slowly and faintly, speaking, not to me, but in the direction in which his eyes were still fixed—"I know you can help me; but——"

He stopped; his face whitened horribly, and the perspiration broke out all over it. He tried to continue; said a word or two, then stopped again. Seriously alarmed about him, I rose from my chair, with the intention of getting him some water from a jug which I saw standing on a side table.

He sprang up at the same moment. All the suspicions I had ever heard whispered against his sanity flashed over my mind in an instant; and I involuntarily stepped back a pace or two.

"Stop," he said, seating himself again; "don't mind me; and don't leave your chair. I want—I wish, if you please, to make a little alteration, before we say anything more. Do you mind sitting in a strong light?"

"Not in the least."

I had hitherto been seated in the shade of his reading-lamp, the only light in the room.

As I answered him, he rose again; and going into another apartment, returned with a large lamp in his hand; then took two candles from the side table, and two others from the chimney-piece; placed them all, to my amazement, together, so as to stand exactly between us; and then tried to light them. His hand trembled so, that he was obliged to give up the attempt, and allow me to come to his assistance. By his direction I took the shade off the reading lamp, after I had lit the other lamp and the four candles. When he sat down again, with this concentration of light between us, his better and gentler manner began to return: and while he now addressed me, he spoke without the slightest hesitation.

"It is useless to ask whether you have heard the reports about me," he said; "I know that you have. My purpose to-night is to give you some reasonable explanation of the conduct which has produced those reports. My secret has been hitherto confided to one person only; I am now about to trust it to your keeping, with a special object which will appear as I go on. First, however, I must begin by telling you exactly what the great difficulty is which obliges me to be still absent from England. I want your advice and your help; and, to conceal nothing from you, I want also to test your forbearance and your friendly sympathy, before I can venture on thrusting my miserable secret into your keeping. Will you pardon this apparent distrust of your frank and open character—this apparent ingratitude for your kindness towards me ever since we first met?"

I begged him not to speak of these things, but to go on.

"You know," he proceeded, "that I am here to recover the body of my Uncle Stephen, and to carry it back with me to our family burial-place in England; and you must also be aware that I have not yet succeeded in discovering his remains. Try to pass over for the present whatever may seem extraordinary and incomprehensible in such a purpose as mine is; and read this newspaper article, where the ink-line is traced. It is the only evidence hitherto obtained on the subject of the fatal duel in which my uncle fell: and I want to hear what course of proceeding the perusal of it may suggest to you as likely to be best on my part."

He handed me an old French newspaper. The substance of what

I read there is still so firmly impressed on my memory, that I am certain of being able to repeat correctly at this distance of time, all the facts which it is necessary for me to communicate to the reader.

The article began, I remember, with editorial remarks on the great curiosity then felt in regard to the fatal duel between the Count St. Lo and Mr. Stephen Monkton, an English gentleman. The writer proceeded to dwell at great length on the extraordinary secrecy in which the whole affair had been involved from first to last; and to express a hope that the publication of a certain manuscript, to which his introductory observations referred, might lead to the production of fresh evidence from other and better informed quarters. The manuscript had been found among the papers of Monsieur Foulon, Mr. Monkton's second, who had died at Paris of a rapid decline, shortly after returning to his home in that city from the scene of the duel. The document was unfinished, having been left incomplete at the very place where the reader would most wish to find it continued. No reason could be discovered for this, and no second manuscript bearing on the all-important subject had been found, after the strictest search among the papers left by the deceased.

The document itself then followed.

It purported to be an agreement privately drawn up between Mr. Monkton's second, Monsieur Foulon, and the Count St. Lo's second, Monsieur Dalville; and contained a statement of all the arrangements for concluding the duel. The paper was dated "Naples, February 22nd"; and was divided into some seven or eight clauses.

The first clause described the origin and nature of the quarrel—a very disgraceful affair on both sides, worth neither remembering nor repeating. The second clause stated that the challenged man having chosen the pistol as his weapon, and the challenger (an excellent swordsman) having, on his side, thereupon insisted that the duel should be fought in such a manner as to make the first fire decisive in its results, the seconds, seeing that fatal consequences must inevitably follow the hostile meeting, determined, first of all, that the duel should be kept a profound secret from everybody, and that the place where it was to be fought should not be made known beforehand, even to the principals themselves. It was added that this excess of precaution had been rendered absolutely necessary, in consequence of a recent address from the Pope to the ruling powers in Italy, commenting on the scandalous frequency of the practice of duelling, and urgently desiring that the laws against duellists should be enforced for the future with the utmost rigour.

The third clause detailed the manner in which it had been arranged that the duel should be fought.

The pistols having been loaded by the seconds on the ground, the combatants were to be placed thirty paces apart, and were to toss up for the first fire. The man who won was to advance ten paces—marked out for him beforehand—and was then to discharge his pistol. If he missed, or failed to disable his opponent, the latter was free to advance, if he chose, the whole remaining twenty paces before he fired in his turn. This arrangement ensured the decisive termination of the duel at the first discharge of the pistols, and both principals and seconds pledged themselves on either side to abide by it.

The fourth clause stated that the seconds had agreed that the duel should be fought *out* of the Neapolitan states, but left themselves to be guided by circumstances as to the exact locality in which it should take place. The remaining clauses, so far as I remember them, were devoted to detailing the different precautions to be adopted for avoiding discovery. The duellists and their seconds were to leave Naples in separate parties; were to change carriages several times; were to meet at a certain town, or, failing that, at a certain post-house on the high road from Naples to Rome; were to carry drawing-books, colour-boxes, and camp-stools, as if they had been artists out on a sketching tour; and were to proceed to the place of the duel on foot, employing no guides, for fear of treachery. Such general arrangements as these, and others for facilitating the flight of the survivors after the affair was over, formed the conclusion of this extraordinary document, which was signed, in initials only, by both the seconds.

Just below the initials, appeared the beginning of a narrative, dated "Paris," and evidently intended to describe the duel itself with extreme minuteness. The handwriting was that of the deceased second.

Monsieur Foulon, the gentleman in question, stated his belief that circumstances might transpire which would render an account by an eye-witness of the hostile meeting between St. Lo and Mr.

Monkton an important document. He proposed, therefore, as one of the seconds, to testify that the duel had been fought in exact accordance with the terms of the agreement, both the principals conducting themselves like men of gallantry and honour(!). And he further announced that, in order not to compromise any one, he should place the paper containing his testimony in safe hands, with strict directions that it was on no account to be opened, except in a case of the last emergency.

After this preamble, Monsieur Foulon related that the duel had been fought two days after the drawing up of the agreement, in a locality to which accident had conducted the duelling party. (The name of the place was not mentioned, nor even the neighbourhood in which it was situated.) The men having been placed according to previous arrangement, the Count St. Lo had won the toss for the first fire, had advanced his ten paces, and had shot his opponent in the body. Mr. Monkton did not immediately fall, but staggered forward some six or seven paces, discharged his pistol ineffectually at the Count, and dropped to the ground a dead man. Monsieur Foulon then stated that he tore a leaf from his pocket-book, wrote on it a brief description of the manner in which Mr. Monkton had died, and pinned the paper to his clothes; this proceeding having been rendered necessary by the peculiar nature of the plan organised on the spot for safely disposing of the dead body. What this plan was, or what was done with the corpse, did not appear, for at this important point the narrative abruptly broke off.

A footnote in the newspaper merely stated the manner in which the document had been obtained for publication, and repeated the announcement contained in the editor's introductory remarks, that no continuation had been found by the persons entrusted with the care of Monsieur Foulon's papers. I have now given the whole substance of what I read, and have mentioned all that was then known of Mr. Stephen Monkton's death.

When I gave the newspaper back to Alfred, he was too much agitated to speak; but he reminded me by a sign that he was anxiously waiting to hear what I had to say. My position was a very trying and a very painful one. I could hardly tell what consequences might not follow any want of caution on my part, and could think at first of no safer plan than questioning him carefully before I committed myself either one way or the other.

"Will you excuse me if I ask you a question or two before I give you my advice?" I said.

He nodded impatiently.

"Yes, yes; any questions you like."

"Were you at any time in the habit of seeing your uncle frequently?"

"I never saw him more than twice in my life; on each occasion, when I was a mere child."

"Then you could have had no very strong personal regard for him?"

"Regard for him! I should have been ashamed to feel any regard for him. He disgraced us wherever he went."

"May I ask if any family motive is involved in your anxiety to recover his remains?"

"Family motives may enter into it among others—but why do you ask?"

"Because, having heard that you employ the police to assist your search, I was anxious to know whether you had stimulated their superiors to make them do their best in your service, by giving some strong personal reasons at headquarters for the very unusual project which has brought you here."

"I give no reasons. I pay for the work I want done, and in return for my liberality I am treated with the most infamous indifference on all sides. A stranger in the country, and badly acquainted with the language, I can do nothing to help myself. The authorities, both at Rome and in this place, pretend to assist me, pretend to search and inquire as I would have them search and inquire, and do nothing more. I am insulted, laughed at, almost to my face."

"Do you not think it possible—mind, I have no wish to excuse the misconduct of the authorities, and do not share in any such opinion myself—but do you not think it likely that the police may doubt whether you are in earnest?"

"Not in earnest!" he cried, starting up and confronting me fiercely, with wild eyes and quickened breath. "Not in earnest! *You* think I'm not in earnest, too. I know you think it, though you tell me you don't. Stop! before we say another word, your own eyes shall convince you. Come here—only for a minute—only for one minute!"

I followed him into his bedroom, which opened out of the sitting-room. At one side of his bed stood a large packing-case of plain wood, upwards of seven feet in length.

"Open the lid, and look in," he said, "while I hold the candle so that you can see."

I obeyed his directions, and discovered, to my astonishment, that the packing-case contained a leaden coffin, magnificently emblazoned with the arms of the Monkton family, and inscribed in old-fashioned letters with the name of "Stephen Monkton," his age and the manner of his death being added underneath.

"I keep his coffin ready for him," whispered Alfred, close at my ear. "Does that look like earnest?"

It looked more like insanity—so like, that I shrank from answering him.

"Yes! yes! I see you are convinced," he continued quickly; "we may go back into the next room, and may talk without restraint on either side now."

On returning to our places, I mechanically moved my chair away from the table. My mind was by this time in such a state of confusion and uncertainty about what it would be best for me to say or do next, that I forgot for the moment the position he had assigned to me when we lit the candles. He reminded me of this directly.

"Don't move away," he said, very earnestly; "keep on sitting in the light; pray do! I'll soon tell you why I am so particular about that. But first give me your advice; help me in my great distress and suspense. Remember, you promised me you would."

I made an effort to collect my thoughts and succeeded. It was useless to treat the affair otherwise than seriously in his presence; it would have been cruel not to have advised him as I best could.

"You know," I said, "that two days after the drawing up of the agreement at Naples, the duel was fought out of the Neapolitan States. This fact has of course led you to the conclusion that all inquiries about localities had better be confined to the Roman territory?"

"Certainly: the search, such as it is, has been made there, and there only. If I can believe the police, they and their agents have inquired for the place where the duel was fought (offering a large reward in my name to the person who can discover it), all along the highroad from Naples to Rome. They have also circulated—at

least, so they tell me—descriptions of the duellists and their seconds; have left an agent to superintend investigations at the post-
house, and another at the town mentioned as meeting-points in the
agreement; and have endeavoured by correspondence with foreign
authorities to trace the Count St. Lo and Monsieur Dalville to their
place or places of refuge. All these efforts, supposing them to have
been really made, have hitherto proved utterly fruitless."

"My impression is," said I, after a moment's consideration, "that
all inquiries made along the highroad, or anywhere near Rome, are
likely to be made in vain. As to the discovery of your uncle's
remains, that is, I think, identical with the discovery of the place
where he was shot; for those engaged in the duel would certainly
not risk detection by carrying a corpse any distance with them in
their flight. The place, then, is all that we want to find out. Now, let
us consider for a moment. The duelling-party changed carriages;
travelled separately, two and two; doubtless took roundabout
roads; stopped at the post-house and the town as a blind; walked,
perhaps, a considerable distance unguided. Depend upon it, such
precautions as these (which we know they must have employed)
left them very little time out of the two days—though they might
start at sunrise, and not stop at nightfall—for straightforward
travelling. My belief therefore is, that the duel was fought somewhere near the Neapolitan frontier; and if I had been the police
agent who conducted the search, I should only have pursued it
parallel with the frontier, starting from west to east till I got up
among the lonely places in the mountains. That is my idea: do you
think it worth anything?"

His face flushed all over in an instant. "I think it an inspiration!" he cried. "Not a day is to be lost in carrying out our plan.
The police are not to be trusted with it. I must start myself, to-
morrow morning; and you——"

He stopped; his face grew suddenly pale; he sighed heavily; his
eyes wandered once more into the fixed look at vacancy; and the
rigid, deathly expression fastened again upon all his features.

"I must tell you my secret before I talk of to-morrow," he
proceeded, faintly. "If I hesitated any longer at confessing everything, I should be unworthy of your past kindness, unworthy of the
help which it is my last hope that you will gladly give me when you
have heard all."

I begged him to wait until he was more composed, until he was better able to speak; but he did not appear to notice what I said. Slowly, and struggling as it seemed against himself, he turned a little away from me; and bending his head over the table, supported it on his hand. The packet of letters with which I had seen him occupied when I came in, lay just beneath his eyes. He looked down on it steadfastly when he next spoke to me.

Chapter Four

"You were born, I believe, in our country," he said; "perhaps therefore you may have heard at some time of a curious old prophecy about our family, which is still preserved among the traditions of Wincot Abbey?"

"I have heard of such a prophecy," I answered; "but I never knew in what terms it was expressed. It professed to predict the extinction of your family, or something of that sort, did it not?"

"No inquiries," he went on, "have traced back that prophecy to the time when it was first made; none of our family records tell us anything of its origin. Old servants and old tenants of ours remember to have heard it from their fathers and grandfathers. The monks, whom we succeeded in the Abbey in Henry the VIII's time, got knowledge of it in some way; for I myself discovered the rhymes in which we know the prophecy to have been preserved from a very remote period, written on a blank leaf of one of the Abbey manuscripts. These are the verses, if verses they deserve to be called.

> *When in Wincot vault a place*
> *Waits for one of Monkton's race;*
> *When that one forlorn shall lie*
> *Graveless under open sky,*
> *Beggared of six feet of earth,*
> *Though lord of acres from his birth—*
> *That shall be a certain sign*
> *Of the end of Monkton's line.*
> *Dwindling ever faster, faster,*
> *Dwindling to the last-left master;*

From mortal ken, from light of day,
Monkton's race shall pass away.

"The prediction seems almost vague enough to have been uttered by an ancient oracle," said I, observing that he waited, after repeating the verses, as if expecting me to say something.

"Vague or not, it is being accomplished," he returned. "I am now the 'Last-left Master'—the last of that elder line of our family at which the prediction points; and the corpse of Stephen Monkton is not in the vaults of Wincot Abbey. Wait, before you exclaim against me! I have more to say about this. Long before the Abbey was ours, when we lived in the ancient manor-house near it (the very ruins of which have long since disappeared), the family-burying place was in the vault under the Abbey chapel. Whether in those remote times the prediction against us was known and dreaded or not, this much is certain: every one of the Monktons (whether living at the Abbey or on the smaller estate in Scotland) was buried in Wincot vault, no matter at what risk or what sacrifice. In the fierce fighting days of the olden time, the bodies of my ancestors who fell in foreign places were recovered and brought back to Wincot, though it often cost, not heavy ransom only but desperate bloodshed as well, to obtain them. This superstition, if you please to call it so, has never died out of the family from that time to the present day; for centuries the succession of the dead in the vault at the Abbey has been unbroken—absolutely unbroken—until now. The place mentioned in the prediction as waiting to be filled, is Stephen Monkton's place; the voice that cries vainly to the earth for shelter is the voice of the dead. As surely as if I saw it, I know that they have left him unburied on the ground where he fell!"

He stopped me before I could utter a word in remonstrance, by slowly rising to his feet, and pointing in the same direction towards which his eyes had wandered a short time since.

"I can guess what you want to ask me," he exclaimed, sternly and loudly; "you want to ask me how I can be mad enough to believe in a doggerel prophecy, uttered in an age of superstition to awe the most ignorant hearers. I answer" (at those words his voice sank suddenly to a whisper), "I answer, because *Stephen Monkton himself stands there at this moment, confirming me in my belief.*"

Whether it was the awe and horror that looked out ghastly from his face as he confronted me, whether it was that I had never hitherto fairly believed in the reports about his madness, and that the conviction of their truth now forced itself upon me on a sudden I know not; but I felt my blood curdling as he spoke, and I knew in my own heart, as I sat there speechless, that I dare not turn round and look where he was still pointing close at my side.

"I see there," he went on in the same whispering voice, "the figure of a dark-complexioned man, standing up with his head uncovered. One of his hands, still clutching a pistol, has fallen to his side; the other presses a bloody handkerchief over his mouth. The spasm of mortal agony convulses his features; but I know them for the features of a swarthy man, who twice frightened me by taking me up in his arms when I was a child, at Wincot Abbey. I asked the nurses at the time who that man was, and they told me it was my uncle, Stephen Monkton. Plainly, as if he stood there living, I see him now at your side, with the death-glare in his great black eyes; and so have I ever seen him since the moment when he was shot; at home and abroad, waking or sleeping, day and night, we are always together wherever I go!"

His whispering tones sank into almost inaudible murmuring as he pronounced these last words. From the direction and expression of his eyes, I suspected that he was speaking to the apparition. If I had beheld it myself at that moment, it would have been, I think, a less horrible sight to witness than to see him, as I saw him now, muttering inarticulately at vacancy. My own nerves were more shaken than I could have thought possible by what had passed. A vague dread of being near him in his present mood came over me, and I moved back a step or two.

He noticed the action instantly.

"Don't go!—pray, pray don't go! Have I alarmed you? Don't you believe me? Do the lights make your eyes ache? I only asked you to sit in the glare of the candles because I could not bear to see the light that always shines from the phantom there at dusk, shining over you as you sat in the shadow. Don't go—don't leave me yet!"

There was an utter forlornness, an unspeakable misery in his face as he said those words, which gave me back my self-possession by the simple process of first moving me to pity. I resumed my chair, and said that I would stay with him as long as he wished.

"Thank you a thousand times! You are patience and kindness itself," he said, going back to his former place, and resuming his former gentleness of manner. "Now that I have got over my first confession of the misery that follows me in secret wherever I go, I think I can tell you calmly all that remains to be told. You see, as I said, my uncle Stephen,"—he turned away his head quickly, and looked down at the table as the name passed his lips—"my uncle Stephen came twice to Wincot while I was a child, and on both occasions frightened me dreadfully. He only took me up in his arms, and spoke to me—very kindly, as I afterwards heard, for *him*—but he terrified me, nevertheless. Perhaps I was frightened at his great stature, his swarthy complexion, and his thick black hair and moustache, as other children might have been; perhaps the mere sight of him had some strange influence on me which I could not then understand, and cannot now explain. However it was, I used to dream of him long after he had gone away; and to fancy that he was stealing on me to catch me up in his arms, whenever I was left in the dark. The servants who took care of me found this out, and used to threaten me with my uncle Stephen whenever I was perverse and difficult to manage. As I grew up, I still retained my vague dread and abhorrence of our absent relative. I always listened intently, yet without knowing why, whenever his name was mentioned by my father or my mother—listened with an unaccountable presentiment that something terrible had happened to him, or was about to happen to me. This feeling only changed when I was left alone in the Abbey; and then it seemed to merge into the eager curiosity which had begun to grow on me rather before that time, about the origin of the ancient prophecy predicting the extinction of our race. Are you following me?"

"I follow every word with the closest attention."

"You must know, then, that I had first found out some fragments of the old rhyme, in which the prophecy occurs, quoted as a curiosity in an antiquarian book in the library. On the page opposite this quotation, had been pasted a rude old woodcut, representing a dark-haired man, whose face was so strangely like what I remembered of my uncle Stephen, that the portrait absolutely startled me. When I asked my father about this—it was then just before his death—he either knew, or pretended to know, nothing of it; and when I afterwards mentioned the prediction he fretfully changed the subject. It was just the same with our chaplain when I

spoke to him. He said the portrait had been done centuries before
my uncle was born; and called the prophecy doggerel and nonsense. I used to argue with him on the latter point, asking why we
Catholics, who believed that the gift of working miracles had never
departed from certain favoured persons, might not just as well
believe that the gift of prophecy had never departed either? He
would not dispute with me; he would only say that I must not
waste time in thinking of such trifles, that I had more imagination
than was good for me, and must suppress instead of exciting it.
Such advice as this only irritated my curiosity. I determined secretly to search through the oldest uninhabited part of the Abbey,
and to try if I could not find out from forgotten family records
what the portrait was, and when the prophecy had been first
written or uttered. Did you ever pass a day alone in the long-
deserted chambers of an ancient house?"

"Never; such solitude as that is not at all to my taste."

"Ah! what a life it was when I began my search. I should like to
live it over again! Such tempting suspense, such strange discoveries, such wild fancies, such enthralling terrors, all belonged to
that life! Only think of breaking open the door of a room which no
living soul had entered before you for nearly a hundred years!
think of the first step forward into a region of airless, awful stillness, where the light falls faint and sickly through closed windows
and rotting curtains! think of the ghostly creaking of the old floor
that cries out on you for treading on it, step as softly as you will!
think of arms, helmets, weird tapestries of bygone days, that seem
to be moving out on you from the walls as you first walk up to
them in the dim light! think of prying into great cabinets and iron-
clasped chests, not knowing what horrors may appear when you
tear them open! or poring over their contents till twilight stole on
you, and darkness grew terrible in the lonely place! of trying to
leave it, and not being able to go, as if something held you; of
wind wailing at you outside; of shadows darkening round you, and
closing you up in obscurity within. Only think of these things, and
you may imagine the fascination of suspense and terror in such a
life as mine was in those past days!"

(I shrunk from imagining that life: it was bad enough to see its
results, as I saw them before me now.)

"Well, my search lasted months and months; then it was suspended a little, then resumed. In whatever direction I pursued it, I

always found something to lure me on. Terrible confessions of past crimes, shocking proofs of secret wickedness that had been hidden securely from all eyes but mine, came to light. Sometimes these discoveries were associated with particular parts of the Abbey, which have had a horrible interest of their own for me ever since. Sometimes with certain old portraits in the picture-gallery, which I actually dreaded to look at, after what I had found out. There were periods when the results of this search of mine so horrified me, that I determined to give it up entirely; but I never could persevere in my resolution, the temptation to go on seemed at certain intervals to get too strong for me, and then I yielded to it again and again. At last I found the book that had belonged to the monks, with the whole of the prophecy written in the blank leaf. This first success encouraged me to get back further yet in the family records. I had discovered nothing hitherto of the identity of the mysterious portrait, but the same intuitive conviction which had assured me of its extraordinary resemblance to my uncle Stephen, seemed also to assure me that he must be more closely connected with the prophecy, and must know more of it than anyone else. I had no means of holding any communication with him, no means of satisfying myself whether this strange idea of mine were right or wrong, until the day when my doubts were settled for ever, by the same terrible proof which is now present to me in this very room."

He paused for a moment, and looked at me intently and suspiciously; then asked if I believed all he had said to me so far. My instant reply in the affirmative seemed to satisfy his doubts, and he went on:

"On a fine evening in February, I was standing alone in one of the deserted rooms of the western turret at the Abbey looking at the sunset. Just before the sun went down, I felt a sensation stealing over me which it is impossible to explain. I saw nothing, heard nothing, knew nothing. This utter self-oblivion came suddenly; it was not fainting, for I did not fall to the ground, did not move an inch from my place. If such a thing could be, I should say it was the temporary separation of soul and body, without death: but all description of my situation at that time is impossible. Call my state what you will, trance or catalepsy, I know that I remained standing by the window utterly unconscious—dead, mind and body—until the sun had set. Then I came to my senses again; and then, when I opened my eyes, there was the apparition of Stephen

Monkton standing opposite to me, faintly luminous, just as it stands opposite me at this very moment by your side."

"Was this before the news of the duel reached England?" I asked.

"*Two weeks before* the news of it reached us at Wincot. And even when we heard of the duel, we did not hear of the day on which it was fought. I only found that out when the document which you have read was published in the French newspaper. The date of that document, you will remember, is February 22nd, and it is stated that the duel was fought two days afterwards. I wrote down in my pocket-book, on the evening when I saw the phantom, the day of the month on which it first appeared to me. That day was the 24th of February."

He paused again, as if expecting me to say something. After the words he had just spoken, what could I say? what could I think?

"Even in the first horror of first seeing the apparition," he went on, "the prophecy against our house came to my mind, and with it the conviction that I beheld before me, in that spectral presence, the warning of my own doom. As soon as I recovered a little, I determined, nevertheless, to test the reality of what I saw—to find out whether I was the dupe of my own diseased fancy, or not. I left the turret; the phantom left it with me. I made an excuse to have the drawing-room at the Abbey brilliantly lighted up—the figure was still opposite me. I walked out into the park—it was there in the clear starlight. I went away from home, and travelled many miles to the sea-side; still the tall dark man in his death agony was with me. After this, I strove against the fatality no more. I returned to the Abbey, and tried to resign myself to my misery. But this was not to be. I had a hope that was dearer to me than my own life; I had one treasure belonging to me that I shuddered at the prospect of losing, and when the phantom presence stood a warning obstacle between me and this one treasure, this dearest hope—then my misery grew heavier than I could bear. You know what I am alluding to; you must have heard often that I was engaged to be married?"

"Yes, often. I have some acquaintance myself with Miss Elmslie."

"You never can know all she has sacrificed for me—never can imagine what I have felt for years and years past"—his voice trembled, and the tears came into his eyes—"but I dare not trust myself to speak of that: the thought of the old happy days in the Abbey almost breaks my heart now. Let me get back to the other subject. I must tell you that I kept the frightful vision which pursued me, at all times, and in all places, a secret from everybody; knowing the vile reports about my having inherited madness from my family, and fearing that an unfair advantage would be taken of any confession that I might make. Though the phantom always stood opposite to me, and therefore always appeared either before or by the side of any person to whom I spoke, I soon schooled myself to hide from others that I was looking at it, except on rare occasions—when I have perhaps betrayed myself to you. But my self-possession availed me nothing with Ada. The day of our marriage was approaching."

He stopped and shuddered. I waited in silence till he had controlled himself.

"Think," he went on, "think of what I must have suffered at looking always on that hideous vision, whenever I looked on my betrothed wife! Think of my taking her hand, and seeming to take it through the figure of the apparition! Think of the calm angel-face and the tortured spectre-face being always together, whenever my eyes met hers! Think of this, and you will not wonder that I betrayed my secret to her. She eagerly entreated to know the worst—nay more, she insisted on knowing it. At her bidding I told all; and then left her free to break our engagement. The thought of death was in my heart as I spoke the parting words—death by my own act, if life still held out after our separation. She suspected that thought; she knew it, and never left me till her good influence had destroyed it for ever. But for her, I should not have been alive now—but for her, I should never have attempted the project which has brought me here."

"Do you mean that it was at Miss Elmslie's suggestion that you came to Naples?" I asked in amazement.

"I mean that what she said, suggested the design which has brought me to Naples," he answered. "While I believed that the phantom had appeared to me as the fatal messenger of death, there was no comfort, there was misery rather in hearing her say that no power on earth should make her desert me, and that she would live for me, and for me only, through every trial. But it was far different when we afterwards reasoned together about the purpose which the apparition had come to fulfil—far different when she showed me that its mission might be for good, instead of for evil; and that the warning it was sent to give, might be to my profit instead of to my loss. At those words, the new idea which gave the new hope of life came to me in an instant. I believed then, what I believe now, that I have a supernatural warrant for my errand here. In that faith I live; without it I should die. *She* never ridiculed it, never scorned it as insanity. Mark what I say! The spirit that appeared to me in the Abbey, that has never left me since, that stands there now by your side, warns me to escape from the fatality which hangs over our race, and commands me, if I would avoid it, to bury the unburied dead. Mortal loves and mortal interests must bow to that awful bidding. The spectre-presence will never leave me till I have sheltered the corpse that cries to the earth to cover it! I dare not return—I dare not marry till I have filled the place that is empty in Wincot vault."

His eyes flashed and dilated; his voice deepened; a fanatic ecstasy shone in his expression as he uttered these words. Shocked and grieved as I was, I made no attempt to remonstrate or to reason with him. It would have been useless to have referred to any of the usual common-places about optical delusions, or diseased imaginations—worse than useless to have attempted to account by natural causes for any of the extraordinary coincidences and events of which he had spoken. Briefly as he had referred to Miss Elmslie, he had said enough to show that the only hope of the poor girl who loved him best and had known him longest of any one, was in humouring his delusions to the last. How faithfully she still clung to the belief that she could restore him! How resolutely was she sacrificing herself to his morbid fancies, in the hope of a happy future that might never come! Little as I knew of Miss Elmslie, the mere thought of her situation, as I now reflected on it, made me feel sick at heart.

"They call me 'Mad Monkton!' " he exclaimed, suddenly breaking the silence between us during the last few minutes.

"Here and in England everybody believes I am out of my senses, except Ada and you. She has been my salvation; and you will be my salvation too. Something told me that, when I first met you walking in the Villa Reale. I struggled against the strong desire that was in me to trust my secret to you; but I could resist it no longer when I saw you to-night at the ball—the phantom seemed to draw me on to you, as you stood alone in the quiet room. Tell me more of that idea of yours about finding the place where the duel was fought. If I set out to-morrow to seek for it myself, where must I go to first?—where?" He stopped; his strength was evidently becoming exhausted, and his mind was growing confused. "What am I to do? I can't remember. You know everything—will you not help me? My misery has made me unable to help myself!"

He stopped, murmured something about failing if he went to the frontier alone, and spoke confusedly of delays that might be fatal; then tried to utter the name of "Ada"; but in pronouncing the first letter his voice faltered, and turning abruptly from me he burst into tears.

My pity for him got the better of my prudence at that moment, and without thinking of responsibilities, I promised at once to do for him whatever he asked. The wild triumph in his expression, as he started up and seized my hand, showed me that I had better have been more cautious; but it was too late now to retract what I had said. The next best thing to do was to try if I could not induce him to compose himself a little, and then to go away and think coolly over the whole affair by myself.

"Yes, yes," he rejoined, in answer to the few words I now spoke to try and calm him, "don't be afraid about me. After what you have said, I'll answer for my own coolness and composure under all emergencies. I have been so long used to the apparition that I hardly feel its presence at all except on rare occasions. Besides, I have here, in this little packet of letters, the medicine for every malady of the sick heart. They are Ada's letters; I read them to calm me whenever my misfortune seems to get the better of my endurance. I wanted that half hour to read them in to-night, before you came, to make myself fit to see you; and I shall go through them again after you are gone. So, once more don't be afraid about me. I know I shall succeed with your help; and Ada shall thank you as you deserve to be thanked when we get back to England. If you hear the fools at Naples talk about my being mad, don't trouble yourself to contradict them: the scandal is so contemptible that it must end by contradicting itself."

I left him, promising to return early the next day.

When I got back to my hotel, I felt that any idea of sleeping, after all that I had seen and heard, was out of the question. So I lit my pipe, and sitting by the window—how it refreshed my mind just then to look at the calm moonlight!—tried to think what it would be best to do. In the first place, any appeal to doctors or to Alfred's friends in England was out of the question. I could not persuade myself that his intellect was sufficiently disordered to justify me, under existing circumstances, in disclosing the secret which he had entrusted to my keeping. In the second place, all attempts on my part to induce him to abandon the idea of searching out his uncle's remains would be utterly useless after what I had incautiously said to him. Having settled these two conclusions, the only really great difficulty which remained to perplex me was whether I was justified in aiding him to execute his extraordinary purpose.

Supposing that with my help he found Mr. Monkton's body, and took it back with him to England, was it right in me thus to lend myself to promoting the marriage which would most likely follow these events—a marriage which it might be the duty of every one to prevent at all hazards? This set me thinking about the extent of his madness, or, to speak more mildly and more correctly, of his delusion. Sane he certainly was on ordinary subjects; nay, in all the narrative parts of what he had said to me on this very evening he had spoken clearly and connectedly. As for the story of the apparition, other men, with intellects as clear as the intellects of their neighbours, had fancied themselves pursued by a phantom, and had even written about it in a high strain of philosophical speculation. It was plain that the real hallucination in the case now before me, lay in Monkton's conviction of the truth of the old prophecy, and in his idea that the fancied apparition was a supernatural warning to him to evade its denunciations. And it was equally clear that both delusions had been produced, in the first instance, by the lonely life he had led, acting on a naturally excitable temperament, which was rendered further liable to moral disease by an hereditary taint of insanity.

Was this curable? Miss Elmslie, who knew him far better than I did, seemed by her conduct to think so. Had I any reason or right to determine off-hand that she was mistaken? Supposing I refused to go to the frontier with him, he would then most certainly depart by himself, to commit all sorts of errors, and perhaps to meet with all sorts of accidents; while I, an idle man, with my time entirely at my own disposal, was stopping at Naples, and leaving him to his fate after I had suggested the plan of his expedition, and had encouraged him to confide in me. In this way I kept turning the subject over and over again in my mind—being quite free, let me add, from looking at it in any other than a practical point of view. I firmly believed, as a derider of all ghost stories, that Alfred was deceiving himself in fancying that he had seen the apparition of his uncle, before the news of Mr. Monkton's death reached England; and I was on this account therefore uninfluenced by the slightest infection of my unhappy friend's delusions, when I at last fairly decided to accompany him in his extraordinary search. Possibly my harum-scarum fondness for excitement at that time, biassed me a little in forming my resolution; but I must add, in common justice to myself, that I also acted from motives of real sympathy for Monkton, and from a sincere wish to allay, if I could, the anxiety of the poor girl who was still so faithfully waiting and hoping for him far away in England.

Certain arrangements preliminary to our departure, which I found myself obliged to make after a second interview with Alfred, betrayed the object of our journey to most of our Neapolitan friends. The astonishment of everybody was of course unbounded, and the nearly universal suspicion that I must be as mad in my way as Monkton himself, showed itself pretty plainly in my presence. Some people actually tried to combat my resolution by telling me what a shameless profligate Stephen Monkton had been—as if I had a strong personal interest in hunting out his remains! Ridicule moved me as little as any arguments of this sort; my mind was made up, and I was as obstinate then as I am now.

In two days' time I had got everything ready, and had ordered the travelling carriage to the door some hours earlier than we had originally settled. We were jovially threatened with "a parting cheer" by all our English acquaintances, and I thought it desirable to avoid this on my friend's account; for he had been more excited, as it was, by the preparations for the journey than I at all liked. Accordingly, soon after sunrise, without a soul in the street to stare at us, we privately left Naples.

Nobody will wonder, I think, that I experienced some difficulty in realising my own position, and shrank instinctively from looking forward a single day into the future, when I now found myself starting, in company with "Mad Monkton," to hunt for the body of a dead duellist all along the frontier line of the Roman states!

Chapter Five

I had settled it in my own mind that we had better make the town of Fondi, close on the frontier, our head-quarters, to begin with; and I had arranged, with the assistance of the Embassy, that the leaden coffin should follow us so far, securely nailed up in its packing case. Besides our passports, we were well furnished with letters of introduction to the local authorities at most of the important frontier towns, and to crown all, we had money enough at our command (thanks to Monkton's vast fortune) to make sure of the services of anyone whom we wanted to assist us, all along our line of search. These various resources ensured us every facility for action—provided always that we succeeded in discovering the body of the dead duellist. But, in the very probable event of our failing to do this, our future prospects—more especially after the responsibility I had undertaken—were of anything but an agreeable nature to contemplate. I confess I felt uneasy, almost hopeless, as we posted, in the dazzling Italian sunshine, along the road to Fondi.

We made an easy two days' journey of it; for I had insisted, on Monkton's account, that we should travel slowly.

On the first day the excessive agitation of my companion a little alarmed me; he showed, in many ways, more symptoms of a disordered mind than I had yet observed in him. On the second day, however, he seemed to get accustomed to contemplate calmly the new idea of the search on which we were bent, and, except on one point, he was cheerful and composed enough. Whenever his dead uncle formed the subject of conversation, he still persisted—on the strength of the old prophecy, and under the influence of the apparition which he saw, or thought he saw, always—in asserting that the corpse of Stephen Monkton, wherever it was, lay yet unburied. On every other topic he deferred to me with the utmost readiness and docility; on this, he maintained his strange opinion with an obstinacy which set reason and persuasion alike at defiance.

On the third day we rested at Fondi. The packing case with the coffin in it, reached us, and was deposited in a safe place under lock and key. We engaged some mules, and found a man to act as guide who knew the country thoroughly. It occurred to me that we had better begin by confiding the real object of our journey only to the most trustworthy people we could find among the better-educated classes. For this reason we followed, in one respect, the example of the duelling-party, by starting, early on the morning of the fourth day, with sketch-books and colour-boxes, as if we were only artists in search of the picturesque.

After travelling some hours in a northerly direction within the Roman frontier, we halted to rest ourselves and our mules at a wild little village, far out of the track of tourists in general.

The only person of the smallest importance in the place was the priest, and to him I addressed my first inquiries, leaving Monkton to await my return with the guide. I spoke Italian quite fluently and correctly enough for my purpose, and was extremely polite and cautious in introducing my business; but, in spite of all the pains I took, I only succeeded in frightening and bewildering the poor priest more and more with every fresh word I said to him. The idea of a duelling-party and a dead man seemed to scare him out of his senses. He bowed, fidgeted, cast his eyes up to heaven, and piteously shrugging his shoulders, told me, with rapid Italian circumlocution, that he had not the faintest idea of what I was talking about. This was my first failure. I confess I was weak enough to feel a little dispirited when I joined Monkton and the guide.

After the heat of the day was over, we resumed our journey.

About three miles from the village, the road, or rather cart-track, branched off in two directions. The path to the right, our guide informed us, led up among the mountains to a convent about six miles off. If we penetrated beyond the convent, we should soon reach the Neapolitan frontier. The path to the left led far inwards on the Roman territory, and would conduct us to a small town where we could sleep for the night. Now the Roman territory presented the first and fittest field for our search, and the convent was always within reach, supposing we returned to Fondi unsuccessful. Besides, the path to the left led over the widest part of the country we were starting to explore; and I was always for vanquishing the greatest difficulty first—so we decided manfully on turning to the left. The expedition in which this resolution involved us lasted a whole week, and produced no results. We discovered absolutely nothing, and returned to our head-quarters at Fondi so completely baffled that we did not know whither to turn our steps next.

I was made much more uneasy by the effect of our failure on Monkton than by the failure itself. His resolution appeared to break down altogether as soon as we began to retrace our steps. He became first fretful and capricious, then silent and desponding. Finally, he sank into a lethargy of body and mind that seriously alarmed me. On the morning after our return to Fondi, he showed a strange tendency to sleep incessantly, which made me suspect the existence of some physical malady in his brain. The whole day he hardly exchanged a word with me, and seemed to be never fairly awake. Early the next morning I went into his room, and found him as silent and lethargic as ever. His servant, who was with us, informed me that Alfred had once or twice before exhibited such physical symptoms of mental exhaustion as we were now observing during his father's lifetime at Wincot Abbey. This piece of information made me feel easier, and left my mind free to return to the consideration of the errand which had brought us to Fondi.

I resolved to occupy the time until my companion got better in prosecuting our search by myself. That path to the right hand which led to the convent, had not yet been explored. If I set off to trace it, I need not be away from Monkton more than one night; and I should at least be able on my return to give him the satisfaction of knowing that one more uncertainty regarding the place of the duel had been cleared up. These considerations decided me. I left a message for my friend, in case he asked where I had gone, and set out once more for the village at which we had halted when starting on our first expedition.

Intending to walk to the convent, I parted company with the guide and the mules where the track branched off, leaving them to go back to the village and await my return.

For the first four miles the path gently ascended through an open country, then became abruptly much steeper, and led me deeper and deeper among thickets and endless woods. By the time my watch informed me that I must have nearly walked my appointed distance, the view was bounded on all sides, and the sky was shut out overhead, by an impervious screen of leaves and branches. I still followed my only guide, the steep path; and in ten minutes, emerging suddenly on a plot of tolerably clear and level ground, I saw the convent before me.

It was a dark, low, sinister-looking place. Not a sign of life or movement was visible anywhere about it. Green stains streaked the once white façade of the chapel in all directions. Moss clustered thick in every crevice of the heavy scowling wall that surrounded the convent. Long lank weeds grew out of the fissures of roof and parapet, and drooping far downward, waved wearily in and out of the barred dormitory windows. The very cross opposite the entrance-gate, with a shocking life-sized figure in wood nailed to it, was so beset at the base with crawling creatures, and looked so slimy green, and rotten all the way up, that I absolutely shrank from it.

A bell-rope with a broken handle hung by the gate. I approached it—hesitated, I hardly knew why—looked up at the convent again, and then walked round to the back of the building, partly to gain time to consider what I had better do next; partly from an unaccountable curiosity that urged me, strangely to myself, to see all I could of the outside of the place before I attempted to gain admission at the gate.

At the back of the convent I found an out-house, built on to the wall—a clumsy, decayed building, with the greater part of the roof fallen in, and with a jagged hole in one of its sides, where in all probability a window had once been. Behind the outhouse the trees grew thicker than ever. As I looked towards them, I could not determine whether the ground beyond me rose or fell—whether it was grassy, or earthy, or rocky. I could see nothing but the all-pervading leaves, brambles, ferns, and long grass.

Not a sound broke the oppressive stillness. No bird's note rose from the leafy wilderness around me; no voices spoke in the convent garden behind the scowling wall; no clock struck in the chapel-tower; no dog barked in the ruined out-house. The dead silence deepened the solitude of the place inexpressibly. I began to feel it weighing on my spirits—the more because woods were never favourite places with me to walk in. The sort of pastoral happiness which poets often represent, when they sing of life in the woods, never, to my mind, has half the charm of life on the mountain or in the plain. When I am in a wood, I miss the boundless loveliness of the sky, and the delicious softness that distance gives to the earthly view beneath. I feel oppressively the change which the free air suffers when it gets imprisoned among leaves; and I am always awed, rather than pleased, by that mysterious still light which shines with such a strange dim lustre in deep places among trees. It may convict me of want of taste and absence of due feeling for the marvellous beauties of vegetation, but I must frankly own that I never penetrate far into a wood without finding that the getting out of it again is the pleasantest part of my walk—the getting out on to the barest down, the wildest hill-side, the bleakest mountain-top— the getting out anywhere so that I can see the sky over me and the view before me as far as my eye can reach.

After such a confession as I have now made, it will appear surprising to no one that I should have felt the strongest possible inclination, while I stood by the ruined out-house, to retrace my steps at once, and make the best of my way out of the wood. I had indeed actually turned to depart, when the remembrance of the errand which had brought me to the convent suddenly stayed my feet. It seemed doubtful whether I should be admitted into the building if I rang the bell; and more than doubtful, if I were let in, whether the inhabitants would be able to afford me any clue to the information of which I was in search. However, it was my duty to Monkton to leave no means of helping him in his desperate object untried; so I resolved to go round to the front of the convent again, and ring the gate-bell at all hazards.

By the merest chance I looked up as I passed the side of the out-house where the jagged hole was, and noticed that it was pierced rather high in the wall.

As I stopped to observe this, the closeness of the atmosphere in the wood seemed to be affecting me more unpleasantly than ever.

I waited a minute and untied my cravat.

Closeness?—Surely it was something more than that. The air was even more distasteful to my nostrils than to my lungs. There was some faint, indescribable smell loading it—some smell of which I had never had any previous experience—some smell which I thought (now that my attention was directed to it) grew more and more certainly traceable to its source the nearer I advanced to the out-house.

By the time I had tried the experiment two or three times, and had made myself sure of this fact, my curiosity became excited. There were plenty of fragments of stone and brick lying about me. I gathered some of them together, and piled them up below the hole, then mounted to the top, and, feeling rather ashamed of what I was doing, peeped into the out-house.

The sight of horror that met my eyes the instant I looked through the hole, is as present to my memory now as if I had beheld it yesterday. I can hardly write of it at this distance of time without a thrill of the old terror running through me again to the heart.

The first impression conveyed to me, as I looked in, was of a long recumbent object, tinged with a lightish blue colour all over, extended on trestles, and bearing a certain hideous, half-formed resemblance to the human face and figure. I looked again, and felt certain of it. There were the prominences of the forehead, nose, and chin, dimly shown as under a veil—there, the round outline of the chest, and the hollow below it—there, the points of the knees, and the stiff, ghastly, upturned feet. I looked again, yet more attentively. My eyes got accustomed to the dim light streaming in through the broken roof; and I satisfied myself, judging by the great length of the body from head to foot, that I was looking at the corpse of a man—a corpse that had apparently once had a sheet spread over it—and that had lain rotting on the trestles under the open sky long enough for the linen to take the livid, light-blue tinge of mildew and decay which now covered it.

How long I remained with my eyes fixed on that dread sight of death, on that tombless, terrible wreck of humanity, poisoning the still air, and seeming even to stain the faint descending light that disclosed it, I know not. I remember a dull, distant sound among the trees, as if the breeze were rising—the slow creeping on of the sound to near the place where I stood—the noiseless, whirling fall of a dead leaf on the corpse below me, through the gap in the out-house roof—and the effect of awakening my energies, of relaxing the heavy strain on my mind, which even the slight change wrought in the scene I beheld by the falling leaf, produced in me immediately. I descended to the ground, and, sitting down on the heap of stones, wiped away the thick perspiration which covered my face, and which I now became aware of for the first time. It was something more than the hideous spectacle unexpectedly offered to my eyes which had shaken my nerves, as I felt that they were shaken now. Monkton's prediction that, if we succeeded in discovering his uncle's body, we should find it unburied, recurred to me the instant I saw the trestles and their ghastly burden. I felt assured on the instant that I had found the dead man—the old prophecy recurred to my memory—a strange yearning sorrow, a vague foreboding of ill, an inexplicable terror, as I thought of the poor lad who was awaiting my return in the distant town, struck through me with a chill of superstitious dread, robbed me of my judgment and resolution, and left me, when I had at last recovered myself, weak and dizzy as if I had just suffered under some pang of overpowering physical pain.

I hastened round to the convent gate, and rang impatiently at the bell—waited a little while, and rang again—then heard footsteps.

In the middle of the gate, just opposite my face, there was a small sliding panel, not more than a few inches long; this was presently pushed aside from within. I saw, through a bit of iron grating, two dull, light grey eyes staring vacantly at me, and heard a feeble, husky voice saying:—

"What may you please to want?"

"I am a traveller——" I began.

"We live in a miserable place. We have nothing to show travellers here."

"I don't come to see anything. I have an important question to ask, which I believe someone in this convent will be able to answer. If you are not willing to let me in, at least come out and speak to me here."

"Are you alone?"

"Quite alone."

"Are there no women with you?"

"None."

The gate was slowly unbarred; and an old Capuchin, very infirm, very suspicious, and very dirty, stood before me. I was far too excited and impatient to waste any time in prefatory phrases; so telling the monk at once how I had looked through the hole in the out-house, and what I had seen inside, I asked him in plain terms who the man had been whose corpse I had beheld, and why the body was left unburied?

The old Capuchin listened to me with watery eyes that twinkled suspiciously. He had a battered tin snuff-box in his hand; and his finger and thumb slowly chased a few scattered grains of snuff round and round the inside of the box all the time I was speaking. When I had done, he shook his head, and said, "that was certainly an ugly sight in the out-house; one of the ugliest sights that ever I had seen in all my life!"

"I don't want to talk of the sight," I rejoined impatiently; "I want to know who the man was, how he died, and why he is not decently buried. Can you tell me?"

The monk's finger and thumb having captured three or four grains of snuff at last, he slowly drew them into his nostrils, holding the box open under his nose the while, to prevent the possibility of wasting even one grain, sniffed once or twice, luxuriously—closed the box—then looked at me again, with his eyes watering and twinkling more suspiciously than before.

"Yes," said the monk, "that's an ugly sight in our out-house—a very ugly sight, certainly!"

I never had more difficulty in keeping my temper in my life, than at that moment. I succeeded, however, in repressing a very disrespectful expression on the subject of monks in general, which was on the tip of my tongue, and made another attempt to conquer the old man's exasperating reserve. Fortunately for my chances of succeeding with him, I was a snuff-taker myself; and I had a box full of excellent English snuff in my pocket, which I now produced as a bribe. It was my last resource.

"I thought your box seemed empty just now," said I; "will you try a pinch out of mine?"

The offer was accepted with an almost youthful alacrity of gesture. The Capuchin took the largest pinch I ever saw held between any man's finger and thumb, inhaled it slowly, without spilling a single grain—half closed his eyes—and, wagging his head gently, patted me paternally on the back.

"Oh! my son!" said the monk, "what delectable snuff! Oh, my son and amiable traveller, give the spiritual father who loves you, yet another tiny, tiny pinch!"

"Let me fill your box for you. I shall have plenty left for myself."

The battered tin snuff-box was given to me before I had done speaking—the paternal hand patted my back more approvingly than ever—the feeble, husky voice grew glib and eloquent in my praise. I had evidently found out the weak side of the old Capuchin; and, on returning him his box, I took instant advantage of the discovery.

"Excuse my troubling you on the subject again," I said, "but I have particular reasons for wanting to hear all that you can tell me in explanation of that horrible sight in the out-house."

"Come in," answered the monk.

He drew me inside the gate, closed it, and then leading the way across a grass-grown courtyard, looking out on a weedy kitchen garden, showed me into a long room with a low ceiling, a dirty dresser, a few rudely-carved stall seats, and one or two grim mildewed pictures for ornaments. This was the sacristy.

"There's nobody here, and it's nice and cool," said the old Capuchin. It was so damp that I actually shivered. "Would you like to see the church?" said the monk; "a jewel of a church, if we could only keep it in repair; but we can't. Ah! malediction and misery, we are too poor to keep our church in repair!"

Here he shook his head, and began fumbling with a large bunch of keys.

"Never mind the church now!" said I. "Can you, or can you not, tell me what I want to know?"

"Everything, from beginning to end—absolutely everything! Why, I answered the gate bell—I always answer the gate bell here," said the Capuchin.

"What, in heaven's name, has the gate bell to do with the unburied corpse in your out-house?"

"Listen, son of mine, and you shall know. Some time ago—some months—ah, me, I'm old; I've lost my memory; I don't know how many months—ah! miserable me, what a very old, old monk I am!" Here he comforted himself with another pinch of my snuff.

"Never mind the exact time," said I. "I don't care about that."

"Good," said the Capuchin. "Now I can go on. Well, let us say, it is some months ago—we in this convent are all at breakfast—wretched, wretched breakfast, son of mine in this convent!—we are at breakfast, and we hear *bang! bang!* twice over. 'Guns,' says I. 'What are they shooting for?' says brother Jeremy. 'Game,' says brother Vincent. 'Aha! game,' says brother Jeremy. 'If I hear more, I shall send out and discover what it means,' says the father superior. We hear no more, and we go on with our wretched breakfasts."

"Where did the report of fire-arms come from?" I inquired.

"From down below, beyond the big trees at the back of the convent, where there's some clear ground—nice ground, if it wasn't for the pools and puddles. But, ah, misery! how damp we are in these parts! how very, very damp!"

"Well, what happened after the report of fire-arms?"

"You shall hear. We are still at breakfast, all silent—for what have we to talk about here? What have we but our devotions, our kitchen garden, and our wretched, wretched bits of breakfasts and dinners? I say we are all silent, when there comes suddenly such a ring at the bell as never was heard before—a very devil of a ring— a ring that caught us all with our bits—our wretched, wretched bits!—in our mouths, and stopped us before we could swallow them. 'Go, brother of mine!' says the father superior to me—'go, it is your duty—go to the gate.' I am brave—a very lion of a Capuchin. I slip out on tip-toe—I wait—I listen—I pull back our little shutter in the gate—I wait, I listen again—I peep through the hole—nothing, absolutely nothing, that I can see. I am brave—I am not to be daunted. What do I do next? I open the gate. Ah! Sacred Mother of Heaven, what do I behold lying all along our threshold? A man—dead!—a big man; bigger than you, bigger than me, bigger than anybody in this convent—buttoned up tight in a fine coat, with black eyes, staring, staring up at the sky; and blood soaking through and through the front of his shirt. What do I do? I scream once—I scream twice—and run back to the father superior!"

All the particulars of the fatal duel which I had gleaned from the French newspaper in Monkton's room at Naples, recurred vividly to my memory. The suspicion that I had felt when I looked into the out-house, became a certainty as I listened to the old monk's last words.

"So far I understand," said I. "The corpse I have just seen in the out-house, is the corpse of the man whom you found dead outside your gate. Now tell me why you have not given the remains decent burial?"

"Wait—wait—wait," answered the Capuchin. "The father superior hears me scream, and comes out; we all run together to the gate; we lift up the big man, and look at him close. Dead! dead as this" (smacking the dresser with his hand). "We look again, and see a bit of paper pinned to the collar of his coat. Aha! son of mine, you start at that. I thought I should make you start at last."

I have started indeed. That paper was doubtless the leaf mentioned in the second's unfinished narrative as having been torn out of his pocket-book, and inscribed with the statement of how the dead man had lost his life. If proof positive were wanted to identify the dead body, here was such proof found.

"What do you think was written on the bit of paper?" continued the Capuchin. "We read, and shudder. This dead man has been killed in a duel—he, the desperate, the miserable, has died in the commission of mortal sin; and the men who saw the killing of him, ask us Capuchins, holy men, servants of Heaven, children of our lord the pope—they ask *us* to give him burial! Oh! but we are outraged when we read that; we groan, we wring our hands, we turn away, we tear our beards, we——"

"Wait one moment," said I, seeing that the old man was heating himself with his narrative, and was likely, until I stopped him, to talk more and more fluently to less and less purpose—"wait a moment. Have you preserved the paper that was pinned to the dead man's coat; and can I look at it?"

The Capuchin seemed on the point of giving me an answer, when he suddenly checked himself. I saw his eyes wander away from my face, and at the same moment heard a door softly opened and closed behind me.

Looking round immediately, I observed another monk in the sacristy—a tall, lean, black-bearded man, in whose presence my old friend with the snuff-box suddenly became quite decorous and devotional to look at. I suspected I was in the presence of the father superior; and I found that I was right the moment he addressed me.

"I am the father superior of this convent," he said in quiet, clear tones, and looking me straight in the face while he spoke, with coldly attentive eyes. "I have heard the latter part of your conversation, and I wish to know why you are so particularly anxious to see the piece of paper that was pinned to the dead man's coat?"

The coolness with which he avowed that he had been listening, and the quietly imperative manner in which he put his concluding questions, perplexed and startled me. I hardly knew at first what tone I ought to take in answering him. He observed my hesitation, and attributing it to the wrong cause, signed to the old Capuchin to retire. Humbly stroking his long grey beard, and furtively consoling himself with a private pinch of the "delectable snuff," my venerable friend shuffled out of the room, making a profound obeisance at the door just before he disappeared.

"Now," said the father superior, as coldly as ever; "I am waiting, sir, for your reply."

"You shall have it in the fewest possible words," said I, answering him in his own tone. "I find, to my disgust and horror, there is an unburied corpse in an out-house attached to this convent. I believe that corpse to be the body of an English gentleman of rank and fortune, who was killed in a duel. I have come into this neighbourhood, with the nephew and only relation of the slain man, for the express purpose of recovering his remains; and I wish to see the paper found on the body, because I believe that paper will identify it to the satisfaction of the relative to whom I have referred. Do you find my reply sufficiently straight-forward? And do you mean to give me permission to look at the paper?"

"I am satisfied with your reply, and see no reason for refusing you a sight of the paper," said the father superior; "but I have something to say first. In speaking of the impression produced on you by beholding the corpse, you used the words 'disgust' and 'horror.' This licence of expression in relation to what you have seen in the precincts of a convent, proves to me that you are out of the pale of the Holy Catholic Church. You have no right, therefore, to expect any explanation; but I will give you one, nevertheless, as a favour. The slain man died, unabsolved, in the commission of mortal sin. We infer so much from the paper which we found on his body; and we know, by the evidence of our own eyes and ears, that he was killed on the territories of the church, and in the act of committing direct violation of those special laws against the crime of duelling, the strict enforcement of which the holy father himself has urged on the faithful throughout his dominions, by letters signed with his own hand. Inside this convent the ground is consecrated; and we Catholics are not accustomed to bury the outlaws of our religion, the enemies of our Holy Father, and the violators of our most sacred laws, in consecrated ground. Outside this convent, we have no rights and no powers; and, if we had both, we should remember that we are monks, not gravediggers, and that the only burial with which we can have any concern, is burial with prayers of the church. That is all the explanation I think it necessary to give. Wait for me here, and you shall see the paper." With those words the father superior left the room as quietly as he had entered it.

I had hardly time to think over this bitter and ungracious explanation, and to feel a little piqued by the language and manner of the person who had given it to me, before the father superior returned with the paper in his hand. He placed it before me on the dresser; and I read hurriedly traced in pencil, the following lines:

"This paper is attached to the body of the late Mr. Stephen Monkton, an Englishman of distinction. He has been shot in a duel, conducted with perfect gallantry and honour on both sides. His body is placed at the door of this convent, to receive burial at the hands of its inmates, the survivors of the encounter being obliged to separate and secure their safety by immediate flight. I, the second of the slain man, and the writer of this explanation, certify, on my word of honour as a gentleman, that the shot which killed my principal on the instant, was fired fairly, in the strictest accordance with the rules laid down beforehand for the conduct of the duel.

(Signed) "F."

"F." I recognised easily enough as the initial letter of Monsieur Foulon's name, the second of Mr. Monkton, who had died of consumption at Paris.

The discovery and the identification were now complete. Nothing remained but to break the news to Alfred, and to get permission to remove the remains in the out-house. I began almost to doubt the evidence of my own senses, when I reflected that the apparent impracticable object with which we had left Naples was already, by the merest chance, virtually accomplished.

"The evidence of the paper is decisive," I said, handing it back. "There can be no doubt that the remains in the out-house are the remains of which we have been in search. May I inquire if any obstacles will be thrown in our way, should the late Mr. Monkton's nephew wish to remove his uncle's body to the family burial-place in England?"

"Where is this nephew?" asked the father superior.

"He is now waiting my return at the town of Fondi."

"Is he in a position to prove his relationship?"

"Certainly; he has papers with him which will place it beyond a doubt."

"Let him satisfy the civil authorities of his claim, and he need expect no obstacle to his wishes from anyone here."

I was in no humour for talking a moment longer with my sour-tempered companion than I could help. The day was wearing on fast; and, whether night overtook me or not, I was resolved never to stop on my return till I got back to Fondi. Accordingly, after telling the father superior that he might expect to hear from me again immediately, I made my bow, and hastened out of the sacristy.

At the convent gate stood my old friend with the tin snuff-box, waiting to let me out.

"Bless you, my son," said the venerable recluse, giving me a farewell pat on the shoulder; "come back soon to your spiritual father who loves you; and amiably favour him with another tiny, tiny pinch of the delectable snuff."

Chapter Six

I returned at the top of my speed to the village where I had left the mules, had the animals saddled immediately, and succeeded in getting back to Fondi a little before sunset.

While ascending the stairs of our hotel, I suffered under the most painful uncertainty as to how I should best communicate the news of my discovery to Alfred. If I could not succeed in preparing him properly for my tidings, the result—with such an organisation as his—might be fatal. On opening the door of his room, I felt by no means sure of myself; and when I confronted him, his manner of receiving me took me so much by surprise that, for a moment or two, I lost my self-possession altogether.

Every trace of the lethargy in which he was sunk when I had last seen him, had disappeared. His eyes were bright, his cheeks deeply flushed. As I entered, he started up, and refused my offered hand.

"You have not treated me like a friend," he said passionately; "you had no right to continue the search unless I searched with you—you had no right to leave me here alone. I was wrong to trust you: you are no better than all the rest of them."

I had by this time recovered a little from my first astonishment, and was able to reply before he could say anything more. It was quite useless, in his present state, to reason with him, or to defend myself. I determined to risk everything, and break my news to him at once.

"You will treat me more justly, Monkton, when you know that I have been doing you good service during my absence," I said.

"Unless I am greatly mistaken, the object for which we have left Naples may be nearer attainment by both of us than——"

The flush left his cheeks almost in an instant. Some expression in my face, or some tone in my voice, of which I was not conscious, had revealed to his nervously-quickened perception more than I had intended that he should know at first. His eyes fixed themselves intently on mine; his hand grasped my arm; and he said to me in an eager whisper:

"Tell me the truth at once. Have you found him?"

It was too late to hesitate. I answered in the affirmative.

"Buried or unburied?"

His voice rose abruptly as he put the question, and his unoccupied hand fastened on my other arm.

"Unburied."

I had hardly uttered the word before the blood flew back into his cheeks; his eyes flashed again as they looked into mine, and he burst into a fit of triumphant laughter, which shocked and startled me inexpressibly.

"What did I tell you? What do you say to the old prophecy now?" he cried, dropping his hold on my arms, and pacing backwards and forwards in the room. "Own you were wrong. Own it, as all Naples shall own it, when once I have got him safe in his coffin!"

His laughter grew more and more violent. I tried to quiet him in vain. His servant and the landlord of the inn entered the room; but they only added fuel to the fire, and I made them go out again. As I shut the door on them, I observed lying on a table near at hand, the packet of letters from Miss Elmslie, which my unhappy friend preserved with such care, and read and re-read with such unfailing devotion. Looking towards me just when I passed by the table, the letters caught his eyes. The new hope for the future, in connection with the writer of them, which my news was already awakening in his heart, seemed to overwhelm him in an instant at sight of the treasured memorials that reminded him of his betrothed wife. His laughter ceased, his face changed, he ran to the table, caught the letters up in his hand, looked from them to me for one moment with an altered expression which went to my heart, then sank down on his knees at the table, laid his face on the letters, and burst into tears. I let the new emotion have its way uninterruptedly, and quitted the room, without saying a word. When I returned, after a lapse of some little time, I found him sitting quietly in his chair, reading one of the letters from the packet which rested on his knee.

His look was kindness itself; his gesture almost womanly in its gentleness as he rose to meet me, and anxiously held out his hand.

He was quite calm enough now to hear in detail all that I had to tell him. I suppressed nothing but the particulars of the state in which I had found the corpse. I assumed no right of direction as to the share he was to take in our future proceedings, with the exception of insisting beforehand that he should leave the absolute superintendence of the removal of the body to me, and that he should be satisfied with a sight of M. Foulon's paper, after receiving my assurance that the remains placed in the coffin were really and truly the remains of which we had been in search.

"Your nerves are not so strong as mine," I said, by way of apology for my apparent dictation; "and for that reason I must beg leave to assume the leadership in all that we have now to do, until I see the leaden coffin soldered down and safe in your possession. After that, I shall resign all my functions to you."

"I want words to thank you for your kindness," he answered. "No brother could have borne with me more affectionately, or helped me more patiently, than you."

He stopped, and grew thoughtful, then occupied himself in tying up slowly and carefully the packet of Miss Elmslie's letters, and then looked suddenly towards the vacant wall behind me, with that strange expression the meaning of which I knew so well. Since we had left Naples, I had purposely avoided exciting him by talking on the useless and shocking subject of the apparition by which he believed himself to be perpetually followed. Just now, however, he seemed so calm and collected—so little likely to be violently agitated by any allusion to the dangerous topic—that I ventured to speak out boldly.

"Does the phantom still appear to you," I asked, "as it appeared at Naples?"

He looked at me, and smiled.

"Did I not tell you that it followed me everywhere?" His eyes wandered back again to the vacant space, and he went on speaking in that direction, as if he had been continuing the conversation with some third person in the room. "We shall part," he said slowly and softly, "when the empty place is filled in Wincot vault.

Then I shall stand with Ada before the altar in the Abbey chapel; and when my eyes meet hers, they will see the tortured face no more."

Saying this, he leaned his head on his hand, sighed, and began repeating softly to himself the lines of the old prophecy:

> *When in Wincot vault a place*
> *Waits for one of Monkton's race:*
> *When that one forlorn shall lie*
> *Graveless under open sky,*
> *Beggared of six feet of earth,*
> *Though lord of acres from his birth—*
> *That shall be a certain sign*
> *Of the end of Monkton's line.*
> *Dwindling ever faster, faster,*
> *Dwindling to the last-left master;*
> *From Mortal ken, from light of day,*
> *Monkton's race shall pass away.*

Fancying that he pronounced the last lines a little incoherently, I tried to make him change the subject. He took no notice of what I said, and went on talking to himself.

"Monkton's race shall pass away!" he repeated; "but not with *me*. The fatality hangs over my head no longer. I shall bury the unburied dead; I shall fill the vacant place in Wincot vault. And then—then the new life, the life with Ada!"—That name seemed to recall him to himself. He drew his travelling desk towards him, placed the packet of letters in it, and then took out a sheet of paper. "I am going to write to Ada," he said, turning to me, "and tell her the good news. Her happiness, when she knows it, will be even greater than mine."

Worn out by the events of the day, I left him writing, and went to bed. I was, however, either too anxious or too tired to sleep. In this waking condition, my mind naturally occupied itself with the discovery at the convent, and with the events to which that discovery would in all probability lead. As I thought on the future, a depression for which I could not account weighed on my spirits. There was not the slightest reason for the vague melancholy forebodings that oppressed me. The remains, to the finding of which my unhappy friend attached so much importance, had been traced; they would certainly be placed at his disposal in a few days; he might take them to England by the first merchant vessel that sailed from Naples; and, the gratification of his strange caprice thus accomplished, there was at least some reason to hope that his mind might recover its tone, and that the new life he would lead at Wincot might result in making him a happy man. Such considerations as these were, in themselves, certainly not calculated to exert any melancholy influence over me; and yet, all through the night, the same inconceivable, unaccountable depression weighed heavily on my spirits—heavily through the hours of darkness—heavily, even when I walked out to breathe the first freshness of the early morning air.

With the day came the all-engrossing business of opening negotiations with the authorities.

Only those who have had to deal with Italian officials can imagine how our patience was tried by everyone with whom we came in contact. We were bandied about from one authority to the other, were stared at, cross-questioned, mystified—not in the least because the case presented any special difficulties or intricacies, but because it was absolutely necessary that every civil dignitary to whom we applied, should assert his own importance by leading us to our object in the most round-about manner possible. After our first day's experience of official life in Italy, I left the absurd formalities, which we had no choice but to perform, to be accomplished by Alfred alone, and applied myself to considering the really serious question of how the remains in the convent outhouse were to be safely removed.

The best plan that suggested itself to me was to write to a friend at Rome, where I knew that it was a custom to embalm the bodies of high dignitaries of the church, and where, I consequently inferred, such chemical assistance as was needed in our emergency might be obtained. I simply stated in my letter that the removal of the body was imperative, then described the condition in which I had found it, and engaged that no expense on our part should be spared if the right person or persons could be found to help us. Here again more difficulties interposed themselves, and more useless formalities were to be gone through; but, in the end, patience, perseverance, and money triumphed, and two men came expressly from Rome to undertake the duties we required of them.

It is unnecessary that I should shock the reader by entering into any detail in this part of my narrative. When I have said that the progress of decay was so far suspended by chemical means as to allow of the remains being placed in the coffin, and to ensure their being transported to England with perfect safety and convenience, I have said enough. After ten days had been wasted in useless delays and difficulties, I had the satisfaction of seeing the convent out-house empty at last; passed through a final ceremony of snuff-taking, or rather, of snuff-giving, with the old Capuchin; and ordered the travelling carriage to be ready at the inn door. Hardly a month had elapsed since our departure, when we entered Naples successful in the achievement of a design, which had been ridiculed as wildly impracticable by every friend of ours who had heard of it.

The first object to be accomplished on our return was to obtain the means of carrying the coffin to England—by sea, as a matter of course. All inquiries after a merchant vessel on the point of sailing for any British port, led to the most unsatisfactory results. There was only one way of ensuring the immediate transportation of the remains to England, and that was to hire a vessel. Impatient to return, and resolved not to lose sight of the coffin till he had seen it placed in Wincot vault, Monkton decided immediately on hiring the first ship that could be obtained. The vessel in port which we were informed could soonest be got ready for sea, was a Sicilian brig; and this vessel my friend accordingly engaged. The best dockyard artisans that could be got were set to work, and the smartest captain and crew to be picked up on an emergency in Naples, were chosen to navigate the brig.

Monkton, after again expressing in the warmest terms his gratitude for the services I had rendered him, disclaimed any intention of asking me to accompany him on the voyage to England. Greatly to his surprise and delight, however, I offered of my own accord to take passage in the brig. The strange coincidences I had witnessed, the extraordinary discovery I had hit on, since our first meeting in Naples, had made his one great interest in life my one great interest for the time being, as well. I shared none of his delusions, poor fellow; but it is hardly an exaggeration to say that my eagerness to follow our remarkable adventure to its end, was as great as his anxiety to see the coffin laid in Wincot vault. Curiosity influenced me, I am afraid, almost as strongly as friendship, when I offered myself as the companion of his voyage home.

We set sail for England on a calm and lovely afternoon.

For the first time since I had known him, Monkton seemed to be in high spirits. He talked and jested on all sorts of subjects, and laughed at me for allowing my cheerfulness to be affected by the dread of sea-sickness. I had really no such fear; it was my excuse to my friend for a return of that unaccountable depression under which I had suffered at Fondi. Everything was in our favour; everybody on board the brig was in good spirits. The captain was delighted with the vessel; the crew, Italians and Maltese, were in high glee at the prospect of making a short voyage on high wages in a well-provisioned ship. I alone felt heavy at heart. There was no valid reason that I could assign to myself for the melancholy that oppressed me, and yet I struggled against it in vain.

Late on our first night at sea, I made a discovery which was by no means calculated to restore my spirits to their usual equilibrium. Monkton was in the cabin, on the floor of which had been placed the packing-case containing the coffin; and I was on deck. The wind had fallen almost to a calm, and I was lazily watching the sails of the brig as they flapped from time to time against the masts, when the captain approached, and, drawing me out of hearing of the man at the helm, whispered in my ear:

"There's something wrong among the men forward. Did you observe how suddenly they all became silent just before sunset?"

I had observed it, and told him so.

"There's a Maltese boy on board," pursued the captain, "who is a smart lad enough, but a bad one to deal with. I have found out that he has been telling the men there is a dead body inside that packing case of your friend's in the cabin."

My heart sank as he spoke. Knowing the superstitious irrationality of sailors—of foreign sailors especially—I had taken care to spread a report on board the brig, before the coffin was shipped, that the packing-case contained a valuable marble statue which Mr. Monkton prized highly, and was unwilling to trust out of his own sight. How could this Maltese boy have discovered that the pretended statue was a human corpse? As I pondered over the question, my suspicions fixed themselves on Monkton's servant, who spoke Italian fluently, and whom I knew to be an incorrigible gossip. The man denied it when I charged him with betraying us, but I have never believed his denial to this day.

"The little imp won't say where he picked up this notion of his about the dead body," continued the captain. "It's not my place to pry into secrets; but I advise you to call the crew aft and contradict the boy, whether he speaks the truth or not. The men are a parcel of fools, who believe in ghosts, and all the rest of it. Some of them say they would never have signed our articles if they had known they were going to sail with a dead man; others only grumble; but I'm afraid we shall have some trouble with them all, in case of rough weather, unless the boy is contradicted by you or the other gentleman. The men say that if either you or your friend tell them on your words of honour that the Maltese is a liar, they will hand him up to be rope's ended accordingly; but that if you won't, they have made up their minds to believe the boy."

Here the captain paused, and awaited my answer. I could give him none. I felt hopeless under our desperate emergency. To get the boy punished by giving my word of honour to support a direct falsehood, was not to be thought of even for a moment. What other means of extrication from this miserable dilemma remained? None that I could think of. I thanked the captain for his attention to our interests, told him I would take time to consider what course I should pursue, and begged that he would say nothing to my friend about the discovery he had made. He promised to be silent, sulkily enough, and walked away from me.

We had expected the breeze to spring up with the morning, but no breeze came. As it wore on towards noon, the atmosphere became insufferably sultry, and the sea looked as smooth as glass. I saw the captain's eye turn often and anxiously to windward. Far away in that direction, and alone in the blue heaven, I observed a little black cloud, and asked if it would bring us any wind.

"More than we want," the captain replied shortly; and then, to my astonishment, ordered the crew aloft to take in sail. The execution of this manoeuvre showed but too plainly the temper of the men; they did their work sulkily and slowly, grumbling and murmuring among themselves. The captain's manner, as he urged them on with oaths and threats, convinced me we were in danger. I looked again to windward. The one little cloud had enlarged to a great bank of murky vapour, and the sea at the horizon had changed in colour.

"The squall will be on us before we know where we are," said the captain. "Go below; you will be only in the way here."

I descended to the cabin, and prepared Monkton for what was coming. He was still questioning me about what I had observed on deck, when the storm burst on us. We felt the little brig strain for an instant as if she would part in two, then she seemed to be swinging round with us, then to be quite still for a moment, trembling in every timber. Last, came a shock which hurled us from our seats, a deafening crash, and a flood of water pouring into the cabin. We clambered, half-drowned, to the deck. The brig had, in the nautical phrase, "broached to," and she now lay on her beam ends.

Before I could make out anything distinctly in the horrible confusion, except the one tremendous certainty that we were entirely at the mercy of the sea, I heard a voice from the fore part of the ship which stilled the clamouring and shouting of the rest of the crew in an instant. The words were in Italian, but I understood their fatal meaning only too easily. We had sprung a leak, and the sea was pouring into the ship's hold like the race of a mill-stream. The captain did not lose his presence of mind in this fresh emergency. He called for his axe to cut away the foremast, and ordering some of the crew to help him, directed the others to rig out the pumps.

The words had hardly passed his lips, before the men broke into open mutiny. With a savage look at me, their ringleader declared that the passengers might do as they pleased, but that he and his messmates were determined to take the boat, and leave the accursed ship, and *the dead man in her,* to go to the bottom together. As he spoke there was a shout among the sailors, and I observed some of them pointing derisively behind me. Looking round, I saw Monkton, who had hitherto kept close at my side, making his way back to the cabin. I followed him directly, but the water and confusion on deck, and the impossibility, from the position of the brig, of moving the feet without the slow assistance of the hands, so impeded my progress that it was impossible for me to overtake him. When I had got below, he was crouched upon the coffin, with the water on the cabin floor whirling and splashing about him, as the ship heaved and plunged. I saw a warning brightness in his eyes, a warning flush on his cheeks, as I approached and said to him:

"There is nothing left for it, Alfred, but to bow to our misfortune, and do the best we can to save our lives."

"Save yours," he cried, waving his hand to me, "for *you* have a future before you. Mine is gone when this coffin goes to the bottom. If this ship sinks, I shall know that the fatality is accomplished, and shall sink with her."

I saw that he was in no state to be reasoned with or persuaded, and raised myself again to the deck. The men were cutting away all obstacles, so as to launch the long boat, placed amidships, over the depressed bulwark of the brig, as she lay on her side; and the captain, after having made a last vain exertion to restore his authority, was looking on at them in silence. The violence of the squall seemed already to be spending itself, and I asked whether there was really no chance for us if we remained by the ship. The captain answered that there might have been the best chance if the men had obeyed his orders, but that now there was none. Knowing that I could place no dependence on the presence of mind of Monkton's servant, I confided to the captain, in the fewest and plainest words, the condition of my unhappy friend, and asked if I might depend on his help. He nodded his head, and we descended together to the cabin. Even at this day, it costs me pain to write of the terrible necessity to which the strength and obstinacy of Monkton's delusion reduced us, in the last resort. We were compelled to secure his hands, and drag him by main force to the deck. The men were on the point of launching the boat, and refused at first to receive us into it.

"You cowards!" cried the captain, "have we got the dead man with us this time? Isn't he going to the bottom along with the brig? Who are you afraid of when we get into the boat?"

This sort of appeal produced the desired effect; the men became ashamed of themselves, and retracted their refusal.

Just as we pushed off from the sinking ship, Alfred made an effort to break from me, but I held him firm, and he never repeated the attempt. He sat by me, with drooping head, still and silent, while the sailors rowed away from the vessel: still and silent, when with one accord they paused at a little distance off, and we all waited and watched to see the brig sink: still and silent, even when that sinking happened, when the labouring hull plunged slowly into a hollow of the sea—hesitated, as it seemed, for one moment—rose a little again—then sank to rise no more.

Sank with her dead freight: sank, and snatched for ever from our power the corpse which we had discovered almost by a miracle—those jealously-preserved remains on the safe keeping of which rested so strangely the hopes and the love-destinies of two living beings! As the last signs of the ship disappeared in the depths of the waters, I felt Monkton trembling all over as he sat close at my side, and heard him repeating to himself, sadly, and many times over, the name of "Ada."

I tried to turn his thoughts to another subject, but it was useless. He pointed over the sea to where the brig had once been, and where nothing was left to look at but the rolling waves.

"The empty place will now remain empty for ever in Wincot vault."

As he said those words, he fixed his eyes for a moment sadly and earnestly on my face, then looked away, leant his cheek upon his hand, and spoke no more.

We were sighted long before nightfall by a trading-vessel, were taken on board, and landed at Cartagena in Spain. Alfred never held up his head, and never once spoke to me of his own accord, the whole time we were at sea in the merchantman. I observed, however, with alarm, that he talked often and incoherently to himself—constantly muttering the lines of the old prophecy—constantly referring to the fatal place that was empty in Wincot vault—constantly repeating in broken accents which it affected me inexpressibly to hear, the name of the poor girl who was awaiting his return to England. Nor were these the only causes for the apprehension that I now felt on his account. Towards the end of our voyage he began to suffer from alternations of fever fits and shivering fits, which I ignorantly imagined to be attacks of ague. I was soon undeceived. We had hardly been a day on shore before he became so much worse that I secured the best medical assistance Cartagena could afford. For a day or two the doctors differed, as usual, about the nature of his complaint, but ere long alarming symptoms displayed themselves. The medical men declared that his life was in danger, and told me that his disease was brain fever.

Shocked and grieved as I was, I hardly knew how to act at first under the fresh responsibility now laid upon me. Ultimately, I decided on writing to the old priest who had been Alfred's tutor, and who, as I knew, still resided at Wincot Abbey. I told this gentleman all that had happened, begged him to break my melancholy news as gently as possible to Miss Elmslie, and assured him of my resolution to remain with Monkton to the last.

After I had despatched my letter, and had sent to Gibraltar to secure the best English medical advice that could be obtained, I felt that I had done my best, and that nothing remained but to wait and hope.

Many a sad and anxious hour did I pass by my poor friend's bedside. Many a time did I doubt whether I had done right in giving any encouragement to his delusion. The reasons for doing so which had suggested themselves to me, after my first interview with him, seemed, however, on reflection, to be valid reasons still. The only way of hastening his return to England and to Miss Elmslie, who was pining for that return, was the way I had taken. It was not my fault that a disaster which no man could foresee, had overthrown all his projects and all mine. But now that the calamity had happened, and was irretrievable, how, in the event of his physical recovery, was his moral malady to be combated?

When I reflected on the hereditary taint in his mental organisation, on that childish fright of Stephen Monkton from which he had never recovered, on the perilously secluded life that he had led at the Abbey, and on his firm persuasion of the reality of the apparition by which he believed himself to be constantly followed, I confess I despaired of shaking his superstitious faith in every word and line of the old family prophecy. If the series of striking coincidences which appeared to attest its truth had made a strong and lasting impression on *me* (and this was assuredly the case), how could I wonder that they had produced the effect of absolute conviction on *his* mind, constituted as it was? If I argued with him, and he answered me, how could I rejoin? If he said, "The prophecy points at the last of the family: *I* am the last of the family. The prophecy mentions an empty place in Wincot vault: there is such an empty place there at the moment. On the faith of the prophecy I told you that Stephen Monkton's body was unburied, and you found that it was unburied"—if he said this, of what use would it be for me to reply, "These are only strange coincidences, after all"?

The more I thought of the task that lay before me, if he recovered, the more I felt inclined to despond. The oftener the English physician who attended on him said to me, "He may get the better of the fever, but he has a fixed idea, which never leaves him night or day, which has unsettled his reason, and which will end in killing him, unless you or some of his friends can remove it"—the oftener I heard this, the more acutely I felt my own powerlessness, the more I shrank from every idea that was connected with the hopeless future.

I had only expected to receive my answer from Wincot in the shape of a letter. It was consequently a great surprise, as well as a great relief, to be informed one day that two gentlemen wished to speak with me, and to find that of these two gentlemen the first was the old priest, and the second a male relative of Mrs. Elmslie.

Just before their arrival the fever-symptoms had disappeared, and Alfred had been pronounced out of danger. Both the priest and his companion were eager to know when the sufferer would be strong enough to travel. They had come to Cartagena expressly to take him home with them, and felt far more hopeful than I did of the restorative effects of his native air. After all the questions connected with the first important point of the journey to England had been asked and answered, I ventured to make some inquiries after Miss Elmslie. Her relative informed me that she was suffering both in body and in mind from excess of anxiety on Alfred's account. They had been obliged to deceive her as to the dangerous nature of his illness, in order to deter her from accompanying the priest and her relation on their mission to Spain.

Slowly and imperfectly, as the weeks wore on, Alfred regained something of his former physical strength, but no alteration appeared in his illness as it affected his mind.

From the very first day of his advance towards recovery, it had been discovered that the brain fever had exercised the strangest influence over his faculties of memory. All recollection of recent events was gone from him. Everything connected with Naples, with me, with his journey to Italy, had dropped in some mysterious manner entirely out of his remembrance. So completely had all late circumstances passed from his memory, that, though he recognised the old priest and his own servant easily on the first days of his convalescence, he never recognised me, but regarded me with such a wistful, doubting expression, that I felt inexpressibly pained when I approached his bedside. All his questions were about Miss Elmslie and Wincot Abbey; and all his talk referred to the period when his father was yet alive.

The doctors augured good rather than ill from this loss of memory of recent incidents, saying that it would turn out to be temporary, and that it answered the first great healing purpose of keeping his mind at ease. I tried to believe them—tried to feel as sanguine, when the day came for his departure, as the old friends felt who were taking him home. But the effort was too much for me. A foreboding that I should never see him again, oppressed my heart, and the tears came into my eyes as I saw the worn figure of my poor friend half helped, half lifted into the travelling carriage, and borne away gently on the road towards home.

He had never recognised me, and the doctors had begged that I would give him, for some time to come, as few opportunities as possible of doing so. But for this request I should have accompanied him to England. As it was, nothing better remained for me to do than to change the scene, and recruit as I best could my energies of body and mind, depressed of late by much watching and anxiety. The famous cities of Spain were not new to me, but I visited them again, and revived old impressions of the Alhambra and Madrid. Once or twice I thought of making a pilgrimage to the East, but late events had sobered and altered me. That yearning unsatisfied feeling which we call "home-sickness," began to prey upon my heart, and I resolved to return to England.

I went back by way of Paris, having settled with the priest that he should write to me at my banker's there, as soon as he could after Alfred had returned to Wincot. If I had gone to the East, the letter would have been forwarded to me. I wrote to prevent this; and, on my arrival at Paris, stopped at the banker's before I went to my hotel.

The moment the letter was put into my hands, the black border on the envelope told me the worst. He was dead.

There was but one consolation—he had died calmly, almost happily, without once referring to those fatal chances which had wrought the fulfilment of the ancient prophecy. "My beloved pupil," the old priest wrote, "seemed to rally a little the first few days after his return, but he gained no real strength, and soon suffered a slight relapse of fever. After this he sank gradually and gently day by day, and so departed from us on the last dread journey. Miss Elmslie (who knows that I am writing this) desires me to express her deep and lasting gratitude for all your kindness to Alfred. She told me when we brought him back, that she had waited for him as his promised wife, and that she would nurse him now as a wife should; and she never left him. His face was turned towards her, his hand was clasped in hers, when he died. It will console you to know that he never mentioned events at Naples, or the shipwreck that followed them, from the day of his return to the day of his death."

Three days after reading the letter I was at Wincot, and heard all the details of Alfred's last moments from the priest. I felt a shock which it would not be very easy for me to analyse or explain, when I heard that he had been buried, at his own desire, in the fatal Abbey vault.

The priest took me down to see the place—a grim, cold, subterranean building, with a low roof, supported on heavy Saxon arches. Narrow niches, with the ends only of coffins visible within them, ran down each side of the vault. The nails and silver ornaments flashed here and there as my companion moved past them with a lamp in his hand. At the lower end of the place he stopped, pointed to a niche, and said: "He lies there, between his father and mother." I looked a little further on, and saw what appeared at first like a long dark tunnel. "That is only an empty niche," said the priest, following me. "If the body of Mr. Stephen Monkton had been brought to Wincot, his coffin would have been placed there."

A chill came over me, and a sense of dread which I am ashamed of having felt now, but which I could not combat then. The blessed light of day was pouring down gaily at the other end of the vault through the open door. I turned my back on the empty niche, and hurried into the sunlight and the fresh air.

As I walked across the grass glade leading down to the vault, I heard the rustle of a woman's dress behind me, and, turning round, saw a young lady advancing, clad in deep mourning. Her sweet, sad face, her manner as she held out her hand, told me who it was in an instant.

"I heard that you were here," she said, "and I wished"—her voice faltered a little. My heart ached as I saw how her lip trembled, but before I could say anything, she recovered herself and went on—"I wished to take your hand, and thank you for your brotherly kindness to Alfred; and I wanted to tell you that I am sure, in all you did, you acted tenderly and considerately for the best. Perhaps you may be soon going away from home again, and we may not meet any more. I shall never, never forget that you were kind to him when he wanted a friend, and that you have the greatest claim of anyone on earth to be gratefully remembered in my thoughts as long as I live."

The inexpressible tenderness of her voice, trembling a little all the while she spoke, the pale beauty of her face, the artless candour in her sad, quiet eyes, so affected me that I could not trust myself to answer her at first, except by gesture. Before I recovered my voice, she had given me her hand once more and had left me.

I never saw her again. The chances and changes of life kept us apart. When I last heard of her, years and years ago, she was faithful to the memory of the dead, and was Ada Elmslie still, for Alfred Monkton's sake.

The Biter Bit

*[Extracted from the Correspondence
of the London Police]*

FROM CHIEF INSPECTOR THEAKSTONE, OF THE DETECTIVE
POLICE, TO SERGEANT BULMER OF THE SAME FORCE

LONDON, *4th July*, 18—.

SERGEANT BULMER,—This is to inform you that you are wanted
to assist in looking up a case of importance, which will require all
the attention of an experienced member of the force. The matter of
the robbery on which you are now engaged, you will please to shift
over to the young man who brings you this letter. You will tell him
all the circumstances of the case, just as they stand; you will put
him up to the progress you have made (if any) towards detecting
the person or persons by whom the money has been stolen; and
you will leave him to make the best he can of the matter now in
your hands. He is to have the whole responsibility of the case, and
the whole credit of his success, if he brings it to a proper issue.

So much for the orders that I am desired to communicate to
you.

A word in your ear, next, about this new man who is to take
your place. His name is Matthew Sharpin; and he is to have the
chance given him of dashing into our office at a jump—supposing
he turns out strong enough to take it. You will naturally ask me
how he comes by this privilege. I can only tell you that he has
some uncommonly strong interest to back him in certain high
quarters which you and I had better not mention except under our
breaths. He has been a lawyer's clerk; and he is wonderfully
conceited in his opinion of himself, as well as mean and underhand

to look at. According to his own account, he leaves his old trade, and joins ours, of his own free will and preference. You will no more believe that than I do. My notion is, that he has managed to ferret out some private information in connection with the affairs of one of his master's clients, which makes him rather an awkward customer to keep in the office for the future, and which, at the same time, gives him hold enough over his employer to make it dangerous to drive him into a corner by turning him away. I think the giving him this unheard-of chance among us, is, in plain words, pretty much like giving him hush-money to keep him quiet. However that may be, Mr. Matthew Sharpin is to have the case now in your hands; and if he succeeds with it, he pokes his ugly nose into our office, as sure as fate. I put you up to this, Sergeant, so that you may not stand in your own light by giving the new man any cause to complain of you at headquarters, and remain yours,

FRANCIS THEAKSTONE.

FROM MR. MATTHEW SHARPIN TO
CHIEF INSPECTOR THEAKSTONE

LONDON, July 5th, 18—.

DEAR SIR,—Having now been favoured with the necessary instructions from Sergeant Bulmer, I beg to remind you of certain directions which I have received, relating to the report of my future proceedings which I am to prepare for examination at headquarters.

The object of my writing, and of your examining what I have written, before you send it in to the higher authorities, is, I am informed, to give me, as an untried hand, the benefit of your advice, in case I want it (which I venture to think I shall not) at any stage of my proceedings. As the extraordinary circumstances of the case on which I am now engaged, make it impossible for me to absent myself from the place where the robbery was committed, until I have made some progress towards discovering the thief, I am necessarily precluded from consulting you personally. Hence the necessity of writing down the various details, which might, perhaps, be better communicated by word of mouth. This, if I am not mistaken, is the position in which we are now placed. I state my own impressions on the subject, in writing, in order that we may clearly understand each other at the outset; and have the honour to remain, your obedient servant,

MATTHEW SHARPIN.

FROM CHIEF INSPECTOR THEAKSTONE TO MR. MATTHEW SHARPIN

LONDON, *5th July,* 18—.

SIR,—You have begun by wasting time, ink, and paper. We both of us perfectly well knew the position we stood in towards each other, when I sent you with my letter to Sergeant Bulmer. There was not the least need to repeat it in writing. Be so good as to employ your pen, in future, on the business actually in hand.

You have now three separate matters on which to write to me. First, You have to draw up a statement of your instructions received from Sergeant Bulmer, in order to show us that nothing has escaped your memory, and that you are thoroughly acquainted with all the circumstances of the case which has been entrusted to you. Secondly, You are to inform me what it is you propose to do. Thirdly, You are to report every inch of your progress (if you make any) from day to day, and, if need be, from hour to hour as well. This is *your* duty. As to what *my* duty may be, when I want you to remind me of it, I will write and tell you so. In the meantime, I remain, yours,

FRANCIS THEAKSTONE.

FROM MR. MATTHEW SHARPIN TO CHIEF INSPECTOR THEAKSTONE

LONDON, *6th July,* 18—.

SIR,—You are rather an elderly person, and, as such, naturally inclined to be a little jealous of men like me, who are in the prime of their lives and their faculties. Under these circumstances, it is my duty to be considerate towards you, and not to bear too hardly on your small failings. I decline, therefore, altogether, to take offence at the tone of your letter; I give you the full benefit of the natural generosity of my nature; I sponge the very existence of your surly communication out of my memory—in short, Chief Inspector Theakstone, I forgive you, and proceed to business.

My first duty is to draw up a full statement of the instructions I have received from Sergeant Bulmer. Here they are at your service, according to my version of them.

At number 13, Rutherford Street, Soho, there is a stationer's shop. It is kept by one Mr. Yatman. He is a married man, but has no family. Besides Mr. and Mrs. Yatman, the other inmates in the house are a young single man named Jay, who lodges in the front room on the second floor—a shopman, who sleeps in one of the attics,—and a servant-of-all-work, whose bed is in the back-kitchen. Once a week a charwoman comes for a few hours in the morning only, to help this servant. These are all the persons who, on ordinary occasions, have means of access to the interior of the house, placed, as a matter of course, at their disposal.

Mr. Yatman has been in business for many years, carrying on his affairs prosperously enough to realise a handsome independence for a person in his position. Unfortunately for himself, he endeavoured to increase the amount of his property by speculating. He ventured boldly in his investments, luck went against him, and rather less than two years ago he found himself a poor man again. All that was saved out of the wreck of his property was the sum of two hundred pounds.

Although Mr. Yatman did his best to meet his altered circumstances, by giving up many of the luxuries and comforts to which he and his wife had been accustomed, he found it impossible to retrench so far as to allow of putting by any money from the income produced by his shop. The business has been declining of late years—the cheap advertising stationers having done it injury with the public. Consequently, up to the last week the only surplus property possessed by Mr. Yatman consisted of the two hundred pounds which had been recovered from the wreck of his fortune. This sum was placed as a deposit in a joint-stock bank of the highest possible character.

Eight days ago, Mr. Yatman and his lodger, Mr. Jay, held a conversation on the subject of the commercial difficulties which are hampering trade in all directions at the present time. Mr. Jay (who lives by supplying the newspapers with short paragraphs relating to accidents, offences, and brief records of remarkable occurrences in general—who is, in short, what they call a penny-a-liner) told his landlord that he had been in the city that day, and had heard unfavourable rumours on the subject of the joint-stock banks. The rumours to which he alluded had already reached the ears of Mr. Yatman from other quarters; and the confirmation of them by his lodger had such an effect on his mind—predisposed as it was to alarm by the experience of his former losses—that he resolved to go at once to the bank and withdraw his deposit.

It was then getting on towards the end of the afternoon; and he arrived just in time to receive his money before the bank closed.

He received the deposit in bank-notes of the following amounts;—one fifty-pound note, three twenty-pound notes, six ten-pound notes, and six five-pound notes. His object in drawing the money in this form was to have it ready to lay out immediately in trifling loans, on good security, among the small tradespeople of his district, some of whom are sorely pressed for the very means of existence at the present time. Investments of this kind seemed to Mr. Yatman to be the most safe and the most profitable on which he could now venture.

He brought the money back in an envelope placed in his breast-pocket; and asked his shopman, on getting home, to look for a small flat tin cash-box, which had not been used for years, and which, as Mr. Yatman remembered it, was exactly of the right size to hold the bank-notes. For some time the cash-box was searched for in vain. Mr. Yatman called to his wife to know if she had any idea where it was. The question was overheard by the servant-of-all-work, who was taking up the tea-tray at the time, and by Mr. Jay, who was coming down stairs on his way out to the theatre. Ultimately the cash-box was found by the shopman. Mr. Yatman placed the bank-notes in it, secured them by a padlock, and put the box in his coat-pocket. It stuck out of the coat pocket a very little, but enough to be seen. Mr. Yatman remained at home, up stairs, all the evening. No visitors called. At eleven o'clock he went to bed, and put the cash-box along with his clothes, on a chair by the bedside.

When he and his wife woke the next morning, the box was gone. Payment of the notes was immediately stopped at the bank of England; but no news of the money has been heard of since that time.

So far, the circumstances of the case are perfectly clear. They point unmistakably to the conclusion that the robbery must have been committed by some person living in the house. Suspicion falls, therefore, upon the servant-of-all-work, upon the shopman, and upon Mr. Jay. The two first knew that the cash-box was being inquired for by their master, but did not know what it was he wanted to put into it. They would assume, of course that it was money. They both had opportunities (the servant, when she took away the tea—and the shopman, when he came, after shutting up, to give the keys of the till to his master) of seeing the cash-box in Mr. Yatman's pocket, and of inferring naturally, from its position there, that he intended to take it into his bedroom with him at night.

Mr. Jay, on the other hand, had been told, during the afternoon's conversation on the subject of joint-stock banks, that his landlord had a deposit of two hundred pounds in one of them. He also knew that Mr. Yatman left him with the intention of drawing that money out; and he heard the inquiry for the cash-box, afterwards, when he was coming down stairs. He must, therefore, have inferred that the money was in the house, and that the cash-box was the receptacle intended to contain it. That he could have had any idea, however, of the place in which Mr. Yatman intended to keep it for the night, is impossible, seeing that he went out before the box was found, and did not return till his landlord was in bed. Consequently, if he committed the robbery, he must have gone into the bedroom purely on speculation.

Speaking of the bedroom reminds me of the necessity of noticing the situation of it in the house, and the means that exist of gaining easy access to it at any hour of the night.

The room in question is the back-room on the first-floor. In consequence of Mrs. Yatman's constitutional nervousness on the subject of fire (which makes her apprehend being burnt alive in her room, in case of accident, by the hampering of the lock if the key is turned in it) her husband has never been accustomed to lock the bedroom door. Both he and his wife are, by their own admission, heavy sleepers. Consequently the risk to be run by any evil-disposed persons wishing to plunder the bedroom, was of the most trifling kind. They could enter the room by merely turning the handle of the door; and if they moved with ordinary caution, there was no fear of their waking the sleepers inside. This fact is of importance. It strengthens our conviction that the money must have been taken by one of the inmates of the house, because it tends to show that the robbery, in this case, might have been committed by persons not possessed of the superior vigilance and cunning of the experienced thief.

Such are the circumstances, as they were related to Sergeant Bulmer, when he was first called in to discover the guilty parties, and, if possible, to recover the lost bank-notes. The strictest inquiry which he could institute, failed of producing the smallest fragment of evidence against any of the persons on whom suspicion naturally fell. Their language and behaviour, on being informed of the robbery, was perfectly consistent with the language and behaviour of innocent people. Sergeant Bulmer felt from the first that this was a case for private inquiry and secret observation. He began by recommending Mr. and Mrs. Yatman to affect a feeling of perfect confidence in the innocence of the persons living under their roof; and he then opened the campaign by employing himself in following the goings and comings and in discovering the friends, the habits, and the secrets of the maid-of-all-work.

Three days and nights of exertion on his own part, and on that of others who were competent to assist his investigations, were enough to satisfy him that there was no sound cause for suspicion against the girl.

He next practised the same precaution in relation to the shopman. There was more difficulty and uncertainty in privately clearing up this person's character without his knowledge, but the obstacles were at last smoothed away with tolerable success; and though there is not the same amount of certainty, in this case, which there was in that of the girl, there is still fair reason for supposing that the shopman has had nothing to do with the robbery of the cash-box.

As a necessary consequence of these proceedings, the range of suspicion now becomes limited to the lodger, Mr. Jay.

When I presented your letter of introduction to Sergeant Bulmer, he had already made some inquiries on the subject of this young man. The result, so far, has not been at all favourable. Mr. Jay's habits are irregular; he frequents public houses, and seems to be familiarly acquainted with a great many dissolute characters; he is in debt to most of the tradespeople whom he employs; he has not paid his rent to Mr. Yatman for the last month; yesterday evening he came home excited by liquor, and last week he was seen talking to a prize-fighter. In short, though Mr. Jay does call himself a journalist, in virtue of his penny-a-line contributions to the newspapers, he is a young man of low tastes, vulgar manners, and bad habits. Nothing has yet been discovered in relation to him, which redounds to his credit in the smallest degree.

I have now reported, down to the very last details, all the particulars communicated to me by Sergeant Bulmer. I believe you will not find an omission anywhere; and I think you will admit, though you are prejudiced against me, that a clearer statement of facts was never laid before you than the statement I have now made. My next duty is to tell you what I propose to do, now that the case is confided to my hands.

In the first place, it is clearly my business to take up the case at the point where Sergeant Bulmer has left it. On his authority, I am justified in assuming that I have no need to trouble myself about the maid-of-all-work and the shopman. Their characters are now to be considered as cleared up. What remains to be privately investigated is the question of the guilt or innocence of Mr. Jay. Before we give up the notes for lost, we must make sure, if we can, that he knows nothing about them.

This is the plan that I have adopted, with the full approval of Mr. and Mrs. Yatman, for discovering whether Mr. Jay is or is not the person who has stolen the cash-box:

I propose, to-day, to present myself at the house in the character of a young man who is looking for lodgings. The back room on the second-floor will be shown to me as the room to let; and I shall establish myself there to-night, as a person from the country who has come to London to look for a situation in a respectable shop or office.

By this means I shall be living next to the room occupied by Mr. Jay. The partition between us is mere lath and plaster. I shall make a small hole in it, near the cornice, through which I can see what Mr. Jay does in his room, and hear every word that is said when any friend happens to call on him. Whenever he is at home, I shall be at my post of observation. Whenever he goes out, I shall be after him. By employing these means of watching him, I believe I may look forward to the discovery of his secret—if he knows anything about the lost bank-notes—as to a dead certainty.

What you may think of my plan of observation I cannot undertake to say. It appears to me to unite the invaluable merits of boldness and simplicity. Fortified by this conviction, I close the present communication with feelings of the most sanguine description in regard to the future, and remain your obedient servant,

MATTHEW SHARPIN.

FROM THE SAME TO THE SAME

7th July.

SIR,—As you have not honoured me with any answer to my last communication, I assume that, in spite of your prejudices against me, it has produced the favourable impression on your mind which I ventured to anticipate. Gratified beyond measure by the token of approval which your eloquent silence conveys to me, I proceed to report the progress that has been made in the course of the last twenty-four hours.

I am now comfortably established next door to Mr. Jay; and I am delighted to say that I have two holes in the partition, instead of one. My natural sense of humour has led me into the pardonable extravagance of giving them appropriate names. One I call my peep-hole, and the other my pipe-hole. The name of the first explains itself; the name of the second refers to a small tin pipe, or tube, inserted in the hole, and twisted so that the mouth of it comes close to my ear, while I am standing at my post of observation. Thus, while I am looking at Mr. Jay through my peep-hole, I can hear every word that may be spoken in his room through my pipe-hole.

Perfect candour—a virtue which I have possessed from my childhood—compels me to acknowledge, before I go any further, that the ingenious notion of adding a pipe-hole to my proposed peep-hole originated with Mrs. Yatman. This lady—a most intelligent and accomplished person, simple, and yet distinguished, in her manners—has entered into all my little plans with an enthusiasm and intelligence which I cannot too highly praise. Mr. Yatman is so cast down by his loss, that he is quite incapable of affording me any assistance. Mrs. Yatman, who is evidently most tenderly attached to him, feels her husband's sad condition of mind even more acutely than she feels the loss of the money; and is mainly stimulated to exertion by her desire to assist in raising him from the miserable state of prostration into which he has now fallen.

"The money, Mr. Sharpin," she said to me yesterday evening, with tears in her eyes, "the money may be regained by rigid economy and strict attention to business. It is my husband's wretched state of mind that makes me so anxious for the discovery of the thief. I may be wrong, but I felt hopeful of success as soon as you entered the house; and I believe, if the wretch who has robbed us is to be found, you are the man to discover him." I accept this gratifying compliment in the spirit in which it was offered—firmly believing that I shall be found, sooner or later, to have thoroughly deserved it.

Let me now return to business; that is to say, to my peep-hole and my pipe-hole.

I have enjoyed some hours of calm observation of Mr. Jay. Though rarely at home, as I understand from Mrs. Yatman, on ordinary occasions, he has been in-doors the whole of this day. That is suspicious, to begin with. I have to report, further that he rose at a late hour this morning (always a bad sign in a young man), and that he lost a great deal of time, after he was up, in yawning and complaining to himself of headache. Like other debauched characters, he ate little or nothing for breakfast. His next proceeding was to smoke a pipe—a dirty clay pipe, which a gentleman would have been ashamed to put between his lips. When he had done smoking, he took out pen, ink, and paper, and sat down to write with a groan—whether of remorse for having taken the bank-notes, or of disgust at the task before him, I am unable to say. After writing a few lines (too far away from my peep-hole to give me a chance of reading over his shoulder), he leaned back in his chair, and amused himself by humming the tunes of certain popular songs. Whether these do, or do not, represent secret signals by which he communicates with his accomplices remains to be seen. After he had amused himself for some time by humming, he got up and began to walk about the room, occasionally stopping to add a sentence to the paper on his desk. Before long, he went to a locked cupboard and opened it. I strained my eyes eagerly, in expectation of making a discovery. I saw him take something carefully out of the cupboard—he turned round—and it was only a pint bottle of brandy! Having drunk some of the liquor, this extremely indolent reprobate lay down on his bed again, and in five minutes was fast asleep.

After hearing him snoring for at least two hours, I was recalled to my peep-hole by a knock at his door. He jumped up and opened it with suspicious activity.

A very small boy, with a very dirty face, walked in, said, "Please, sir, they're waiting for you," sat down on a chair, with his legs a long way from the ground, and instantly fell asleep! Mr. Jay swore an oath, tied a wet towel round his head, and going back to his paper, began to cover it with writing as fast as his fingers could move the pen. Occasionally getting up to dip the towel in water and tie it on again, he continued at this employment for nearly three hours; then folded up the leaves of writing, woke the boy, and gave them to him, with this remarkable expression:—"Now, then, young sleepy-head, quick—march! If you see the governor, tell him to have the money ready when I call for it." The boy grinned, and disappeared. I was sorely tempted to follow "sleepy-head," but, on reflection, considered it safest still to keep my eye on the proceedings of Mr. Jay.

In half an hour's time, he put on his hat and walked out. Of course, I put on my hat and walked out also. As I went down stairs, I passed Mrs. Yatman going up. The lady has been kind enough to undertake, by previous arrangement between us, to search Mr. Jay's room, while he is out of the way, and while I am necessarily engaged in the pleasing duty of following him wherever he goes. On the occasion to which I now refer, he walked straight to the nearest tavern, and ordered a couple of mutton chops for his dinner. I placed myself in the next box to him, and ordered a couple of mutton chops for my dinner. Before I had been in the room a minute, a young man of highly suspicious manners and appearance, sitting at a table opposite, took his glass of porter in his hand and joined Mr. Jay. I pretended to be reading the newspaper, and listened, as in duty bound, with all my might.

"Jack has been here inquiring after you," says the young man.

"Did he leave any message?" asks Mr. Jay.

"Yes," says the other. "He told me, if I met with you, to say that he wished very particularly to see you to-night; and that he would give you a look in, at Rutherford Street, at seven o'clock."

"All right," says Mr. Jay. "I'll get back in time to see him."

Upon this, the suspicious-looking young man finished his porter, and saying that he was rather in a hurry, took leave of his friend (perhaps I should not be wrong if I said his accomplice) and left the room.

At twenty-five minutes and a half past six—in these serious cases it is important to be particular about time—Mr. Jay finished his chops and paid his bill. At twenty-six minutes and three-quarters I finished my chops and paid mine. In ten minutes more I was inside the house in Rutherford Street, and was received by Mrs. Yatman in the passage. That charming woman's face exhibited an expression of melancholy and disappointment which it quite grieved me to see.

"I am afraid, Ma'am," says I, "that you have not hit on any little criminating discovery in the lodger's room?"

She shook her head and sighed. It was a soft, languid, fluttering sigh;—and, upon my life, it quite upset me. For the moment I forgot business, and burned with envy of Mr. Yatman.

"Don't despair, Ma'am," I said, with an insinuating mildness which seemed to touch her. "I have heard a mysterious conversation—I know of a guilty appointment—and I expect great things from my Peep-hole and my Pipe-hole to-night. Pray, don't be alarmed, but I think we are on the brink of a discovery."

Here my enthusiastic devotion to business got the better of my tender feelings. I looked—winked—nodded—left her.

When I got back to my observatory, I found Mr. Jay digesting his mutton chops in an arm-chair, with his pipe in his mouth. On his table were two tumblers, a jug of water, and the pint bottle of brandy. It was then close upon seven o'clock. As the hour struck, the person described as "Jack" walked in.

He looked agitated—I am happy to say he looked violently agitated. The cheerful glow of anticipated success diffused itself (to use a strong expression) all over me, from head to foot. With breathless interest I looked through my Peep-hole, and saw the visitor—the "Jack" of this delightful case—sit down, facing me, at the opposite side of the table to Mr. Jay. Making allowance for the difference in expression which their countenances just now happened to exhibit, these two abandoned villains were so much alike in other respects as to lead at once to the conclusion that they were brothers. Jack was the cleaner man and the better dressed of the two. I admit that, at the outset. It is, perhaps, one of my failings to push justice and impartiality to their utmost limits. I am no Pharisee; and where Vice has its redeeming point, I say, let Vice have its due—yes, yes, by all manner of means, let Vice have its due.

"What's the matter now, Jack?" says Mr. Jay.

"Can't you see it in my face?" says Jack. "My dear fellow, delays are dangerous. Let us have done with suspense, and risk it the day after to-morrow."

"So soon as that?" cried Mr. Jay, looking very much astonished. "Well, I'm ready, if you are. But, I say, Jack, is Somebody Else ready too? Are you quite sure of that?"

He smiled as he spoke—a frightful smile—and laid a very strong emphasis on those two words, "Somebody Else." There is evidently a third ruffian, a nameless desperado, concerned in the business.

"Meet us to-morrow," says Jack, "and judge for yourself. Be in the Regent's Park at eleven in the morning, and look out for us at the turning that leads to the Avenue Road."

"I'll be there," says Mr. Jay. "Have a drop of brandy and water? What are you getting up for? You're not going already?"

"Yes, I am," says Jack. "The fact is, I'm so excited and agitated that I can't sit still anywhere for five minutes together. Ridiculous as it may appear to you, I'm in a perpetual state of nervous flutter. I can't, for the life of me, help fearing that we shall be found out. I fancy that every man who looks twice at me in the street is a spy——"

At those words, I thought my legs would have given way under me. Nothing but strength of mind kept me at my Peep-hole—nothing else, I give you my word of honour.

"Stuff and nonsense!" cried Mr. Jay, with all the effrontery of a veteran in crime. "We have kept the secret up to this time, and we will manage cleverly to the end. Have a drop of brandy and water, and you will feel as certain about it as I do."

Jack steadily refused the brandy and water, and steadily persisted in taking his leave.

"I must try if I can't walk it off," he said. "Remember to-morrow morning—eleven o'clock, Avenue Road side of the Regent's Park."

With those words he went out. His hardened relative laughed desperately, and resumed the dirty clay pipe.

I sat down on the side of my bed, actually quivering with excitement.

It is clear to me that no attempt has yet been made to change the stolen bank-notes; and I may add that Sergeant Bulmer was of that opinion also, when he left the case in my hands. What is the natural conclusion to draw from the conversation which I have just set down? Evidently, that the confederates meet to-morrow to take their respective shares in the stolen money, and to decide on the safest means of getting the notes changed the day after. Mr. Jay is, beyond a doubt, the leading criminal in this business, and he will probably run the chief risk—that of changing the fifty-pound note. I shall, therefore, still make it my business to follow him—attending at the Regent's Park to-morrow, and doing my best to hear what is said there. If another appointment is made for the day after, I shall, of course, go to it. In the meantime, I shall want the immediate assistance of two competent persons (supposing the rascals separate after their meeting) to follow the two minor criminals. It is only fair to add, that, if the rogues all retire together, I shall probably keep my ɪ .bordinates in reserve. Being naturally ambitious, I desire, if possible, to have the whole credit of discovering this robbery to myself.

8th July.

I have to acknowledge, with thanks, the speedy arrival of my two subordinates—men of very average abilities, I am afraid; but, fortunately, I shall always be on the spot to direct them.

My first business this morning was, necessarily, to prevent mistakes by accounting to Mr. and Mrs. Yatman for the presence of two strangers on the scene. Mr. Yatman (between ourselves, a poor feeble man) only shook his head and groaned. Mrs. Yatman (that superior woman) favoured me with a charming look of intelligence.

"Oh, Mr. Sharpin!" she said, "I am so sorry to see those two men! Your sending for their assistance looks as if you were beginning to be doubtful of success."

I privately winked at her (she is very good in allowing me to do so without taking offence), and told her, in my facetious way, that she laboured under a slight mistake.

"It is because I am sure of success, Ma'am, that I send for them. I am determined to recover the money, not for my own sake only, but for Mr. Yatman's sake—and for yours."

I laid a considerable amount of stress on those last three words. She said, "Oh, Mr. Sharpin!" again—and blushed of a heavenly red—and looked down at her work. I could go to the world's end with that woman, if Mr. Yatman would only die.

I sent off the two subordinates to wait, until I wanted them, at the Avenue Road gate of the Regent's Park. Half an hour afterwards I was following in the same direction myself, at the heels of Mr. Jay.

The two confederates were punctual to the appointed time, I blush to record it, but it is nevertheless necessary to state, that the third rogue—the nameless desperado of my report, or if you prefer it, the mysterious "Somebody Else" of the conversation between the two brothers—is a woman! and, what is worse, a young woman! and what is more lamentable still, a nice-looking woman! I have long resisted a growing conviction, that, wherever there is mischief in this world, an individual of the fair sex is inevitably certain to be mixed up in it. After the experience of this morning, I can struggle against that sad conclusion no longer.—I give up the sex—excepting Mrs. Yatman, I give up the sex.

The man named "Jack" offered the woman his arm. Mr. Jay placed himself on the other side of her. The three then walked away slowly among the trees. I followed them at a respectful distance. My two subordinates, at a respectful distance also, followed me.

It was, I deeply regret to say, impossible to get near enough to them to overhear their conversation, without running too great a risk of being discovered. I could only infer from their gestures and actions that they were all three talking with extraordinary earnestness on some subject which deeply interested them. After having been engaged in this way a full quarter of an hour, they suddenly turned round to retrace their steps. My presence of mind did not forsake me in this emergency. I signed to the two subordinates to walk on carelessly and pass them, while I myself slipped dexterously behind a tree. As they came by me, I heard "Jack" address these words to Mr. Jay:—

"Let us say half-past ten to-morrow morning. And mind you come in a cab. We had better not risk taking one in this neighbourhood."

Mr. Jay made some brief reply, which I could not overhear. They walked back to the place at which they had met, shaking hands there with an audacious cordiality which it quite sickened me to see. They then separated. I followed Mr. Jay. My subordinates paid the same delicate attention to the other two.

Instead of taking me back to Rutherford Street, Mr. Jay led me to the Strand. He stopped at a dingy, disreputable-looking house, which, according to the inscription over the door, was a newspaper office, but which, in my judgment, had all the external appearance of a place devoted to the reception of stolen goods.

After remaining inside for a few minutes, he came out, whistling with his finger and thumb in his waistcoat pocket. A less discreet man than myself would have arrested him on the spot. I remembered the necessity of catching the two confederates, and the importance of not interfering with the appointment that had been made for the next morning. Such coolness at this, under trying circumstances, is rarely to be found, I should imagine, in a young beginner, whose reputation as a detective policeman is still to make.

From the house of suspicious appearance, Mr. Jay betook himself to a cigar-divan, and read the magazines over a cheroot. I sat at a table near him, and read the magazines likewise over a cheroot. From the divan he strolled to the tavern and had his chops. I strolled to the tavern and had my chops. When he had done, he went back to his lodging. When I had done, I went back to mine. He was overcome with drowsiness early in the evening and went to bed. As soon as I heard him snoring, I was overcome with drowsiness, and went to bed also.

Early in the morning my two subordinates came to make their report.

They had seen the man named "Jack" leave the woman near the gate of an apparently respectable villa-residence, not far from the Regent's Park. Left to himself, he took a turning to the right, which led to a sort of suburban street, principally inhabited by shopkeepers. He stopped at the private door of one of the houses, and let himself in with his own key—looking about him as he opened the door, and staring suspiciously at my men as they lounged along on the opposite side of the way. These were all the particulars which the subordinates had to communicate. I kept them in my room to attend on me, if needful, and mounted to my Peep-hole to have a look at Mr. Jay.

He was occupied in dressing himself, and was taking extraordinary pains to destroy all traces of the natural slovenliness of his appearance. This was precisely what I expected. A vagabond like Mr. Jay knows the importance of giving himself a respectable look when he is going to run the risk of changing a stolen bank-note. At five minutes past ten o'clock, he had given the last brush to his shabby hat and the last scouring with bread-crumb to his dirty gloves. At ten minutes past ten he was in the street, on his way to the nearest cab-stand, and I and my subordinates were close on his heels.

He took a cab, and we took a cab. I had not overheard them appoint a place of meeting, when following them in the Park on the previous day; but I soon found that we were proceeding in the old direction of the Avenue Road gate.

The cab in which Mr. Jay was riding turned into the Park slowly. We stopped outside, to avoid exciting suspicion. I got out to follow the cab on foot. Just as I did so, I saw it stop, and detected the two confederates approaching it from among the trees. They got in, and the cab was turned about directly. I ran back to my own cab, and told the driver to let them pass him, and then to follow as before.

The man obeyed my directions, but so clumsily as to excite their suspicions. We had been driving after them about three minutes (returning along the road by which we had advanced) when I looked out of the window to see how far they might be ahead of us. As I did this, I saw two hats popped out of the windows of their cab, and two faces looking back at me. I sank into my place in a cold sweat;—the expression is coarse, but no other form of words can describe my condition at that trying moment.

"We are found out!" I said faintly to my two subordinates. They stared at me in astonishment. My feelings changed instantly from the depth of despair to the height of indignation.

"It is the cabman's fault. Get out, one of you," I said, with dignity—"get out and punch his head."

Instead of following my directions (I should wish this act of disobedience to be reported at head-quarters) they both looked out of the window. Before I could pull them back, they both sat down again. Before I could express my just indignation, they both grinned, and said to me, "Please to look out, sir!"

I did look out. The thieves' cab had stopped.

Where?

At a church door!!!

What effect this discovery might have had upon the ordinary run of men, I don't know. Being of a strong religious turn myself, it filled me with horror. I have often read of the unprincipled cunning of criminal persons; but I never before heard of three thieves attempting to double on their pursuers by entering a church! The sacrilegious audacity of that proceeding is, I should think, unparalleled in the annals of crime.

I checked my grinning subordinates by a frown. It was easy to see what was passing in their superficial minds. If I had not been able to look below the surface, I might, on observing two nicely-dressed men and one nicely-dressed woman enter a church before eleven in the morning on a week day, have come to the same hasty conclusion at which my inferiors had evidently arrived. As it was, appearances had no power to impose on *me*. I got out, and, followed by one of my men, entered the church. The other man I sent round to watch the vestry door. You may catch a weasel asleep—but not your humble servant, Matthew Sharpin!

We stole up the gallery stairs, diverged to the organ loft and peered through the curtains in front. There they were all three, sitting in a pew below—yes, incredible as it may appear, sitting in a pew below!

Before I could determine what to do, a clergyman made his appearance in full canonicals, from the vestry door, followed by a clerk. My brain whirled, and my eyesight grew dim. Dark remembrances of robberies committed in vestries floated through my mind. I trembled for the excellent man in full canonicals—I even trembled for the clerk.

The clergyman placed himself inside the altar rails. The three desperadoes approached him. He opened his book, and began to read. What?—you will ask.

I answer, without the slightest hesitation, the first lines of the Marriage Service.

My subordinate had the audacity to look at me, and then to stuff his pocket-handkerchief into his mouth. I scorned to pay any attention to him. After I had discovered that the man "Jack" was the bridegroom, and that the man Jay acted the part of father, and gave away the bride, I left the church, followed by my man, and joined the other subordinate outside the vestry door. Some people in my position would now have felt rather crestfallen, and would have begun to think that they had made a very foolish mistake. Not the faintest misgiving of any kind troubled me. I did not feel in the slightest degree depreciated in my own estimation. And even now, after a lapse of three hours, my mind remains, I am happy to say, in the same calm and hopeful condition.

As soon as I and my subordinates were assembled together outside the church, I intimated my intention of still following the other cab, in spite of what had occurred. My reason for deciding on this course will appear presently. The two subordinates were astonished at my resolution. One of them had the impertinence to say to me: —

"If you please, sir, who is it that we are after? A man who has stolen money, or a man who has stolen a wife?"

The other low person encouraged him by laughing. Both have deserved an official reprimand; and both, I sincerely trust, will be sure to get it.

When the marriage ceremony was over, the three got into their cab; and once more our vehicle (neatly hidden round the corner of the church, so that they could not suspect it to be near them) started to follow theirs.

We traced them to the terminus of the South-Western Railway. The newly-married couple took tickets for Richmond—paying their fare with a half-sovereign, and so depriving me of the pleasure of arresting them, which I should certainly have done, if they had offered a bank-note. They parted from Mr. Jay, saying, "Remember the address,—14 Babylon Terrace. You dine with us to-morrow week." Mr. Jay accepted the invitation, and added, jocosely, that he was going home at once to get off his clean clothes, and to be comfortable and dirty again for the rest of the day. I have to report that I saw him home safely, and that he is comfortable and dirty again (to use his own disgraceful language) at the present moment.

Here the affair rests, having by this time reached what I may call its first stage.

I know very well what persons of hasty judgment will be inclined to say of my proceedings thus far. They will assert that I have been deceiving myself all through, in the most absurd way; they will declare that the suspicious conversations which I have reported, referred solely to the difficulties and dangers of successfully carrying out a runaway match; and they will appeal to the scene in the church, as offering undeniable proof of the correctness of their assertions. So let it be. I dispute nothing up to this point. But I ask a question, out of the depths of my own sagacity as a man of the world, which the bitterest of my enemies will not, I think, find it particularly easy to answer.

Granted the fact of the marriage, what proof does it afford me of the innocence of the three persons concerned in that clandestine transaction? It gives me none. On the contrary, it strengthens my suspicions against Mr. Jay and his confederates, because it suggests a distinct motive for their stealing the money. A gentleman who is going to spend his honeymoon at Richmond wants money; and a gentleman who is in debt to all his tradespeople wants money. Is this an unjustifiable imputation of bad motives? In the name of outraged morality, I deny it. These men have combined together, and have stolen a woman. Why should they not combine together, and steal a cash-box? I take my stand on the logic of rigid virtue; and I defy all the sophistry of vice to move me an inch out of my position.

Speaking of virtue, I may add that I have put this view of the case to Mr. and Mrs. Yatman. That accomplished and charming woman found it difficult, at first, to follow the close chain of my reasoning. I am free to confess that she shook her head, and shed tears, and joined her husband in premature lamentation over the loss of the two hundred pounds. But a little careful explanation on my part, and a little attentive listening on hers, ultimately changed her opinion. She now agrees with me, that there is nothing in this unexpected circumstance of the clandestine marriage which absolutely tends to divert suspicion from Mr. Jay, or Mr. "Jack," or the runaway lady. "Audacious hussy" was the term my fair friend used in speaking of her, but let that pass. It is more to the purpose to record that Mrs. Yatman has not lost confidence in me and that Mr. Yatman promises to follow her example, and do his best to look hopefully for future results.

I have now, in the new turn that circumstances have taken, to wait advice from your office. I pause for fresh orders with all the composure of a man who has got two strings to his bow. When I traced the three confederates from the church door to the railway terminus, I had two motives for doing so. First, I followed them as a matter of official business, believing them still to have been guilty of the robbery. Secondly, I followed them as a matter of private speculation, with a view of discovering the place of refuge to which the runaway couple intended to retreat, and of making my information a marketable commodity to offer to the young lady's family and friends. Thus, whatever happens, I may congratulate myself beforehand on not having wasted my time. If the office approves of my conduct, I have my plan ready for further proceedings. If the office blames me, I shall take myself off, with my marketable information, to the genteel villa-residence in the neighbourhood of the Regent's Park. Any way, the affair puts money into my pocket, and does credit to my penetration as an uncommonly sharp man.

I have only one word more to add, and it is this:—If any individual ventures to assert that Mr. Jay and his confederates are innocent of all share in the stealing of the cash-box, I, in return, defy that individual—though he may even be Chief Inspector Theakstone himself—to tell me who has committed the robbery at Rutherford Street, Soho.

I have the honour to be,
Your very obedient servant,
MATTHEW SHARPIN.

FROM CHIEF INSPECTOR THEAKSTONE TO SERGEANT BULMER

Birmingham, July 9th.

SERGEANT BULMER,—That empty-headed puppy, Mr. Matthew Sharpin, has made a mess of the case at Rutherford Street, exactly as I expected he would. Business keeps me in this town; so I write to you to set the matter straight. I enclose, with this, the pages of feeble scribble-scrabble which the creature, Sharpin, calls a report. Look them over; and when you have made your way through all the gabble, I think you will agree with me that the conceited booby has looked for the thief in every direction but the right one. You can lay your hand on the guilty person in five minutes, now. Settle the case at once; forward your report to me at this place; and tell Mr. Sharpin that he is suspended till further notice.

Yours,
FRANCIS THEAKSTONE.

FROM SERGEANT BULMER TO CHIEF INSPECTOR THEAKSTONE

London, July 10th.

INSPECTOR THEAKSTONE,—Your letter and enclosure came safe to hand. Wise men, they say, may always learn something, even from a fool. By the time I had got through Sharpin's maundering report of his own folly, I saw my way clear enough to the end of the Rutherford Street case, just as you thought I should. In half an hour's time I was at the house. The first person I saw there was Mr. Sharpin himself.

"Have you come to help me?" says he.

"Not exactly," says I. "I've come to tell you that you are suspended till further notice."

"Very good," says he, not taken down, by so much as a single peg, in his own estimation. "I thought you would be jealous of me. It's very natural; and I don't blame you. Walk in, pray, and make yourself at home. I'm off to do a little detective business on my own account, in the neighbourhood of the Regent's Park. Ta-ta, sergeant, ta-ta!"

With those words he took himself out of the way—which was exactly what I wanted him to do.

As soon as the maid-servant had shut the door, I told her to inform her master that I wanted to say a word to him in private. She showed me into the parlour behind the shop; and there was Mr. Yatman, all alone, reading the newspaper.

"About this matter of the robbery, sir," says I.

He cut me short, peevishly enough—being naturally a poor, weak, womanish sort of man. "Yes, yes, I know," says he. "You have come to tell me that your wonderfully clever man, who has bored holes in my second-floor partition, has made a mistake, and is off the scent of the scoundrel who has stolen my money."

"Yes, sir," says I. "That *is* one of the things I came to tell you. But I have got something else to say, besides that."

"Can you tell me who the thief is?" says he, more pettish than ever.

"Yes, sir," says I, "I think I can."

He put down the newspaper, and began to look rather anxious and frightened.

"Not my shopman?" says he. "I hope, for the man's own sake, it's not my shopman."

"Guess again, sir," says I.

"That idle slut, the maid?" says he.

"She is idle, sir," says I, "and she is also a slut; my first inquiries about her proved as much as that. But she's not the thief."

"Then in the name of heaven, who is?" says he.

"Will you please to prepare yourself for a very disagreeable surprise, sir?" says I. "And in case you lose your temper, will you excuse my remarking that I am the stronger man of the two, and that, if you allow yourself to lay hands on me, I may unintentionally hurt you, in pure self-defence?"

He turned as pale as ashes, and pushed his chair two or three feet away from me.

"You have asked me to tell you, sir, who has taken your money," I went on. "If you insist on my giving you an answer——"

"I do insist," he said faintly. "Who has taken it?"

"Your wife has taken it," I said very quietly, and very positively at the same time.

He jumped out of the chair as if I had put a knife into him, and struck his fist on the table, so heavily that the wood cracked again.

"Steady, sir," says I. "Flying into a passion won't help you to the truth."

"It's a lie!" says he, with another smack of his fist on the table— "a base, vile, infamous lie! How dare you——"

He stopped, and fell back into the chair again, looked about him in a bewildered way, and ended by bursting out crying.

"When your better sense comes back to you, sir," says I, "I am sure you will be gentleman enough to make an apology for the language you have just used. In the meantime, please to listen, if you can, to a word of explanation. Mr. Sharpin has sent in a report to our inspector, of the most irregular and ridiculous kind; setting down, not only all his own foolish doings and sayings, but the doings and sayings of Mrs. Yatman as well. In most cases, such a document would have been fit for the waste-paper basket; but, in this particular case, it so happens that Mr. Sharpin's budget of nonsense leads to a certain conclusion, which the simpleton of a writer has been quite innocent of suspecting from the beginning to the end. Of that conclusion I am so sure, that I will forfeit my place, if it does not turn out that Mrs. Yatman has been practising upon the folly and conceit of this young man, and that she has tried to shield herself from discovery by purposely encouraging him to suspect the wrong persons. I tell you that confidently; and I will even go further. I will undertake to give a decided opinion as to why Mrs. Yatman took the money, and what she has done with it, or with a part of it. Nobody can look at that lady, sir, without being struck by the great taste and beauty of her dress——"

As I said those last words, the poor man seemed to find his powers of speech again. He cut me short directly, as haughtily as if he had been a duke instead of a stationer.

"Try some other means of justifying your vile calumny against my wife," says he. "Her milliner's bill for the past year, is on my file of receipted accounts at this moment."

"Excuse me, sir," says I, "but that proves nothing. Milliners, I must tell you, have a certain rascally custom which comes within the daily experience of our office. A married lady who wishes it, can keep two accounts at her dressmaker's; one is the account which her husband sees and pays; the other is the private account, which contains all the extravagant items, and which the wife pays secretly, by instalments, whenever she can. According to our usual experience, these instalments are mostly squeezed out of the house-keeping money. In your case, I suspect no instalments have been paid; proceedings have been threatened; Mrs. Yatman, knowing your altered circumstances, has felt herself driven into a corner; and she has paid her private account out of your cash-box."

"I won't believe it," says he. "Every word you speak is an abominable insult to me and to my wife."

"Are you man enough, sir," says I, taking him up short, in order to save time and words, "to get that receipted bill you spoke of just now off the file, and come with me at once to the milliner's shop where Mrs. Yatman deals?"

He turned red in the face at that, got the bill directly, and put on his hat. I took out of my pocket-book the list containing the numbers of the lost notes, and we left the house together immediately.

Arrived at the milliner's (one of the expensive West-end houses, as I expected), I asked for a private interview, on important business, with the mistress of the concern. It was not the first time that she and I had met over the same delicate investigation. The moment she set eyes on me, she sent for her husband. I mentioned who Mr. Yatman was, and what we wanted.

"This is strictly private?" inquires her husband. I nodded my head.

"And confidential?" says the wife. I nodded again.

"Do you see any objection, dear, to obliging the sergeant with a sight of the books?" says the husband.

"None in the world, love, if you approve of it," says the wife.

All this while poor Mr. Yatman sat looking the picture of astonishment and distress, quite out of place at our polite conference. The books were brought—and one minute's look at the pages in which Mrs. Yatman's name figured was enough, and more than enough, to prove the truth of every word I had spoken.

There, in one book, was the husband's account, which Mr. Yatman had settled. And there, in the other, was the private account, crossed off also; the date of settlement being the very day after the loss of the cash-box. This said private account amounted to the sum of a hundred and seventy-five pounds, odd shillings; and it extended over a period of three years. Not a single instalment had been paid on it. Under the last line was an entry to this effect: "Written to for the third time, June 23rd." I pointed to it, and asked the milliner if that mean "last June." Yes, it did mean last June; and she now deeply regretted to say that it had been accompanied by a threat of legal proceedings.

"I thought you gave good customers more than three years credit?" says I.

The milliner looks at Mr. Yatman, and whispers to me—"Not when a lady's husband gets into difficulties."

She pointed to the account as she spoke. The entries after the time when Mr. Yatman's circumstances became involved were just as extravagant, for a person in his wife's situation, as the entries for the year before that period. If the lady had economised in other things, she had certainly not economised in the matter of dress.

There was nothing left now but to examine the cash-book, for form's sake. The money had been paid in notes, the amounts and numbers of which exactly tallied with the figures set down in my list.

After that, I thought it best to get Mr. Yatman out of the house immediately. He was in such a pitiable condition, that I called a cab and accompanied him home in it. At first he cried and raved like a child: but I soon quieted him—and I must add, to his credit, that he made me a most handsome apology for his language, as the cab drew up at his house door. In return, I tried to give him some advice about how to set matters right, for the future, with his wife. He paid very little attention to me, and went upstairs muttering to himself about a separation. Whether Mrs. Yatman will come cleverly out of the scrape or not, seems doubtful. I should say, myself, that she will go into screeching hysterics, and so frighten the poor man into forgiving her. But this is no business of ours. So far as we are concerned, the case is now at an end; and the present report may come to a conclusion along with it.

I remain, accordingly, yours to command,

THOMAS BULMER.

P.S.—I have to add, that, on leaving Rutherford Street, I met Mr. Matthew Sharpin coming to pack up his things.

"Only think!" says he, rubbing his hands in great spirits, "I've been to the genteel villa-residence; and the moment I mentioned my business, they kicked me out directly. There were two witnesses of the assault; and it's worth a hundred pounds to me, if it's worth a farthing."

"I wish you joy of your luck," says I.

"Thank you," says he. "When may I pay you the same compliment on finding the thief?"

"Whenever you like," says I, "for the thief is found."

"Just what I expected," says he. "I've done all the work; and now you cut in, and claim all the credit—Mr. Jay of course?"

"No," says I.

"Who is it then?" says he.

"Ask Mrs. Yatman," says I. "She's waiting to tell you."

"All right! I'd much rather hear it from that charming woman than from you," says he, and goes into the house in a mighty hurry.

What do you think of that, Inspector Theakstone? Would you like to stand in Mr. Sharpin's shoes? I shouldn't, I can promise you!

FROM·CHIEF INSPECTOR THEAKSTONE TO MR. MATTHEW SHARPIN

July 12th.

SIR,—Sergeant Bulmer has already told you to consider yourself suspended until further notice. I have now authority to add, that your services as a member of the Detective Police are positively declined. You will please to take this letter as notifying officially your dismissal from the force.

I may inform you, privately, that your rejection is not intended to cast any reflections on your character. It merely implies that you are not quite sharp enough for our purpose. If we are to have a new recruit among us, we should infinitely prefer Mrs. Yatman.

Your obedient servant,

FRANCIS THEAKSTONE.

NOTE ON THE PRECEDING CORRESPONDENCE, ADDED BY MR. THEAKSTONE

The Inspector is not in a position to append any explanations of importance to the last of the letters. It has been discovered that Mr. Matthew Sharpin left the house in Rutherford Street five minutes after his interview outside of it with Sergeant Bulmer—his manner expressing the liveliest emotions of terror and astonishment, and his left cheek displaying a bright patch of red, which might have been the result of a slap on the face from a female hand. He was also heard, by the shopman at Rutherford Street, to use a very shocking expression in reference to Mrs. Yatman; and was seen to clench his fist vindictively, as he ran round the corner of the street. Nothing more has been heard of him; and it is conjectured that he has left London with the intention of offering his valuable services to the provincial police.

On the interesting domestic subject of Mr. and Mrs. Yatman still less is known. It has, however, been positively ascertained that the medical attendant of the family was sent for in a great hurry, on the day when Mr. Yatman returned from the milliner's shop. The neighbouring chemist received, soon afterwards, a prescription of a soothing nature to make up for Mrs. Yatman. The day after, Mr. Yatman purchased some smelling-salts at the shop, and afterwards appeared at the circulating library to ask for a novel, descriptive of high life, that would amuse an invalid lady. It has been inferred from these circumstances, that he has not thought it desirable to carry out his threat of separating himself from his wife—at least in the present (presumed) condition of that lady's sensitive nervous system.

A CATALOG OF SELECTED
DOVER BOOKS
IN ALL FIELDS OF INTEREST

A CATALOG OF SELECTED DOVER
BOOKS IN ALL FIELDS OF INTEREST

100 BEST-LOVED POEMS, Edited by Philip Smith. "The Passionate Shepherd to His Love," "Shall I compare thee to a summer's day?" "Death, be not proud," "The Raven," "The Road Not Taken," plus works by Blake, Wordsworth, Byron, Shelley, Keats, many others. 96pp. 5$\frac{5}{16}$ x 8$\frac{1}{4}$. 0-486-28553-7

100 SMALL HOUSES OF THE THIRTIES, Brown-Blodgett Company. Exterior photographs and floor plans for 100 charming structures. Illustrations of models accompanied by descriptions of interiors, color schemes, closet space, and other amenities. 200 illustrations. 112pp. 8$\frac{3}{8}$ x 11. 0-486-44131-8

1000 TURN-OF-THE-CENTURY HOUSES: With Illustrations and Floor Plans, Herbert C. Chivers. Reproduced from a rare edition, this showcase of homes ranges from cottages and bungalows to sprawling mansions. Each house is meticulously illustrated and accompanied by complete floor plans. 256pp. 9$\frac{3}{8}$ x 12$\frac{1}{4}$.
0-486-45596-3

101 GREAT AMERICAN POEMS, Edited by The American Poetry & Literacy Project. Rich treasury of verse from the 19th and 20th centuries includes works by Edgar Allan Poe, Robert Frost, Walt Whitman, Langston Hughes, Emily Dickinson, T. S. Eliot, other notables. 96pp. 5$\frac{5}{16}$ x 8$\frac{1}{4}$. 0-486-40158-8

101 GREAT SAMURAI PRINTS, Utagawa Kuniyoshi. Kuniyoshi was a master of the warrior woodblock print — and these 18th-century illustrations represent the pinnacle of his craft. Full-color portraits of renowned Japanese samurais pulse with movement, passion, and remarkably fine detail. 112pp. 8$\frac{3}{8}$ x 11. 0-486-46523-3

ABC OF BALLET, Janet Grosser. Clearly worded, abundantly illustrated little guide defines basic ballet-related terms: arabesque, battement, pas de chat, relevé, sissonne, many others. Pronunciation guide included. Excellent primer. 48pp. 4$\frac{3}{16}$ x 5$\frac{3}{4}$.
0-486-40871-X

ACCESSORIES OF DRESS: An Illustrated Encyclopedia, Katherine Lester and Bess Viola Oerke. Illustrations of hats, veils, wigs, cravats, shawls, shoes, gloves, and other accessories enhance an engaging commentary that reveals the humor and charm of the many-sided story of accessorized apparel. 644 figures and 59 plates. 608pp. 6$\frac{1}{8}$ x 9$\frac{1}{4}$.
0-486-43378-1

ADVENTURES OF HUCKLEBERRY FINN, Mark Twain. Join Huck and Jim as their boyhood adventures along the Mississippi River lead them into a world of excitement, danger, and self-discovery. Humorous narrative, lyrical descriptions of the Mississippi valley, and memorable characters. 224pp. 5$\frac{5}{16}$ x 8$\frac{1}{4}$. 0-486-28061-6

ALICE STARMORE'S BOOK OF FAIR ISLE KNITTING, Alice Starmore. A noted designer from the region of Scotland's Fair Isle explores the history and techniques of this distinctive, stranded-color knitting style and provides copious illustrated instructions for 14 original knitwear designs. 208pp. 8$\frac{3}{8}$ x 10$\frac{7}{8}$. 0-486-47218-3

Browse over 9,000 books at www.doverpublications.com

ALICE'S ADVENTURES IN WONDERLAND, Lewis Carroll. Beloved classic about a little girl lost in a topsy-turvy land and her encounters with the White Rabbit, March Hare, Mad Hatter, Cheshire Cat, and other delightfully improbable characters. 42 illustrations by Sir John Tenniel. 96pp. 5$\frac{3}{16}$ x 8¼. 0-486-27543-4

AMERICA'S LIGHTHOUSES: An Illustrated History, Francis Ross Holland. Profusely illustrated fact-filled survey of American lighthouses since 1716. Over 200 stations — East, Gulf, and West coasts, Great Lakes, Hawaii, Alaska, Puerto Rico, the Virgin Islands, and the Mississippi and St. Lawrence Rivers. 240pp. 8 x 10¾. 0-486-25576-X

AN ENCYCLOPEDIA OF THE VIOLIN, Alberto Bachmann. Translated by Frederick H. Martens. Introduction by Eugene Ysaye. First published in 1925, this renowned reference remains unsurpassed as a source of essential information, from construction and evolution to repertoire and technique. Includes a glossary and 73 illustrations. 496pp. 6⅛ x 9¼. 0-486-46618-3

ANIMALS: 1,419 Copyright-Free Illustrations of Mammals, Birds, Fish, Insects, etc., Selected by Jim Harter. Selected for its visual impact and ease of use, this outstanding collection of wood engravings presents over 1,000 species of animals in extremely lifelike poses. Includes mammals, birds, reptiles, amphibians, fish, insects, and other invertebrates. 284pp. 9 x 12. 0-486-23766-4

THE ANNALS, Tacitus. Translated by Alfred John Church and William Jackson Brodribb. This vital chronicle of Imperial Rome, written by the era's great historian, spans A.D. 14-68 and paints incisive psychological portraits of major figures, from Tiberius to Nero. 416pp. 5$\frac{3}{16}$ x 8¼. 0-486-45236-0

ANTIGONE, Sophocles. Filled with passionate speeches and sensitive probing of moral and philosophical issues, this powerful and often-performed Greek drama reveals the grim fate that befalls the children of Oedipus. Footnotes. 64pp. 5$\frac{3}{16}$ x 8 ¼. 0-486-27804-2

ART DECO DECORATIVE PATTERNS IN FULL COLOR, Christian Stoll. Reprinted from a rare 1910 portfolio, 160 sensuous and exotic images depict a breathtaking array of florals, geometrics, and abstracts — all elegant in their stark simplicity. 64pp. 8⅜ x 11. 0-486-44862-2

THE ARTHUR RACKHAM TREASURY: 86 Full-Color Illustrations, Arthur Rackham. Selected and Edited by Jeff A. Menges. A stunning treasury of 86 full-page plates span the famed English artist's career, from Rip Van Winkle (1905) to masterworks such as Undine, A Midsummer Night's Dream, and Wind in the Willows (1939). 96pp. 8⅜ x 11. 0-486-44685-9

THE AUTHENTIC GILBERT & SULLIVAN SONGBOOK, W. S. Gilbert and A. S. Sullivan. The most comprehensive collection available, this songbook includes selections from every one of Gilbert and Sullivan's light operas. Ninety-two numbers are presented uncut and unedited, and in their original keys. 410pp. 9 x 12. 0-486-23482-7

THE AWAKENING, Kate Chopin. First published in 1899, this controversial novel of a New Orleans wife's search for love outside a stifling marriage shocked readers. Today, it remains a first-rate narrative with superb characterization. New introductory Note. 128pp. 5$\frac{3}{16}$ x 8¼. 0-486-27786-0

BASIC DRAWING, Louis Priscilla. Beginning with perspective, this commonsense manual progresses to the figure in movement, light and shade, anatomy, drapery, composition, trees and landscape, and outdoor sketching. Black-and-white illustrations throughout. 128pp. 8⅜ x 11. 0-486-45815-6

Browse over 9,000 books at www.doverpublications.com

THE BATTLES THAT CHANGED HISTORY, Fletcher Pratt. Historian profiles 16 crucial conflicts, ancient to modern, that changed the course of Western civilization. Gripping accounts of battles led by Alexander the Great, Joan of Arc, Ulysses S. Grant, other commanders. 27 maps. 352pp. 5⅜ x 8½. 0-486-41129-X

BEETHOVEN'S LETTERS, Ludwig van Beethoven. Edited by Dr. A. C. Kalischer. Features 457 letters to fellow musicians, friends, greats, patrons, and literary men. Reveals musical thoughts, quirks of personality, insights, and daily events. Includes 15 plates. 410pp. 5⅜ x 8½. 0-486-22769-3

BERNICE BOBS HER HAIR AND OTHER STORIES, F. Scott Fitzgerald. This brilliant anthology includes 6 of Fitzgerald's most popular stories: "The Diamond as Big as the Ritz," the title tale, "The Offshore Pirate," "The Ice Palace," "The Jelly Bean," and "May Day." 176pp. 5⅜ x 8½. 0-486-47049-0

BESLER'S BOOK OF FLOWERS AND PLANTS: 73 Full-Color Plates from Hortus Eystettensis, 1613, Basilius Besler. Here is a selection of magnificent plates from the *Hortus Eystettensis,* which vividly illustrated and identified the plants, flowers, and trees that thrived in the legendary German garden at Eichstätt. 80pp. 8⅜ x 11.
0-486-46005-3

THE BOOK OF KELLS, Edited by Blanche Cirker. Painstakingly reproduced from a rare facsimile edition, this volume contains full-page decorations, portraits, illustrations, plus a sampling of textual leaves with exquisite calligraphy and ornamentation. 32 full-color illustrations. 32pp. 9⅜ x 12¼. 0-486-24345-1

THE BOOK OF THE CROSSBOW: With an Additional Section on Catapults and Other Siege Engines, Ralph Payne-Gallwey. Fascinating study traces history and use of crossbow as military and sporting weapon, from Middle Ages to modern times. Also covers related weapons: balistas, catapults, Turkish bows, more. Over 240 illustrations. 400pp. 7¼ x 10⅛. 0-486-28720-3

THE BUNGALOW BOOK: Floor Plans and Photos of 112 Houses, 1910, Henry L. Wilson. Here are 112 of the most popular and economic blueprints of the early 20th century — plus an illustration or photograph of each completed house. A wonderful time capsule that still offers a wealth of valuable insights. 160pp. 8⅜ x 11.
0-486-45104-6

THE CALL OF THE WILD, Jack London. A classic novel of adventure, drawn from London's own experiences as a Klondike adventurer, relating the story of a heroic dog caught in the brutal life of the Alaska Gold Rush. Note. 64pp. 5³⁄₁₆ x 8¼.
0-486-26472-6

CANDIDE, Voltaire. Edited by Francois-Marie Arouet. One of the world's great satires since its first publication in 1759. Witty, caustic skewering of romance, science, philosophy, religion, government — nearly all human ideals and institutions. 112pp. 5³⁄₁₆ x 8¼. 0-486-26689-3

CELEBRATED IN THEIR TIME: Photographic Portraits from the George Grantham Bain Collection, Edited by Amy Pastan. With an Introduction by Michael Carlebach. Remarkable portrait gallery features 112 rare images of Albert Einstein, Charlie Chaplin, the Wright Brothers, Henry Ford, and other luminaries from the worlds of politics, art, entertainment, and industry. 128pp. 8⅜ x 11. 0-486-46754-6

CHARIOTS FOR APOLLO: The NASA History of Manned Lunar Spacecraft to 1969, Courtney G. Brooks, James M. Grimwood, and Loyd S. Swenson, Jr. This illustrated history by a trio of experts is the definitive reference on the Apollo spacecraft and lunar modules. It traces the vehicles' design, development, and operation in space. More than 100 photographs and illustrations. 576pp. 6¾ x 9¼. 0-486-46756-2

Browse over 9,000 books at www.doverpublications.com

A CHRISTMAS CAROL, Charles Dickens. This engrossing tale relates Ebenezer Scrooge's ghostly journeys through Christmases past, present, and future and his ultimate transformation from a harsh and grasping old miser to a charitable and compassionate human being. 80pp. 5‰ x 8¼. 0-486-26865-9

COMMON SENSE, Thomas Paine. First published in January of 1776, this highly influential landmark document clearly and persuasively argued for American separation from Great Britain and paved the way for the Declaration of Independence. 64pp. 5‰ x 8¼. 0-486-29602-4

THE COMPLETE SHORT STORIES OF OSCAR WILDE, Oscar Wilde. Complete texts of "The Happy Prince and Other Tales," "A House of Pomegranates," "Lord Arthur Savile's Crime and Other Stories," "Poems in Prose," and "The Portrait of Mr. W. H." 208pp. 5‰ x 8¼. 0-486-45216-6

COMPLETE SONNETS, William Shakespeare. Over 150 exquisite poems deal with love, friendship, the tyranny of time, beauty's evanescence, death, and other themes in language of remarkable power, precision, and beauty. Glossary of archaic terms. 80pp. 5‰ x 8¼. 0-486-26686-9

THE COUNT OF MONTE CRISTO: Abridged Edition, Alexandre Dumas. Falsely accused of treason, Edmond Dantès is imprisoned in the bleak Chateau d'If. After a hair-raising escape, he launches an elaborate plot to extract a bitter revenge against those who betrayed him. 448pp. 5‰ x 8¼. 0-486-45643-9

CRAFTSMAN BUNGALOWS: Designs from the Pacific Northwest, Yoho & Merritt. This reprint of a rare catalog, showcasing the charming simplicity and cozy style of Craftsman bungalows, is filled with photos of completed homes, plus floor plans and estimated costs. An indispensable resource for architects, historians, and illustrators. 112pp. 10 x 7. 0-486-46875-5

CRAFTSMAN BUNGALOWS: 59 Homes from "The Craftsman," Edited by Gustav Stickley. Best and most attractive designs from Arts and Crafts Movement publication — 1903–1916 — includes sketches, photographs of homes, floor plans, descriptive text. 128pp. 8¼ x 11. 0-486-25829-7

CRIME AND PUNISHMENT, Fyodor Dostoyevsky. Translated by Constance Garnett. Supreme masterpiece tells the story of Raskolnikov, a student tormented by his own thoughts after he murders an old woman. Overwhelmed by guilt and terror, he confesses and goes to prison. 480pp. 5‰ x 8¼. 0-486-41587-2

THE DECLARATION OF INDEPENDENCE AND OTHER GREAT DOCUMENTS OF AMERICAN HISTORY: 1775-1865, Edited by John Grafton. Thirteen compelling and influential documents: Henry's "Give Me Liberty or Give Me Death," Declaration of Independence, The Constitution, Washington's First Inaugural Address, The Monroe Doctrine, The Emancipation Proclamation, Gettysburg Address, more. 64pp. 5‰ x 8¼. 0-486-41124-9

THE DESERT AND THE SOWN: Travels in Palestine and Syria, Gertrude Bell. "The female Lawrence of Arabia," Gertrude Bell wrote captivating, perceptive accounts of her travels in the Middle East. This intriguing narrative, accompanied by 160 photos, traces her 1905 sojourn in Lebanon, Syria, and Palestine. 368pp. 5⅜ x 8½. 0-486-46876-3

A DOLL'S HOUSE, Henrik Ibsen. Ibsen's best-known play displays his genius for realistic prose drama. An expression of women's rights, the play climaxes when the central character, Nora, rejects a smothering marriage and life in "a doll's house." 80pp. 5‰ x 8¼. 0-486-27062-9

CATALOG OF DOVER BOOKS

DOOMED SHIPS: Great Ocean Liner Disasters, William H. Miller, Jr. Nearly 200 photographs, many from private collections, highlight tales of some of the vessels whose pleasure cruises ended in catastrophe: the *Morro Castle, Normandie, Andrea Doria, Europa,* and many others. 128pp. 8⅞ x 11¼.　　　　0-486-45366-9

THE DORÉ BIBLE ILLUSTRATIONS, Gustave Doré. Detailed plates from the Bible: the Creation scenes, Adam and Eve, horrifying visions of the Flood, the battle sequences with their monumental crowds, depictions of the life of Jesus, 241 plates in all. 241pp. 9 x 12.　　　　0-486-23004-X

DRAWING DRAPERY FROM HEAD TO TOE, Cliff Young. Expert guidance on how to draw shirts, pants, skirts, gloves, hats, and coats on the human figure, including folds in relation to the body, pull and crush, action folds, creases, more. Over 200 drawings. 48pp. 8¼ x 11.　　　　0-486-45591-2

DUBLINERS, James Joyce. A fine and accessible introduction to the work of one of the 20th century's most influential writers, this collection features 15 tales, including a masterpiece of the short-story genre, "The Dead." 160pp. 5³⁄₁₆ x 8¼.
0-486-26870-5

EASY-TO-MAKE POP-UPS, Joan Irvine. Illustrated by Barbara Reid. Dozens of wonderful ideas for three-dimensional paper fun — from holiday greeting cards with moving parts to a pop-up menagerie. Easy-to-follow, illustrated instructions for more than 30 projects. 299 black-and-white illustrations. 96pp. 8⅜ x 11.
0-486-44622-0

EASY-TO-MAKE STORYBOOK DOLLS: A "Novel" Approach to Cloth Dollmaking, Sherralyn St. Clair. Favorite fictional characters come alive in this unique beginner's dollmaking guide. Includes patterns for Pollyanna, Dorothy from *The Wonderful Wizard of Oz,* Mary of *The Secret Garden,* plus easy-to-follow instructions, 263 black-and-white illustrations, and an 8-page color insert. 112pp. 8¼ x 11.　0-486-47360-0

EINSTEIN'S ESSAYS IN SCIENCE, Albert Einstein. Speeches and essays in accessible, everyday language profile influential physicists such as Niels Bohr and Isaac Newton. They also explore areas of physics to which the author made major contributions. 128pp. 5 x 8.　　　　0-486-47011-3

EL DORADO: Further Adventures of the Scarlet Pimpernel, Baroness Orczy. A popular sequel to *The Scarlet Pimpernel,* this suspenseful story recounts the Pimpernel's attempts to rescue the Dauphin from imprisonment during the French Revolution. An irresistible blend of intrigue, period detail, and vibrant characterizations. 352pp. 5³⁄₁₆ x 8¼.　　　　0-486-44026-5

ELEGANT SMALL HOMES OF THE TWENTIES: 99 Designs from a Competition, Chicago Tribune. Nearly 100 designs for five- and six-room houses feature New England and Southern colonials, Normandy cottages, stately Italianate dwellings, and other fascinating snapshots of American domestic architecture of the 1920s. 112pp. 9 x 12.　　　　0-486-46910-7

THE ELEMENTS OF STYLE: The Original Edition, William Strunk, Jr. This is the book that generations of writers have relied upon for timeless advice on grammar, diction, syntax, and other essentials. In concise terms, it identifies the principal requirements of proper style and common errors. 64pp. 5⅜ x 8½.　0-486-44798-7

THE ELUSIVE PIMPERNEL, Baroness Orczy. Robespierre's revolutionaries find their wicked schemes thwarted by the heroic Pimpernel — Sir Percival Blakeney. In this thrilling sequel, Chauvelin devises a plot to eliminate the Pimpernel and his wife. 272pp. 5³⁄₁₆ x 8¼.　　　　0-486-45464-9

Browse over 9,000 books at www.doverpublications.com

AN ENCYCLOPEDIA OF BATTLES: Accounts of Over 1,560 Battles from 1479 B.C. to the Present, David Eggenberger. Essential details of every major battle in recorded history from the first battle of Megiddo in 1479 B.C. to Grenada in 1984. List of battle maps. 99 illustrations. 544pp. 6½ x 9¼. 0-486-24913-1

ENCYCLOPEDIA OF EMBROIDERY STITCHES, INCLUDING CREWEL, Marion Nichols. Precise explanations and instructions, clearly illustrated, on how to work chain, back, cross, knotted, woven stitches, and many more — 178 in all, including Cable Outline, Whipped Satin, and Eyelet Buttonhole. Over 1400 illustrations. 219pp. 8⅜ x 11¼. 0-486-22929-7

ENTER JEEVES: 15 Early Stories, P. G. Wodehouse. Splendid collection contains first 8 stories featuring Bertie Wooster, the deliciously dim aristocrat and Jeeves, his brainy, imperturbable manservant. Also, the complete Reggie Pepper (Bertie's prototype) series. 288pp. 5⅜ x 8½. 0-486-29717-9

ERIC SLOANE'S AMERICA: Paintings in Oil, Michael Wigley. With a Foreword by Mimi Sloane. Eric Sloane's evocative oils of America's landscape and material culture shimmer with immense historical and nostalgic appeal. This original hardcover collection gathers nearly a hundred of his finest paintings, with subjects ranging from New England to the American Southwest. 128pp. 10⅝ x 9. 0-486-46525-X

ETHAN FROME, Edith Wharton. Classic story of wasted lives, set against a bleak New England background. Superbly delineated characters in a hauntingly grim tale of thwarted love. Considered by many to be Wharton's masterpiece. 96pp. 5³⁄₁₆ x 8 ¼. 0-486-26690-7

THE EVERLASTING MAN, G. K. Chesterton. Chesterton's view of Christianity — as a blend of philosophy and mythology, satisfying intellect and spirit — applies to his brilliant book, which appeals to readers' heads as well as their hearts. 288pp. 5⅜ x 8½. 0-486-46036-3

THE FIELD AND FOREST HANDY BOOK, Daniel Beard. Written by a co-founder of the Boy Scouts, this appealing guide offers illustrated instructions for building kites, birdhouses, boats, igloos, and other fun projects, plus numerous helpful tips for campers. 448pp. 5³⁄₁₆ x 8¼. 0-486-46191-2

FINDING YOUR WAY WITHOUT MAP OR COMPASS, Harold Gatty. Useful, instructive manual shows would-be explorers, hikers, bikers, scouts, sailors, and survivalists how to find their way outdoors by observing animals, weather patterns, shifting sands, and other elements of nature. 288pp. 5⅜ x 8½. 0-486-40613-X

FIRST FRENCH READER: A Beginner's Dual-Language Book, Edited and Translated by Stanley Appelbaum. This anthology introduces 50 legendary writers — Voltaire, Balzac, Baudelaire, Proust, more — through passages from *The Red and the Black, Les Misérables, Madame Bovary,* and other classics. Original French text plus English translation on facing pages. 240pp. 5⅜ x 8½. 0-486-46178-5

FIRST GERMAN READER: A Beginner's Dual-Language Book, Edited by Harry Steinhauer. Specially chosen for their power to evoke German life and culture, these short, simple readings include poems, stories, essays, and anecdotes by Goethe, Hesse, Heine, Schiller, and others. 224pp. 5⅜ x 8½. 0-486-46179-3

FIRST SPANISH READER: A Beginner's Dual-Language Book, Angel Flores. Delightful stories, other material based on works of Don Juan Manuel, Luis Taboada, Ricardo Palma, other noted writers. Complete faithful English translations on facing pages. Exercises. 176pp. 5⅜ x 8½. 0-486-25810-6

Browse over 9,000 books at www.doverpublications.com

FIVE ACRES AND INDEPENDENCE, Maurice G. Kains. Great back-to-the-land classic explains basics of self-sufficient farming. The one book to get. 95 illustrations. 397pp. 5⅜ x 8½.   0-486-20974-1

FLAGG'S SMALL HOUSES: Their Economic Design and Construction, 1922, Ernest Flagg. Although most famous for his skyscrapers, Flagg was also a proponent of the well-designed single-family dwelling. His classic treatise features innovations that save space, materials, and cost. 526 illustrations. 160pp. 9⅜ x 12¼.
0-486-45197-6

FLATLAND: A Romance of Many Dimensions, Edwin A. Abbott. Classic of science (and mathematical) fiction — charmingly illustrated by the author — describes the adventures of A. Square, a resident of Flatland, in Spaceland (three dimensions), Lineland (one dimension), and Pointland (no dimensions). 96pp. 5³⁄₁₆ x 8¼.
0-486-27263-X

FRANKENSTEIN, Mary Shelley. The story of Victor Frankenstein's monstrous creation and the havoc it caused has enthralled generations of readers and inspired countless writers of horror and suspense. With the author's own 1831 introduction. 176pp. 5³⁄₁₆ x 8¼.   0-486-28211-2

THE GARGOYLE BOOK: 572 Examples from Gothic Architecture, Lester Burbank Bridaham. Dispelling the conventional wisdom that French Gothic architectural flourishes were born of despair or gloom, Bridaham reveals the whimsical nature of these creations and the ingenious artisans who made them. 572 illustrations. 224pp. 8⅜ x 11.   0-486-44754-5

THE GIFT OF THE MAGI AND OTHER SHORT STORIES, O. Henry. Sixteen captivating stories by one of America's most popular storytellers. Included are such classics as "The Gift of the Magi," "The Last Leaf," and "The Ransom of Red Chief." Publisher's Note. 96pp. 5³⁄₁₆ x 8¼.   0-486-27061-0

THE GOETHE TREASURY: Selected Prose and Poetry, Johann Wolfgang von Goethe. Edited, Selected, and with an Introduction by Thomas Mann. In addition to his lyric poetry, Goethe wrote travel sketches, autobiographical studies, essays, letters, and proverbs in rhyme and prose. This collection presents outstanding examples from each genre. 368pp. 5⅜ x 8½.   0-486-44780-4

GREAT EXPECTATIONS, Charles Dickens. Orphaned Pip is apprenticed to the dirty work of the forge but dreams of becoming a gentleman — and one day finds himself in possession of "great expectations." Dickens' finest novel. 400pp. 5³⁄₁₆ x 8¼.
0-486-41586-4

GREAT WRITERS ON THE ART OF FICTION: From Mark Twain to Joyce Carol Oates, Edited by James Daley. An indispensable source of advice and inspiration, this anthology features essays by Henry James, Kate Chopin, Willa Cather, Sinclair Lewis, Jack London, Raymond Chandler, Raymond Carver, Eudora Welty, and Kurt Vonnegut, Jr. 192pp. 5⅜ x 8½.   0-486-45128-3

HAMLET, William Shakespeare. The quintessential Shakespearean tragedy, whose highly charged confrontations and anguished soliloquies probe depths of human feeling rarely sounded in any art. Reprinted from an authoritative British edition complete with illuminating footnotes. 128pp. 5³⁄₁₆ x 8¼.   0-486-27278-8

THE HAUNTED HOUSE, Charles Dickens. A Yuletide gathering in an eerie country retreat provides the backdrop for Dickens and his friends — including Elizabeth Gaskell and Wilkie Collins — who take turns spinning supernatural yarns. 144pp. 5⅜ x 8½.   0-486-46309-5

Browse over 9,000 books at www.doverpublications.com

HEART OF DARKNESS, Joseph Conrad. Dark allegory of a journey up the Congo River and the narrator's encounter with the mysterious Mr. Kurtz. Masterly blend of adventure, character study, psychological penetration. For many, Conrad's finest, most enigmatic story. 80pp. 5³⁄₁₆ x 8¼. 0-486-26464-5

HENSON AT THE NORTH POLE, Matthew A. Henson. This thrilling memoir by the heroic African-American who was Peary's companion through two decades of Arctic exploration recounts a tale of danger, courage, and determination. "Fascinating and exciting." — *Commonweal.* 128pp. 5⅜ x 8½. 0-486-45472-X

HISTORIC COSTUMES AND HOW TO MAKE THEM, Mary Fernald and E. Shenton. Practical, informative guidebook shows how to create everything from short tunics worn by Saxon men in the fifth century to a lady's bustle dress of the late 1800s. 81 illustrations. 176pp. 5⅜ x 8½. 0-486-44906-8

THE HOUND OF THE BASKERVILLES, Arthur Conan Doyle. A deadly curse in the form of a legendary ferocious beast continues to claim its victims from the Baskerville family until Holmes and Watson intervene. Often called the best detective story ever written. 128pp. 5³⁄₁₆ x 8¼. 0-486-28214-7

THE HOUSE BEHIND THE CEDARS, Charles W. Chesnutt. Originally published in 1900, this groundbreaking novel by a distinguished African-American author recounts the drama of a brother and sister who "pass for white" during the dangerous days of Reconstruction. 208pp. 5⅜ x 8½. 0-486-46144-0

THE HUMAN FIGURE IN MOTION, Eadweard Muybridge. The 4,789 photographs in this definitive selection show the human figure — models almost all undraped — engaged in over 160 different types of action: running, climbing stairs, etc. 390pp. 7⅞ x 10⅝. 0-486-20204-6

THE IMPORTANCE OF BEING EARNEST, Oscar Wilde. Wilde's witty and buoyant comedy of manners, filled with some of literature's most famous epigrams, reprinted from an authoritative British edition. Considered Wilde's most perfect work. 64pp. 5³⁄₁₆ x 8¼. 0-486-26478-5

THE INFERNO, Dante Alighieri. Translated and with notes by Henry Wadsworth Longfellow. The first stop on Dante's famous journey from Hell to Purgatory to Paradise, this 14th-century allegorical poem blends vivid and shocking imagery with graceful lyricism. Translated by the beloved 19th-century poet, Henry Wadsworth Longfellow. 256pp. 5³⁄₁₆ x 8¼. 0-486-44288-8

JANE EYRE, Charlotte Brontë. Written in 1847, *Jane Eyre* tells the tale of an orphan girl's progress from the custody of cruel relatives to an oppressive boarding school and its culmination in a troubled career as a governess. 448pp. 5³⁄₁₆ x 8¼. 0-486-42449-9

JAPANESE WOODBLOCK FLOWER PRINTS, Tanigami Kônan. Extraordinary collection of Japanese woodblock prints by a well-known artist features 120 plates in brilliant color. Realistic images from a rare edition include daffodils, tulips, and other familiar and unusual flowers. 128pp. 11 x 8¼. 0-486-46442-3

JEWELRY MAKING AND DESIGN, Augustus F. Rose and Antonio Cirino. Professional secrets of jewelry making are revealed in a thorough, practical guide. Over 200 illustrations. 306pp. 5⅜ x 8½. 0-486-21750-7

JULIUS CAESAR, William Shakespeare. Great tragedy based on Plutarch's account of the lives of Brutus, Julius Caesar and Mark Antony. Evil plotting, ringing oratory, high tragedy with Shakespeare's incomparable insight, dramatic power. Explanatory footnotes. 96pp. 5³⁄₁₆ x 8¼. 0-486-26876-4

Browse over 9,000 books at www.doverpublications.com